THE
DESIGNERS

ROWAN

Lisa Richardson

Martin Storey

Sarah Hatton

Marie Wallin

Jennie Atkinson

Galina Carroll

Emma Wright

Georgia Farrell

ROWAN

STORY

·················

KINSHIP

A collection of 22 designs for women.

·················

R O W A N

ALMONDBURY
Cocoon
Martin Storey
110

6

OXTON
Kid Classic
Sarah Hatton
124

8

GRANSMOOR

Hemp Tweed

Lisa Richardson

132

WEETON
SCARF

Alpaca Merino DK

Lisa Richardson

161

FARNLEY
Big Wool
Emma Wright
149

SYKES
Kid Classic
Martin Storey
156

HUTTON
SCARF

Felted Tweed, Kidsilk Haze
Lisa Richardson
163

15

BRADSHAW
Kid Classic
Martin Storey
148

FOSS
Kid Classic
Galina Carroll
130

FUMBER
Felted Tweed
Marie Wallin
116

BUTTRICK
Hemp Tweed
Martin Storey
114

THACKREY
SCARF
Felted Tweed
Martin Storey
155

COWLAM

Hemp Tweed

Lisa Richardson

120

FISHLAKE
Felted Tweed
Marie Wallin
128

BIELBY
Felted Tweed Aran
Martin Storey
127

WILSHAW
Big Wool
Georgia Farrell
165

36

LUND
Pure Wool Superwash DK
Sarah Hatton
140

MARR
Alpaca Merino DK
Lisa Richardson
143

EASTBURY

Alpaca Merino DK

Emma Wright

158

Photographer: Moy Williams. **Styling:** Lisa Richardson. **Hair & Make Up:** Michaela Taylor (Boss Models).
Models: Simiatu Morris, & Elizabeth Tierney. **Location:** Haworth, York.

FEATURE

Designer Profile

GEORGIA
FARRELL

Words by Rosee Woodland

ROWAN

Georgia Farrell doesn't see buildings. At least not in the way you or I might see buildings.

Where our eyes register bricks and wood, stone and steel, the 25-year-old knitwear designer perceives stitch patterns; knits and purls, cables and colour work.

Now designing independently, and for Rowan, Georgia's obsession with translating modern architecture into knitting designs began at London Metropolitan University, where she studied textiles.

"Our studios were based on the edge of the City and the East End, near Whitechapel. Every day I would walk from Liverpool Street station and see buildings like the Gherkin and the Heron Tower. I was constantly drawn to very strong, angular, geometric patterns.

"In my final year, I was part of the Future Fashion Studio, where one of my tutors was a knit specialist and the other an architect. Maybe this had some impact on me too!

"I began looking at tessellating patterns and mathematics and combining them with elements, shapes and lines from buildings I had found.

"It became my design style and it has only grown stronger since. Almost everything I design now is linked back to architecture in some way, whether it's a tessellating pattern that clads a building, or the lines and structure of a tower block."

Some of us struggle to appreciate the concrete and steel materials beloved of many modern architects, but Georgia finds them fascinating. And while she admits her shelves are full of architectural magazines and books, she finds there's nothing quite like putting one foot in front of the other to find inspiration.

With the heart of London just a short train ride from her home in Essex, she still regularly travels into the capital, searching for fresh ideas.

"I try to make time when travelling, whether it's just on the journey into London or a weekend break in a new city, to look up and see what I can find.

"I like walking around a building, getting different angles and compositions and collections of surfaces, patterns and lines."

Georgia interprets these patterns to create knitted swatches, playing with different mixtures of stitches until she has a perfect representation of the original building, created with humble yarn and needles.

"It's at this point that I start to consider what the final outcome will be; a garment, a hat, a scarf, or even a cushion or a blanket.

"I usually sketch the final outcome, and then

01. Londone buildings.
02. Georgia Farrell.
03. Wilshaw from Kinship by Georgia Farrell

begin working on a schematic while I finish the final tension swatch. Then the pattern writing begins; the technical part that takes it from a concept to a real hand knit design that people can make themselves."

So what is it about modern architecture that Georgia finds so appealing?

"I guess it stems from my love of geometry and maths. I love tessellating patterns with strong bold geometric shapes, and modern architecture is like an everyday visual representation of geometry.

"Modern architecture reflects my style, both personally and as a designer. I want my knitwear to have a strong, modern aesthetic, just the way I like my architecture.

"I don't just find inspiration in shiny, fancy glass skyscrapers though. I also love Brutalist-style concrete buildings like the Barbican Estate in London, one of my favourite places to wander on a Sunday in the City."

Georgia's work was first spotted by Rowan in a student showcase at the Knitting and Stitching Show at London's iconic Alexandra Palace.

Appropriately, her first design for Rowan, the Arrow Hat and Snood in Rowan Cocoon, was inspired by another capital landmark. The textured arrow motif on these chunky accessories mimics that found on the Leadenhall building, instantly recognisable by its sloping glass facade, and better known to many as the Cheesegrater.

"I had seen it from afar and was really struck by it then but I recently found myself standing at the bottom of it, gazing up, on a cold foggy Sunday in January and it just blew me away!", she exclaims, describing it as her current favourite building.

Georgia is a big fan of chunky yarns like Cocoon and Big Wool for garments. For homeware she favours Pure Wool Superwash DK and Worsted. Recently though, she's been trying out new ideas in Kid Classic and Hemp Tweed, pushing the edge of her comfort zone.

Translating a rigid, giant structure into a smaller-scale, drapey piece of cloth must be challenging, but it's a test of skill and ingenuity that this ambitious and experimental designer relishes.

"It's quite a nice juxtaposition, and sometimes a factor that I'm quite glad of because who wants to wear a stiff angular box instead of a soft cosy jumper?

"I often use very simple square silhouettes, oversized and boxy with almost never any waist shaping. This allows the structural geometric lines and patterns to flow over the knitting without being distorted and interfered with.

"It's also an aesthetic and stylistic choice for me. These are the kind of garments that I love to wear and so I'm drawn to these shapes when designing. One thing I do a lot when swatching and designing is to use smaller needles than the recommended needle size to get a neater, crisper, cleaner finish to my geometric textured patterns."

So, with a clear vision of her design style and a sketchpad brimful of ideas, what's next for Essex's new rising star?

"At the moment I'm working with the brilliant Quail Studio and Rowan on a book. It's a collection of 12 designs, mostly women's garments with a few fun accessories, in my signature style; featuring textured stitch patterns all inspired by architecture.

"I am so lucky to have been given the creative freedom and support to realise this project and I can't wait to share it with everyone."

Georgia Farrell's first book will be out later this year. You can find more of her work at www.georgiafarrell.co.uk.

04. Criss cross cushion.
05. Criss cross cushion inspiration.
06. Le Prisme.
07. Torte jacket inspired by Le Prisme.

TRAVEL JOURNAL

Kinship Story

Words by Katie Calvert

....

ROWAN

"One may guess the power of the north wind blowing over the edge, by the excessive slant of a few stunted firs at the end of the house; and by a range of gaunt thorns all stretching their limbs one way, as if craving alms of the sun."
Wuthering Heights

Across the world, the Brontës and Haworth, located in the heart of Yorkshire, are synonymous with literary success and a strong sense of heritage. Similarly, Rowan is well known for its dedication to its Yorkshire heritage and history, so it is rather apt that for Magazine 62, Lisa Richardson chose Haworth to photograph Kinship.

The most famous of the Brontës are the three youngest sisters who's short, but fruitful, lives were spent mainly in Haworth. Predominantly home educated and given access to a wide range of writers and poets to read, the sisters, Charlotte, Emily and Anne, held a deep affinity towards their home, incorporating their surroundings into their work and detailing their homesickness in poetry. They first found publication under the male pseudonyms of Currer, Ellis and Acton Bell, producing a book of poems. Upon release, their poems sold few copies, and, although they were well received by a handful of reviewers, more focus was placed on their unusual pen names. History, however, has been kinder, and whilst Charlotte is considered the lesser of the three poets, Emily, in particular, has been praised for her ability as a poet of original power and genius. As novelists, they have found further recognition and respect among a wider audience. Whilst still alive, Charlotte was able to enjoy literary success for her novel Jane Eyre. Emily's only novel, Wuthering Heights, is similarly recognisable, with powerful descriptions of the dramatic moorland that the sisters would have been able to experience and explore, just as visitors can today. Anne's work has not had quite the same level of recognition

that it deserves, due in part to Charlotte's refusal of re-publication after Anne's death. However, what links each writer's work is a deeply emotive narrative, unlike anything that you'd imagine women of that period would be writing.

The years 2016 to 2020 celebrate the bicentenaries of the births of Charlotte, Emily and Anne as well as Branwell, their equally talented brother, but with less credence due to his wayward behaviour. On the BBC, last Christmas, 'To Walk Invisible' detailed their work and their battle for recognition as female writers. This programme recreates and visualises clearly the raw feel and look of Haworth as it was, with much of this remaining the same today. Although, it only takes a read of some of their work to garner a glimpse of what life in Haworth was really like for the Brontës.

At the centre of Haworth is a plethora of independent shops and appealing cafes, leading up through a steep, cobbled street, which gives way to stunning views. Along this route, you are brought to the churchyard and the church, where the Brontës father, Patrick, a published poet himself, would have given sermons. This church is situated in front of the Parsonage, from which the Brontës could view the wild, evocative Yorkshire moorland. The Rowan team sampled a few of these lovely outlets. Sitting just below the Parsonage, Villette Coffee House has an exquisite selection of Yorkshire cakes and pastries. Opposite, the appropriately titled Cobbles and Clay is a café and pottery painting studio. At the centre sits Cabinet of Curiosities. Originally a druggists and apothecary store, where Branwell Brontë purchased the laudanum that would contribute to his untimely death, it has been beautifully restored. Painted black and gold on the outside, it is a stand out feature on Main Street. The inside is no less vivid, with antique fittings and handmade candles, soaps and bath powders to entice.

01. Marr photography in progress.
02. Howarth.
03. Bronte Parsonage Museum.
04. Foss photography in progress.

05

The Black Bull's interiors, adjacent to the church, have been used as a backdrop for some of the garments. This pub is one of Haworth's oldest drinking establishments, once frequented by Branwell. Not far from here is the Old White Lion hotel a classic British pub, where Lisa and the rest of the team stayed overnight. Located just a short walk away from the Parsonage, the hotel also features an award winning restaurant, Gimmerton, serving fresh, local produce, in keeping with Haworth's speciality for independence.

Although the Brontë Parsonage, the original home of the family and now a museum, is one of the most visited literary sites in the world, attracting hundreds of thousands of visitors per year, Haworth still preserves its rugged, natural beauty. The Bronte Society is one of the oldest literary societies, and retaining that heritage is vital. There may be nothing more that can be published by the sisters, but their legacy continues to be far reaching.

Haworth is at the epicentre of Brontë country, but Rowan, situated in Huddersfield, West Yorkshire, and with a history that spans almost 40 years in this northern town, has the privilege of living amongst this literary heritage. A number of museums in the surrounding area hold special links to the Brontës who reimagined them and the people they encountered in a number of their novels. This landscape, which comprises of West Yorkshire and the East Lancashire Pennines in Northern England, is dominated by Millstone Grit, a dark sandstone, which gives the scenery its

air of bleakness and desolation, often described in their work.

Kinship has been created to celebrate Rowan's wonderful Yorkshire heritage. Whilst this is something that Rowan has visited in the past, here, against the breathtaking Yorkshire scenery of a culturally rich Haworth, Rowan has found a setting that allows them to display the designs with just the right mix of beauty and heritage. Added to that, Haworth today is twinned with Machu Picchu in Peru. An area that specialises in Alpaca wool, it is fitting that Rowan should incorporate Alpaca Merino DK into this collection, including designs such as Weeton and Marr, and then showcase it on the streets of Haworth. As many of our Rowan knitters already know, this is a super soft, extra lightweight yarn, with a chainette construction that gives the finished fabric a beautifully soft, weightless feel to knit and wear. The designs featured include simple to knit textures and Fairisle, mixed with modern cables and combined with traditional Arans. Shades of grey, dove and cream compliment the wild moorland and stone backdrops to this charmingly quaint village. It is easy to imagine wrapping yourself in any one of the garments or cosy scarves to keep out the biting cold of the Yorkshire moors. So take part in a Brontë walk, wearing your Rowan knit and look out onto the bleak beauty, whilst imagining what it would have been like to grow up with these moors as a vast and expansive back garden in which to play, as the Brontës would have done.

05. Buttrick photography in progress.
06. Cowlam photography in progress.
07. Haworth.
08. Moy, Lisa & Chris.
09. Fishlake photography in progress.

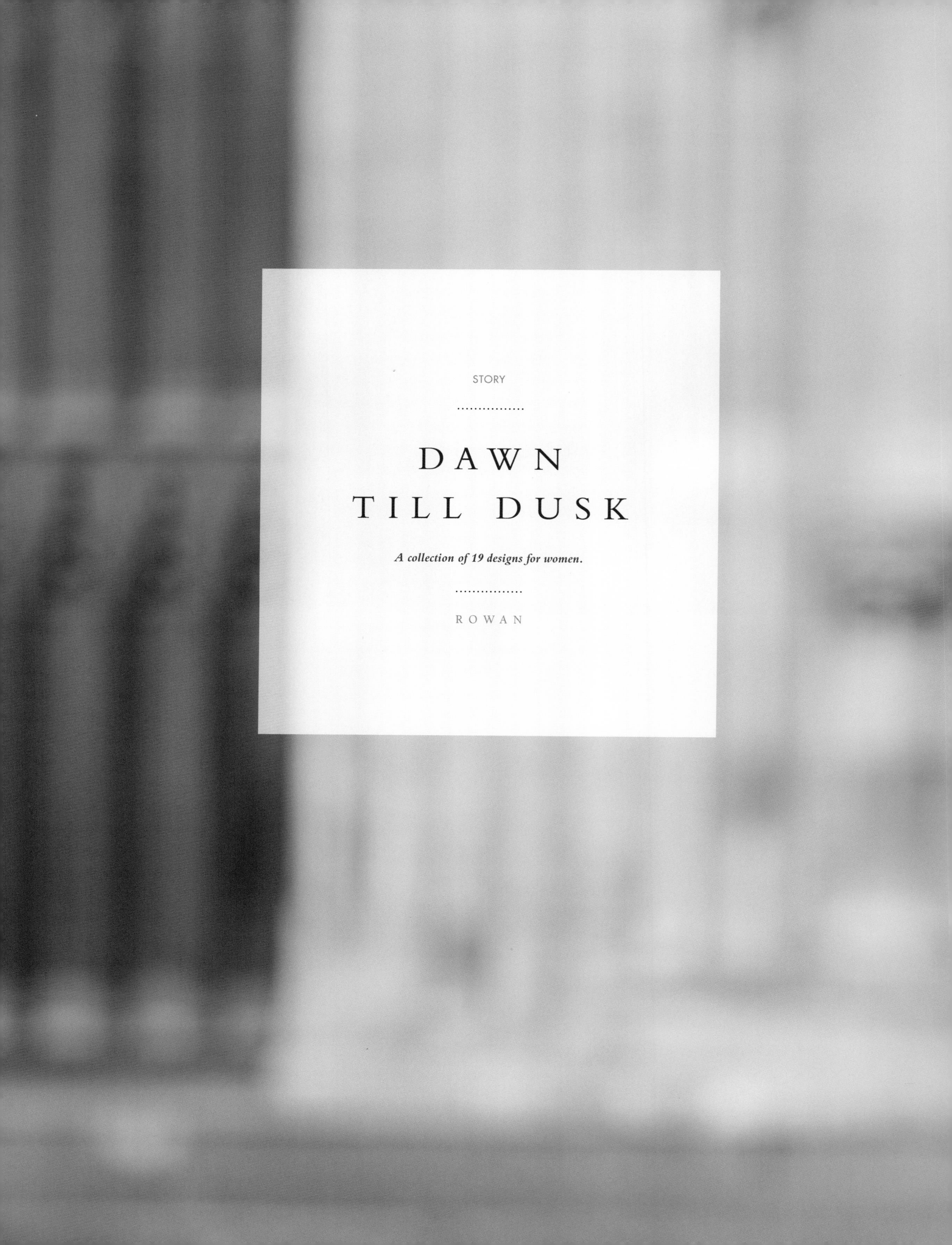

STORY

··············

DAWN TILL DUSK

A collection of 19 designs for women.

··············

ROWAN

55

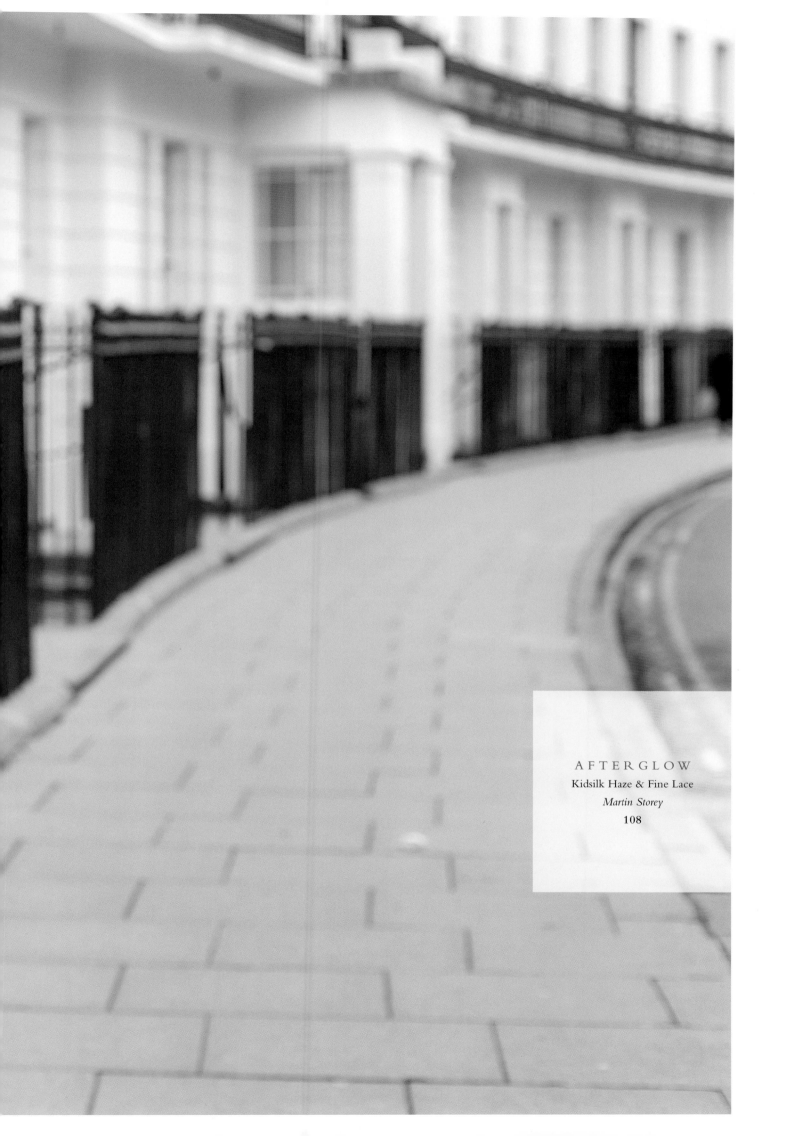

AFTERGLOW
Kidsilk Haze & Fine Lace
Martin Storey
108

SUNSET
Kidsilk Haze
Marie Wallin
162

NIGHTFALL
Kid Classic
Martin Storey
146

EVE
Alpaca Merino DK
Jennie Atkinson
142

ECLIPSE
Kidsilk Haze & Fine Lace
Martin Storey
164

HUTTON
Felted Tweed, Kidsilk Haze
Lisa Richardson
163

TWILIGHT
Kidsilk Haze, Fine Lace
Lisa Richardson
138

67

EVENING
Kid Classic
Martin Storey
119

70

VEILED
Kid Classic
Martin Storey
164

AFTERGLOW
Kidsilk Haze & Fine Lace
Martin Storey
108

DUSKY
SCARF
Kidsilk Haze & Fine Lace
Martin Storey
112

MELLOW
Kid Classic
Sarah Hatton
134

MIDNIGHT
Kidsilk Haze, Fine Lace
Lisa Richardson
160

GLOAMING
Kidsilk Haze, Fine Lace
Lisa Richardson
117

TWILIGHT
Kidsilk Haze, Fine Lace
Lisa Richardson
138

80

VEILED
Kid Classic
Martin Storey
164

SUBDUED
Alpaca Merino DK
Emma Wright
113

DAYBREAK
Kid Classic
Marie Wallin
122

Photographer: Moy Williams. **Styling:** Lisa Richardson. **Hair & Make Up:** Michaela Taylor (Boss Models).
Models: Elizabeth Tierney & Kirstie Bennet. **Location:** York.

FROM ONE DRIZZLY ISLAND TO ANOTHER....

Words by Rosee Woodland

....

What makes a knitting shop special? Is it the yarns they sell? The customers they serve? Rosee Woodland spoke to the owners of two coastal stores with loyal followings, and more than a little in common, despite the ocean between them.

Monica Hardman's Shoreham-by-Sea yarn store is a treasure trove for Rowan fans.

As the first independent yarn store in the UK to stock Rowan handknitting yarns, she carries the full range, and has every Rowan magazine from issue 1 to 61, providing a one-stop shop and reference archive to boot!

Taught to knit at the age of seven by her grandmother and mother, Monica admits she's been "obsessed" ever since.

She began her business with a club for machine knitters in her home in 1972. Six years after opening her first machine knitting shop in 1977, she expanded into the historic three-storey home of Shoreham Knitting and Needlecraft and began selling handknit yarns.

Around the same time, Monica stumbled across a newspaper interview with Rowan founder Stephen Sheard and liked what she read. She has sold Rowan yarns and patterns ever since.

Running a business from a tall, old building has its challenges, with a lot of walking up and down stairs for Monica and her team!

"The building dates to the 17th century but was rebuilt in 1919," the 71-year-old explains.

"You can see in the yard the remains of when it was very old. It was a wine merchant originally. It has a cellar and there is a beautiful archway,

where the coaches used to go in."

This charming building is also the home of English Yarns, the shop's website, which started off in 1996 with a rather spectacular order from a New York customer who spent £3,000 on Rowan yarn.

"It went into three massive boxes!" exclaims Monica. "We were so worried, but it got there. And she's still a customer."

The English Yarns website now offers a range of Rowan patterns as free downloads and Monica is always happy to talk to customers via email or telephone.

"We're a specialist company and we give people the best customer service", says Monica. "If customers are going to trust you, they need to know that you're going to give them the outstanding service that they need."

Monica's favourite Rowan yarns mirror those of her customers; Felted Tweed, Kidsilk Haze, Handknit DK Cotton, Kid Classic and Pure Wool Worsted.

"Rowan's designs are very British and that is the classic look that people love," says Monica. "What gives people the buzz is seeing a design in the Rowan magazine and re-creating it."

With plans to streamline some of the store's ordering systems, there may even be a little extra knitting time in Monica's future. Does she have a favourite design? "A little jacket that I wear more than anything else. It's called Emmeline. It's in Kid Classic and is by Sarah Dallas."

It's a timeless design in a timeless yarn, an appropriate choice for a woman who, like many of her customers, has been with Rowan from day one.

Shoreham-by-Sea Yarn Store will soon be refurbished and become a flagship store for Rowan.

01. From the exterior, you can see the shape of the original 17th century building, complete with archway for merchant's coaches.
02. The shop's shelves are stuffed with goodies for Rowan fans.
03. Monica and staff celebrating their 40th Anniversary in 2012.
04. Monica (centre) and shop staff are joined by Rowan Brand Manager David MacLeod (far left).
05. Teaching the next generation of knitters at a summer workshop, held on the shop's doorstep.

118
CHURCHMOUSE YARNS & TEAS

Take a trip some 4,826 miles west to Bainbridge Island, off the coast of Seattle, and you'll find Churchmouse Yarns & Teas.

Geographically, it's half a world away from Shoreham-by-Sea, but owners Kit Hutchin and John Koval share much in common with Monica Hardman.

Growing up in chilly northern Canada, Kit's English and Irish grandmothers gave her a love of wool, good shortbread and tea with milk.

Like Monica, she learned to knit when she was seven, and never stopped, and, in 2000, after leaving her job as copy director in fashion retail (she says it was a "dream job, it just wasn't my dream"), she took the plunge and opened Churchmouse, with husband John coming on board full-time ten years later.

"I envisioned an English village shop filled with traditional English woolly wools, and a pantry filled with good everyday teas and pottery from Stoke-on-Trent on a kitchen dresser. Goods from one drizzly island to another," says Kit.

John adds: "We always felt that people could buy yarn anywhere, the difference is how they feel when they buy it from us.

"The store is designed with a residential feel, antique English pine cupboards, an Irish kitchen dresser, Yorkshire mill tables, cozy lamps. We want people to feel at home."

The Bainbridge Island community, half an hour from Seattle by ferry, embraced the shop immediately. And following the launch of their website in 2010, John and Kit now have customers from all over the world.

"Every spring, we put a map up in the shop so visitors can put a pin where they're from; last year we had every state in the US and every continent." John explains.

Like Monica, Kit is a "fiercely proud" owner of Rowan magazine number 1.

"It was love at first sight", she says. " I loved the landscape, history and tradition, but always also loved the relevant—and even forward— fashion styling.

"We think of several Rowan yarns as the 'canon'; Kidsilk Haze, Felted Tweed, Kid Classic, and 'newer' ones like Cocoon, Fine Lace. We've continued to publish Churchmouse Classics patterns in all of these. Almost half of Churchmouse published patterns use Rowan yarns, so anyone who downloads one of ours will see the yarns we like to use."

Like Monica, Kit's favourite pattern is a Rowan classic; Martha, by Sarah Hatton.

"Virtually everyone on staff and many, many customers knitted one, " says John. "We even had a 'show us your Martha' event in the store!"

Next on the cards for Churchmouse is a minor shop revamp and the continued expansion of their online community, plus more retreats on their tiny island.

"We love to share our home", Kit adds.

And if you can't stop by in person to Shoreham-by-Sea or Bainbridge Island, rest assured you'll always find a warm online welcome from these dedicated Rowan fans.

Shoreham Knitting and Needlecraft
19 East Street, Shoreham-by-Sea,
BN43 5ZE, UK.
www.englishyarns.co.uk

Churchmouse Yarns & Teas
118 Madrone Lane N, Bainbridge Island,
WA 98110, USA.
www.churchmouseyarns.com

11. Churchmouse Teas and Brown Betties.
Photo: Mike Seidel.
12. Make yourself at home.
13. Try me on. A Churchmouse Better-Than-Basic Pullover in Rowan Kid Classic adorns the dress form. On the shelves behind it are folded samples using Rowan yarns. *Photo: Mike Seidel.*

ROWAN

SUBSCRIPTION

Rowan Subscription includes...

Rowan's Knitting & Crochet Magazine

twice a year (RRP £25)

Newsletter twice a year

Subscribers pattern brochure

Welcome or renewal gift of yarn (RRP £20)

Purchase back issues of our magazines

Subscribe for £25.00

Postage charges: UK £5 • Europe £10 • North America £10 • Rest of World £20

To join or renew ...

www.knitrowan.com | ☎ *0333 200 6466*

Don't forget to quote code *SUBS6217★* for an exclusive 10% discount off your membership

★Valid until 1st March 2018

ROWAN
Style
edit

AW 17

what is the 'rowan style edit'?

taking current rowan designs, quail studio re-style the collection to offer a different take on the original rowan photography. drawing upon street-style trends, styling choices are aimed to allow you to take your wardrobe favourites and pair them with your handknitted garment to get the complete look!

launched twice a year, for the spring/summer and autumn/winter seasons, selected designs will feature seasonal trends, as well as timeless classics.

quail studio brings the designs to life with technical hints & tips and catwalk videos for each of the designs in the style edit collection.

watch out on social media for behind the scenes sneak peeks and release date information.

@rowanyarns
@quail_studio

q u a i l s t u d i o

101

LONGWOOD. (H.56.)

ROWAN
valley tweed
50g

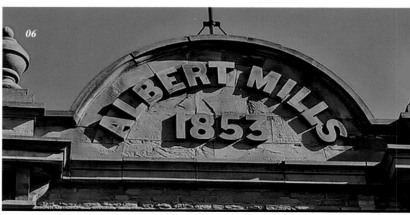

ALBERT MILLS
1853

YARN IN THE VALLEY

Words by Sarah Brook

....

ROWAN

The history of Rowan is woven deeply into its location, primarily being founded above a grocery store in Almondbury, Huddersfield, before moving to a disused textile mill just on the outskirts of Holmfirth, and finally resting at Brooke's Mill in Huddersfield, itself another historical landmark of West Yorkshire's landscape. The initial naming of the company stems from the inspiration from the beautiful Rowan trees, which so freely adorn the local riverbanks around this corner of the county, and it is with this natural beauty in mind that we can so easily understand why Rowan's co-founder Stephen Sheard put so much importance on the colour palettes offered, and how this became so fundamental to the yarn and design collections over the years.

The town and district of Huddersfield itself commands a place which is deeply embedded in the history of the textile industry. Formerly property of the Crown, 1599 saw the manor purchased by William Ramsden, whose family was to prove to be key in the development of the strength of textiles in the area. Part of this support was the building of the Cloth Hall, or textile market, in 1766, Sir John Ramsden's Canal in 1780 and, finally, help in bringing the all-important railway to Huddersfield in the 1840s. The town was a major part of the thriving wool and cotton trades of the time, beginning with small scale family operations of weaving in cottages, helped by a plentiful supply of wool and the soft water of the rivers Colne and Holme, which is perfect for cloth production. This moved swiftly on to larger, mill-based businesses with the emergence of the industrial revolution of the late 18th and 19th centuries, when the district became a beacon of industrial wealth, resulting in a plethora of beautiful Victorian buildings, which can still be seen today. It does, therefore, seem fitting that the Rowan brand we see today, celebrating wool and cotton fibre as much as it does design, should be based in an area boasting so much heritage within the industry.

In the mid 20th century, there was a marked decline in demand for UK products and many of the once bustling mills were forced into closure. In present times, there remains a strong textile tradition within the Huddersfield area, with high-quality, niche mills remaining as part of a modern outlook on demand.

One such example is Brierley Brothers Ltd, who command the respect of being one of today's leading spinners of woollen textile yarns in the UK. Located at Albert Mills, Lockwood, which was originally built as a steam-powered "woollen manufactory" in 1853, the company showcases a rich heritage in supplying high quality, whilst incorporating modern innovation processes. The company is proud to only spin using the finest traceable wools and fibres, which allows it to provide a fibre content guarantee and quality assurances based on the aim of excellence. It is also a member of the Campaign for Wool, an initiative which champions natural products through the promotion of Britain's native breeds as a sustainable and socially responsible resource.

August 2017 sees the introduction of our Valley Tweed, 100% wool tweed yarn, spun and dyed by Brierley Brothers Ltd at Albert mills in Yorkshire, only a few miles down the road from the home of Rowan. The spinners have used their expertise to create an airy and light yarn, featuring a beautiful colour effect brought about by the incorporation of an extra thread of lambswool. A selection of earthy, natural shades make up a colour palette inspired by and named after the surrounding valleys and features of the Yorkshire landscape, which also features as the setting for the Valley Tweed collection. Photographed in the Colne Valley, on the Pennine Way and on Marsden Moor, it fits perfectly with the celebration of local heritage, fine, locally sourced yarn and, of course, design.

01. The old spinning mills. *Image from Kirklees Image Archive: www.kirkleesimages.org.uk*
02. Rowan Yarn, Valley Tweed spun by Brierley Brothers Ltd.
03. Marsden Moor.
04. The machines in action at Brierley Brothers Ltd.
05. Pennine Way.
06. Brierley Brothers Ltd.

WHAT'S NEW

Rowan brochures are available

from Rowan stockists

View the collections online:

www.knitrowan.com

....

R O W A N

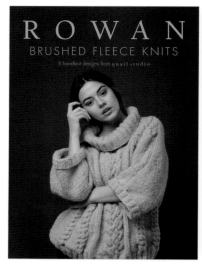

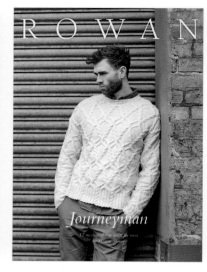

B R U S H E D F L E E C E K N I T S

8 designs from Quail Studio for Rowan.
Featuring Cardigans, Sweaters and
Accessories.
Knit that perfect cosy wardrobe staple
using the delightfully soft and luxurious
Rowan Brushed Fleece yarn.
ZB219
Autumn Winter 2017

J O U R N E Y M A N

A collection of 12 'modern classic' knits
for men designed by Martin Storey.
The perfect man's knit-wardrobe of casual
crew necks, shawl collar jackets, easy soft
rib & slip stitch sweaters, textured slipover
and cosy textured scarves.
ZB220
Autumn Winter 2017

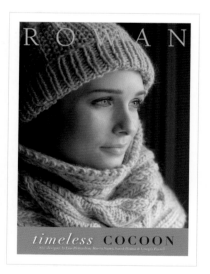

V A L L E Y T W E E D

Designed by Rowan featuring 7 designs
for women.
ZB221
Autumn Winter 2017

C A S H M E R E T W E E D

A collection of 7 modern Scandinavian
& Icelandic inspired knits for women by
Martin Storey.
This collection includes updated fairisle-
yoke sweaters, colour block rib and cable
sweaters, fairisle sleeve scarf and hat.
ZB228
Autumn Winter 2017

T I M E L E S S C O C O O N

Designed by Lisa Richardson, Sarah
Hatton, Brandon Mably & Georgia
Farrell, featuring 6 designs for women.
Easy to intermediate knits detailing
cables, two colour fairisles Stocking
stitch and ribs..
ZB222
Autumn Winter 2017

T I M E L E S S W O R S T E D

A collection of 7 women's bold, graphic
statement and must-have aran knits by
Martin Storey.
A chunky aran jacket, cable cowl,
asymmetric colour block sweater and
quirky 'Rowan' intarsia-lettered sweater
and cardigan all feature.
ZB223
Autumn Winter 2017

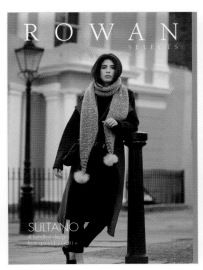

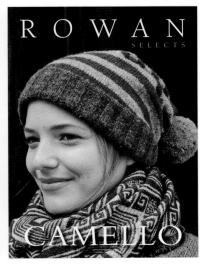

TIMELESS DK

A collection of 6 women's timeless-knits all worked in simple and clean silhouettes designed by Martin Storey.
A twinset-look cardigan, slipover, turtle neck sweater, weekend cardigan and a deep v-neck sweater form the basics of this collection.
ZB224
Autumn Winter 2017

ROWAN SELECTS ROWAN FINEST

Designed by Martin Storey, Sarah Hatton & Amy Herzog featuring 6 designs for women.
ZB225
Autumn Winter 2017

ROWAN SELECTS SULTANO

Sultano has it all, a pure luxury feel accompanied by an elegant colour pallet. This collection of 4 designs brings to life the yarn with a chic, stylish feel that will certainly complete your outfit.
ZB229
Autumn Winter 2017

ROWAN SELECTS CAMELLO

Designed by Lisa Richardson & Sarah Hatton featuring 8 designs for women.
ZB227
Autumn Winter 2017

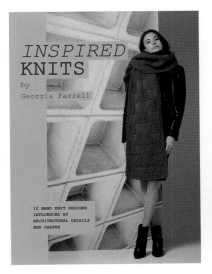

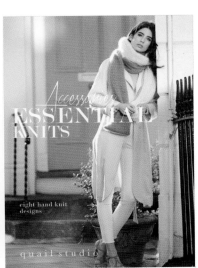

NORTH SEA

8 handknit designs by Marie Wallin. North Sea' is a celebration of the traditional fisherman knit. The collection features cabling and celtic twists, complimented by Nordic inspired Fairisles.
Using Rowan's Felted Tweed and Valley Tweed.
968-0-9927978-7-4
Autumn Winter 2017

CUTE COMFORT KNITS

A collection of 10 knitting projects by Jem Weston.
Ranging from simple blankets, cables and colourwork, these projects will make you want to snuggle up on the sofa with your knitting.
Using Rowan's Felted Tweed, Summerlite DK, Kid classic, Pure Wool Superwash Worsted, Cocoon & Big wool
978-0-9956266-0-7
Autumn Winter 2017

INSPIRED KNITS

A collection of 12 designs inspired by Georgia's love of architecture.
Using Rowan's Pure Wool Superwash, Felted Tweed, Kid Classic, Hemp Tweed, Brushed Fleece, Cocoon & Big Wool
978-0-9935908-2-5
Autumn Winter 2017

ESSENTIAL ACCESSORIES

The fourth in the series of Essential knits from q u a i l s t u d i o comes the Accessories collection. Designed to be an appealing collection where each design is wearable, and can be styled in different ways – completing your essential wardrobe.
Using Rowan's Cocoon, Felted Tweed, Big Wool, Softyak DK, Kidsilk Haze & Baby Merino Silk DK.
978-0-9935908-3-2
Autumn Winter 2017

EVENTIDE

Lisa Richardson

Main image page **76, 77**

● ●

SIZE

To fit bust

81-86	91-97	102-107	112-117	122-127	cm
32-34	36-38	40-42	44-46	48-50	in

Actual bust measurement of garment

100	111	121	129	140	cm
39½	43½	47½	51	55	in

YARN

Kid Classic

10	11	12	13	14	x 50gm

(photographed in Feather 828)

NEEDLES

1 pair 4½mm (no 7) (US 7) needles
1 pair 5mm (no 6) (US 8) needles

BEADS – approx 1440 [1570: 1650: 1840: 2150] beads (ref Debbie Abrahams size 6, colour 563)

TENSION

19 sts and 25 rows to 10 cm measured over beaded st st using 5mm (US 8) needles.

SPECIAL ABBREVIATION

bead 1 = place a bead by taking yarn to RS of work and slipping bead up next to st just worked, slip next st purlwise from left needle to right needle and take yarn back to **WS** of work, leaving bead sitting in front of slipped st on **RS**.

Beading note: Before starting to knit, thread beads onto yarn. To do this, thread a fine sewing needle (one that will easily pass through the beads) with sewing thread. Knot ends of thread and then pass end of yarn through this loop. Thread a bead onto sewing thread and then gently slide it along and onto knitting yarn. Continue in this way until required number of beads are on yarn. Do not place beads on edge 2 sts of rows as this will interfere with seaming.

BACK

Using 4½mm (US 7) needles cast on 95 [105: 115: 123: 133] sts.
Row 1 (RS): P1 [1: 1: 0: 0], K3, *P2, K3, rep from * to last 1 [1: 1: 0: 0] st, P1 [1: 1: 0: 0].
Row 2: K1 [1: 1: 0: 0], P3, *K2, P3, rep from * to last 1 [1: 1: 0: 0] st, K1 [1: 1: 0: 0].
These 2 rows form rib.
Work in rib for a further 14 rows, ending with **RS** facing for next row.
Change to 5mm (US 8) needles.
Beg and ending rows as indicated and repeating the 44 row patt repeat throughout, cont in patt from chart as folls:
Cont straight until back meas 56 [56.5: 57: 57.5: 58] cm, ending with RS facing for next row.
Shape armholes
Keeping patt correct, cast off 4 [5: 6: 7: 8] sts at beg of next 2 rows. 87 [95: 103: 109: 117] sts.
Dec 1 st at each end of next 5 [5: 7: 7: 7] rows, then on foll 4 [6: 6: 6: 6] alt rows.
69 [73: 77: 83: 91] sts.
Cont straight until armhole meas 22 [23.5: 25: 26.5: 28] cm, ending with RS facing for next row.
Shape shoulders and back neck
Next row (RS): Cast off 4 [5: 5: 6: 7] sts, patt until there are 19 [20: 21: 23: 25] sts on right needle and turn, leaving rem sts on a holder.
Work each side of neck separately.
Dec 1 st at neck edge of next 4 rows **and at same time** cast off 5 [5: 5: 6: 7] sts at beg of 2nd row, then 5 [5: 6: 6: 7] sts at beg of foll alt row.
Work 1 row.
Cast off rem 5 [6: 6: 7: 7] sts.
With RS facing, rejoin yarn and cast off centre 23 [23: 25: 25: 27] sts, then patt to end.
Complete to match first side, reversing shapings.

POCKET LININGS (make 2)

Using 5mm (US 8) needles cast on 29 [29: 31: 31: 31] sts.
Beg with a K row, work in st st for 36 [36: 38: 38: 38] rows, ending with RS facing for next row.
Break yarn and leave sts on a holder.

LEFT FRONT

Using 4½mm (US 7) needles cast on 60 [65: 70: 74: 79] sts.

Row 1 (RS): P1 [1: 1: 0: 0], K3, *P2, K3, rep from * to last st, K1.
Row 2: K1, P3, *K2, P3, rep from * to last 1 [1: 1: 0: 0] st, K1 [1: 1: 0: 0].
These 2 rows form rib.
Work in rib for a further 13 rows, ending with **WS** facing for next row.
Row 16 (WS): Rib 15 and slip these 15 sts onto a holder (for front band), M1, rib to end.
46 [51: 56: 60: 65] sts.
Change to 5mm (US 8) needles.
Beg and ending rows as indicated, cont in patt from chart as folls:
Cont straight until left front meas 21 [22: 22: 24: 25] cm, ending with RS facing for next row.
Place pocket
Next row (RS): Patt 5 [7: 8: 9: 11] sts, slip next 29 [29: 31: 31: 31] sts onto a holder (for pocket top) and, in their place, patt across 29 [29: 31: 31: 31] sts of first pocket lining, patt 12 [15: 17: 20: 23] sts.
Cont straight until 40 [38: 38: 34: 32] rows less have been worked than on back to beg of armhole shaping, ending with RS facing for next row.
Shape front slope
Keeping patt correct, dec 1 st at end of next and 6 [6: 6: 5: 5] foll 6th rows. 39 [44: 49: 54: 59] sts.
Work 3 [1: 1: 3: 1] rows, ending with RS facing for next row.
Shape armhole
Keeping patt correct, cast off 4 [5: 6: 7: 8] sts at beg of next row. 35 [39: 43: 47: 51] sts.
Work 1 row.
Dec 1 st at armhole edge of next 5 [5: 7: 7: 7] rows, then on foll 4 [6: 6: 6: 6] alt rows **and at same time** dec 1 st at front slope edge of next [3rd: 3rd: next: 3rd] and 1 [1: 2: 3: 2] foll 6th rows, then on 0 [1: 0: 0: 0] foll 8th row.
24 [25: 27: 30: 35] sts.
Dec 1 st at front slope edge **only** on 2nd [8th: 2nd: 6th: 2nd] and 0 [0: 0: 0: 4] foll 6th rows, then on 4 [3: 4: 4: 2] foll 8th rows. 19 [21: 22: 25: 28] sts.
Cont straight until left front matches back to beg of shoulder shaping, ending with RS facing for next row.
Shape shoulder
Cast off 4 [5: 5: 6: 7] sts at beg of next and foll 0 [2: 1: 2: 2] alt rows, then 5 [-: 6: -: -] sts at beg of

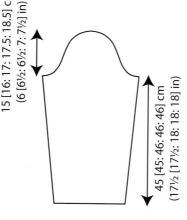

15 [16: 17: 17.5: 18.5] cm
(6 [6½: 6½: 7: 7½] in)

45 [45: 46: 46: 46] cm
(17½ [17½: 18: 18: 18] in)

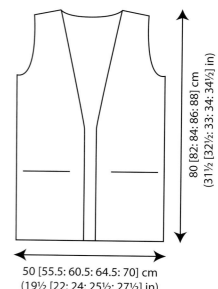

80 [82: 84: 86: 88] cm
(31½ [32½: 33: 34: 34½] in)

50 [55.5: 60.5: 64.5: 70] cm
(19½ [22: 24: 25½: 27½] in)

foll 2 [-: 1: -: -] alt rows.
Work 1 row.
Cast off rem 5 [6: 6: 7: 7] sts.

RIGHT FRONT
Using 4½mm (US 7) needles cast on 60 [65: 70:
74: 79] sts.
Row 1 (RS): K4, ★P2, K3, rep from ★ to last 1 [1:
1: 0: 0] st, P1 [1: 1: 0: 0].
Row 2: K1 [1: 1: 0: 0], P3, ★K2, P3, rep from ★ to
last st, K1.
These 2 rows form rib.
Work in rib for a further 13 rows, ending with
WS facing for next row.
Row 16 (WS): Rib to last 15 sts, M1 and turn,
leaving rem 15 sts on a holder (for front band).
46 [51: 56: 60: 65] sts.
Change to 5mm (US 8) needles.
Beg and ending rows as indicated, cont in patt
from chart as folls:
Cont straight until right front meas 21 [22: 22:
24: 25] cm, ending with RS facing for next row.
Place pocket
Next row (RS): Patt 12 [15: 17: 20: 23] sts, slip
next 29 [29: 31: 31: 31] sts onto a holder (for
pocket top) and, in their place, patt across 29 [29:
31: 31: 31] sts of second pocket lining, patt 5 [7: 8:
9: 11] sts.
Complete to match left front, reversing shapings.

SLEEVES
Using 4½mm (US 7) needles cast on 41 [43: 45:
45: 47] sts.
Row 1 (RS): K2 [0: 0: 0: 0], P2 [0: 1: 1: 2], ★K3,
P2, rep from ★ to last 2 [3: 4: 4: 0] sts, K2 [3: 3: 3:
0], P0 [0: 1: 1: 0].
Row 2: P2 [0: 0: 0: 0], K2 [0: 1: 1: 2], ★P3, K2, rep
from ★ to last 2 [3: 4: 4: 0] sts, P2 [3: 3: 3: 0], K0 [0:
1: 1: 0].
These 2 rows form rib.
Work in rib for a further 10 rows, ending with
RS facing for next row.
Change to 5mm (US 8) needles.
Beg and ending rows as indicated, cont in patt
from chart as folls:
Inc 1 st at each end of 5th [5th: 5th: 3rd: 3rd] and
every foll 6th [6th: 6th: 4th: 4th] row to 49 [59:
67: 51: 59] sts, then on every foll 8th [8th: 8th:
6th: 6th] row until there are 65 [69: 73: 77: 81] sts,
taking inc sts into patt.
Cont straight until sleeve meas 45 [45: 46: 46: 46] cm,
ending with RS facing for next row.
Shape top
Keeping patt correct, cast off 4 [5: 6: 7: 8] sts at beg
of next 2 rows. 57 [59: 61: 63: 65] sts.
Dec 1 st at each end of next 3 rows, then on foll 2
alt rows, then on 3 foll 4th rows.
41 [43: 45: 47: 49] sts.
Work 1 row.
Dec 1 st at each end of next and every foll alt row
until 31 sts rem, then on foll 7 rows, ending with
RS facing for next row.
Cast off rem 17 sts.

MAKING UP
Press as described on the information page.
Join both shoulder seams using back stitch, or
mattress stitch if preferred.
Left front band
Slip 15 sts on left front holder onto 4½mm (US 7)
needles and rejoin yarn with RS facing.
Row 1 (RS): K4, ★P2, K3, rep from ★ to last st, K1.
Row 2: K1, ★P3, K2, rep from ★ to last 4 sts, P3,
K1.

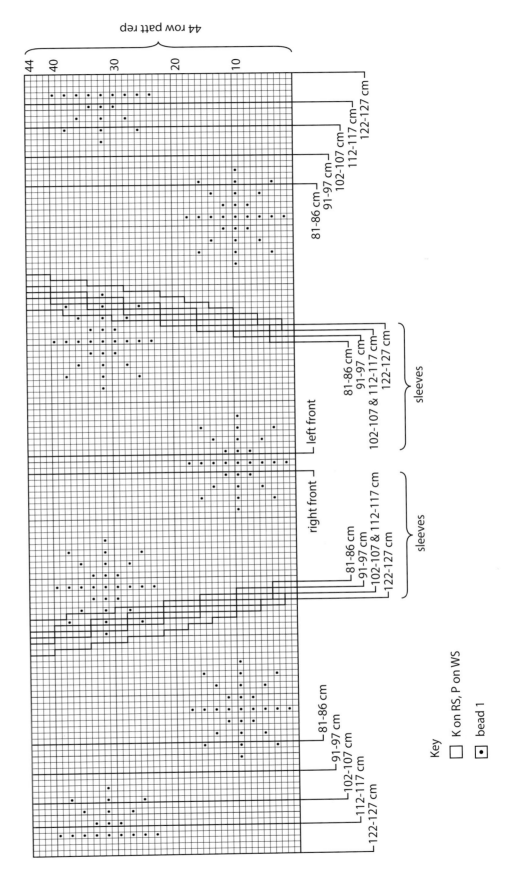

Key
☐ K on RS, P on WS
• bead 1

107

These 2 rows form rib.

Cont in rib until band, when slightly stretched, fits up left front opening edge, up left front slope and across to centre back neck, ending with RS facing for next row.

Cast off in rib.

Right front band

Slip 15 sts on right front holder onto 4½mm (US 7) needles and rejoin yarn with **WS** facing.

Beg with row 2, work in rib as given for left front band until this band, when slightly stretched, fits up right front opening edge, up right front slope and across to centre back neck, ending with RS facing for next row.

Cast off in rib.

Slip st bands in place, joining cast-off ends at centre back neck.

Pocket tops (both alike)

Slip 29 [29: 31: 31: 31] sts on pocket holder onto 4½mm (US 7) needles and rejoin yarn with RS facing.

Row 1 (RS): K15 [15: 5: 5: 5], M1, (K7, M1) 0 [0: 3: 3: 3] times, K14 [14: 5: 5: 5]. 30 [30: 35: 35: 35] sts.

Beg with row 2, work in rib as given for left front band for 9 rows, ending with RS facing for next row.

Cast off in rib.

See information page for finishing instructions, setting in sleeves using the set-in method.

AFTERGLOW

Martin Storey

Main image page **56, 72**

● ● ●

BEADS – approx 610 (650: 670: 700: 720] beads (ref Debbie Abrahams size 6, colour 563)

TENSION

24 sts and 33 rows to 10 cm measured over st st using 3¼mm (US 3) needles and one strand of each of yarns A and B held together. Beaded patt panel (81 sts) meas 31 cm.

SPECIAL ABBREVIATION

bead 1 = place a bead by taking yarn to RS of work and slipping bead up next to st just worked, slip next st purlwise from left needle to right needle and take yarn back to WS of work, leaving bead sitting in front of slipped st on RS.

Beading note: Before starting to knit front of garment, thread beads onto yarn. To do this, thread a fine sewing needle (one that will easily pass through the beads) with sewing thread. Knot ends of thread and then pass end of yarn through this loop. Thread a bead onto sewing thread and then gently slide it along and onto knitting yarn. Continue in this way until required number of beads are on yarn. Do not place beads on edge 3 sts of rows as this will interfere with seaming.

BACK

Using 2¾mm (US 2) needles and one strand each of yarns A and B held together cast on 110 [122: 134: 146: 158] sts.

Row 1 (RS): K2, *P2, K2, rep from * to end.
Row 2: P2, *K2, P2, rep from * to end.

These 2 rows form rib.

Work in rib for a further 4 rows, inc 1 st at end of last row and ending with RS facing for next row. 111 [123: 135: 147: 159] sts.

Change to 3¼mm (US 3) needles.

Beg with a K row, work in st st throughout as folls: Work 10 [14: 18: 24: 28] rows, ending with RS facing for next row.

Dec 1 st at each end of next and foll 10th row, then on 4 foll 8th rows. 99 [111: 123: 135: 147] sts.

Work 13 rows, ending with RS facing for next row.

Inc 1 st at each end of next and 4 foll 6th rows. 109 [121: 133: 145: 157] sts.

Cont straight until back meas 35 [35.5: 36: 36.5:

SIZE

To fit bust

81-86 91-97 102-107 112-117 122-127 cm
32-34 36-38 40-42 44-46 48-50 in

Actual bust measurement of garment

91 101 111 121 131 cm
36 40 43½ 47½ 51½ in

YARN

Kidsilk Haze and Fine Lace

A KSH Pearl 590

5 6 6 7 8 x 25gm

B Lace Cameo 920

3 3 3 4 4 x 50gm

NEEDLES

1 pair 2¾mm (no 12) (US 2) needles
1 pair 3¼mm (no 10) (US 3) needles

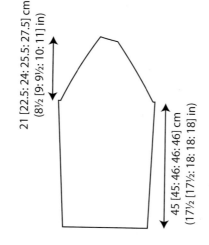

21 [22.5: 24: 25.5: 27.5] cm
(8½ [9: 9½: 10: 11] in)

45 [45: 46: 46: 46] cm
(17½ [17½: 18: 18: 18] in)

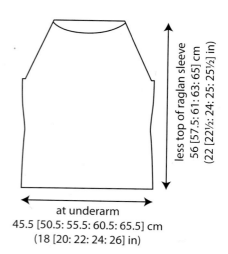

less top of raglan sleeve
56 [57.5: 61: 63: 65] cm
(22 [22½: 24: 25: 25½] in)

at underarm
45.5 [50.5: 55.5: 60.5: 65.5] cm
(18 [20: 22: 24: 26] in)

37] cm, ending with RS facing for next row.

Shape raglan armholes
Cast off 3 sts at beg of next 2 rows.
103 [115: 127: 139: 151] sts.
Next row (RS): K2, sl 1, K1, psso, K to last 4 sts, K2tog, K2.
Next row: (P2, P2tog) 0 [0: 0: 1: 1] times, P to last 0 [0: 0: 4: 4] sts, (P2tog tbl, P2) 0 [0: 0: 1: 1] times.
101 [113: 125: 135: 147] sts.
Working all raglan armhole decreases as set by last 2 rows, dec 1 st at each end of 3rd [3rd: 3rd: next: next] and foll 0 [0: 0: 4: 8] rows, then on 6 [2: 0: 0: 0] foll 4th rows, then on foll 19 [29: 36: 37: 38] alt rows. 49 [49: 51: 51: 53] sts.
Work 1 row, ending with RS facing for next row.
Break yarn and leave rem sts on a holder (for neckband).

FRONT
Using 2¾mm (US 2) needles and one strand each of yarns A and B held together cast on 118 [130: 142: 154: 166] sts.
Work in rib as given for back for 6 rows, dec 1 st at end of last row and ending with RS facing for next row. 117 [129: 141: 153: 165] sts.
Change to 3¼mm (US 3) needles.
Now work in patt, placing chart as folls:
Row 1 (RS): K18 [24: 30: 36: 42], work next 81 sts as row 1 of chart, K18 [24: 30: 36: 42].
Row 2: P18 [24: 30: 36: 42], work next 81 sts as row 2 of chart, P18 [24: 30: 36: 42].
These 2 rows set the sts – central 81 sts in patt from chart with st st at sides.
Repeating the 28 row chart repeat throughout, cont as now set as folls:
Work 8 [12: 16: 22: 26] rows, ending with RS facing for next row.
Dec 1 st at each end of next and foll 10th row, then on 4 foll 8th rows.

105 [117: 129: 141: 153] sts.
Work 13 rows, ending with RS facing for next row.
Inc 1 st at each end of next and 4 foll 6th rows.
115 [127: 139: 151: 163] sts.
Cont straight until front matches back to beg of raglan armhole shaping, ending with RS facing for next row.

Shape raglan armholes
Keeping patt correct, cast off 3 sts at beg of next 2 rows. 109 [121: 133: 145: 157] sts.
Next row (RS): K2, sl 1, K1, psso, patt to last 4 sts, K2tog, K2.
Next row: P3 [3: 3: 2: 2], (P2tog) 0 [0: 0: 1: 1] times, patt to last 3 [3: 3: 4: 4] sts, (P2tog tbl) 0 [0: 0: 1: 1] times, P3 [3: 3: 2: 2].
107 [119: 131: 141: 153] sts.
Working all raglan armhole decreases as set by last 2 rows, dec 1 st at each end of 3rd [3rd: 3rd: next: next] and foll 0 [0: 0: 4: 8] rows, then on 6 [2: 0: 0: 0] foll 4th rows, then on foll 12 [22: 28: 29: 29] alt rows. 69 [69: 73: 73: 77] sts.
Work 1 row, ending with RS facing for next row.
Shape front neck
Next row (RS): K2, sl 1, K1, psso, patt 8 [8: 10: 10: 12] sts and turn, leaving rem sts on a holder.
11 [11: 13: 13: 15] sts.
Work each side of neck separately.
Keeping patt and raglan armhole decreases correct as set, dec 1 st at neck edge of next 5 [5: 6: 6: 6] rows, then on foll 0 [0: 0: 0: 1] alt row **and at same time** dec 1 st at raglan armhole edge of 2nd and foll 1 [1: 2: 2: 3] alt rows. 4 sts.
Work 0 [0: 1: 1: 1] row, ending with RS facing for next row.
Next row (RS): K1, sl 1, K2tog, psso. 2 sts.
Work 1 row.
Next row: K2tog and fasten off.
With RS facing, slip centre 45 sts onto a holder, rejoin yarns and patt to last 4 sts, K2tog, K2.

11 [11: 13: 13: 15] sts.
Complete to match first side, reversing shapings.

SLEEVES
Using 2¾mm (US 2) needles and one strand each of yarns A and B held together cast on 54 [58: 62: 62: 62] sts.
Work in rib as given for back for 6 rows, inc [dec: dec: dec: inc] 1 st at end of last row and ending with RS facing for next row. 55 [57: 61: 61: 63] sts.
Change to 3¼mm (US 3) needles.
Beg with a K row, work in st st throughout as folls:
Inc 1 st at each end of 9th [7th: 7th: 7th: 5th] and every foll 10th [8th: 8th: 8th: 6th] row to 73 [61: 73: 93: 79] sts, then on every foll 12th [10th: 10th: –: 8th] row until there are 79 [83: 89: –: 99] sts.
Cont straight until sleeve meas 45 [45: 46: 46: 46] cm, ending with RS facing for next row.
Shape raglan
Cast off 3 sts at beg of next 2 rows.
73 [77: 83: 87: 93] sts.
Working all raglan decreases in same way as raglan armhole decreases, dec 1 st at each end of next and 6 foll 4th rows, then on every foll alt row until 23 sts rem.
Work 1 row, ending with RS facing for next row.
Left sleeve only
Dec 1 st at each end of next row, then cast off 4 sts at beg of foll row. 17 sts.
Dec 1 st at beg of next row, then cast off 5 sts at beg of foll row. 11 sts.
Rep last 2 rows once more.
Right sleeve only
Cast off 5 sts at beg and dec 1 st at end of next row. 17 sts.
Work 1 row.
Rep last 2 rows twice more.
Both sleeves
Cast off rem 5 sts.

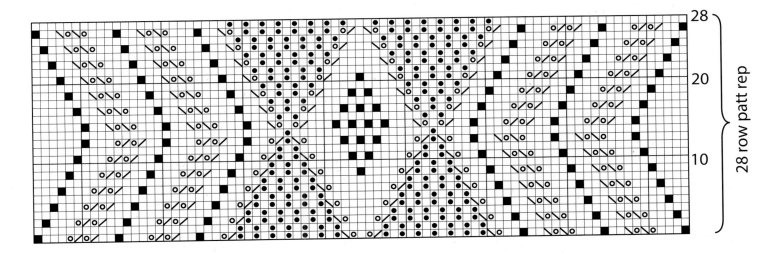

Key

☐ K on RS, P on WS

⦿ P on RS, K on WS

⊡ yfwd

⧄ K2tog

⧅ sl1, K1, psso

■ bead1

Press as described on the information page.
Join both front and right back raglan seams using back stitch, or mattress stitch if preferred.

Neckband

With RS facing, using 2¾mm (US 2) needles and one strand each of yarns A and B held together, pick up and knit 17 sts from top of left sleeve, and 7 [7: 8: 8: 11] sts down left side of front neck, K across 45 sts on front holder as folls: K8, (K2tog, K7) 3 times, K2tog, K8, pick up and knit 7 [7: 8: 8: 11] sts up right side of front neck, and 17 sts from top of right sleeve, then K across 49 [49: 51: 51: 53] sts on back holder. 138 [138: 142: 142: 150] sts.
Beg with row 2, work in rib as given for back for 7 rows, ending with RS facing for next row.
Cast off in rib.
See information page for finishing instructions.

ALMONDBURY

Martin Storey

Main image page **4, 6, 7**

● ● ●

SIZE

To fit bust

81–86	91–97	102–107	112–117	122–127	cm
32–34	36–38	40–42	44–46	48–50	in

Actual bust measurement of garment

135	143	154	164	177	cm
53	56½	60½	64½	69½	in

YARN

Cocoon

A Shale 804

6	6	7	8	8	x 100gm

B Scree 803

6	7	7	8	9	x 100gm

C Frost 806

6	6	7	8	8	x 100gm

NEEDLES

1 pair 6mm (no 4) (US 10) needles
1 pair 7mm (no 2) (US 10½) needles
Cable needle

TENSION

23 sts and 19½ rows to 10 cm measured over patt using 7mm (US 10½) needles.

SPECIAL ABBREVIATIONS

C12B = slip next 6 sts onto cable needle and leave at back of work, K6, then K6 from cable needle;
C12F = slip next 6 sts onto cable needle and leave at front of work, K6, then K6 from cable needle;
C6B = slip next 3 sts onto cable needle and leave at back of work, K3, then K3 from cable needle;
C6F = slip next 3 sts onto cable needle and leave at front of work, K3, then K3 from cable needle.

Pattern note: When working patt from chart for body do NOT work part cables along side seam edges. If there are insufficient sts to work the complete cable, work edge sts of rows in rev st st. When joining sections to work back, you may prefer to work on a circular needle due to number of sts.

BODY (worked in one piece, beg at front hem edges)

Left front

Using 6mm (US 10) needles and yarn A cast on 78 [83: 89: 95: 102] sts.
Beg and ending rows as indicated, cont in patt from chart for body as folls:
Work chart rows 1 to 6, ending with RS facing for next row.
Change to 7mm (US 10½) needles.
Now repeating chart rows **7 to 46 throughout**, cont in patt from chart as folls:
Work 44 [44: 44: 52: 52] rows, ending with RS facing for next row.
Break off yarn A and join in yarn B.
Work 48 [48: 48: 54: 54] rows, ending with RS

Body Chart

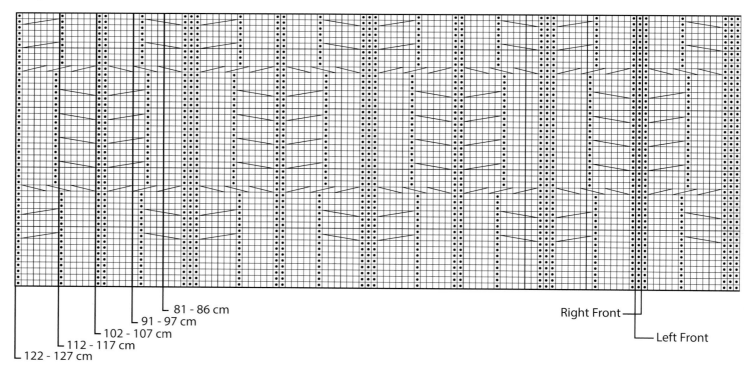

└ 81 - 86 cm
└ 91 - 97 cm
└ 102 - 107 cm
└ 112 - 117 cm
└ 122 - 127 cm

Right Front ┘
└ Left Front

facing for next row.
Break off yarn B and join in yarn C.
Work 47 [47: 47: 53: 53] rows, ending with **WS** facing for next row.★★
Break yarn and leave sts on a holder.
Right front
Work as given for left front to ★★.
Join for back
Next row (WS): Patt to last st of right front, K tog last st of right front with first st of left front,

patt to end of left front sts.
155 [165: 177: 189: 203] sts.
Place markers at both ends of last row to denote shoulder fold line. (Fronts should meas approx 75 [75: 75: 85: 85] cm.)
Work 48 [48: 48: 54: 54] rows, ending with RS facing for next row.
Break off yarn C and join in yarn B.
Work 48 [48: 48: 54: 54] rows, ending with RS facing for next row.

Break off yarn B and join in yarn A.
Work 44 [44: 44: 52: 52] rows, ending after chart row 46 and with RS facing for next row.
Change to 6mm (US 10) needles.
Now work chart rows 1 to 6 once more, ending with RS facing for next row.
Cast off in patt.

SLEEVES
Using 6mm (US 10) needles and yarn A cast on 97 [99: 101: 101: 103] sts.
Beg and ending rows as indicated, cont in patt from chart for sleeve as folls:
Work chart rows 1 to 6, ending with RS facing for next row.
Change to 7mm (US 10½) needles.
Now repeating chart rows **7 to 46 throughout**, cont in patt from chart as folls:
Inc 1 st at each end of next and foll 3 [8: 8: 8: 8] alt rows, then on 2 [0: 0: 0: 0] foll 4th rows, taking inc sts into patt. 109 [117: 119: 119: 121] sts.
Work 3 [1: 1: 1: 1] rows, ending with RS facing for next row.
Break off yarn A and join in yarn B.
Inc 1 st at each end of next and foll 0 [0: 3: 11: 11] alt rows, then on 5 [5: 4: 0: 0] foll 4th rows, taking inc sts into patt. 121 [129: 135: 143: 145] sts.
Work 3 [3: 1: 1: 1] rows, ending with RS facing for next row.
Break off yarn B and join in yarn C.
Inc 1 st at each end of next [next: 3rd: 3rd: next] and foll 0 [0: 0: 0: 3] alt rows, then on 2 [2: 2: 2: 1] foll 4th rows, taking inc sts into patt.
127 [135: 141: 149: 155] sts.
Work 5 rows, ending with RS facing for next row. (Sleeve should meas approx 32 [32: 33: 33: 33] cm.)
Shape top
Keeping patt correct, cast off 10 [11: 11: 12: 13] sts at beg of next 4 [6: 2: 4: 8] rows, then 11 [12: 12: 13: -] sts at beg of foll 4 [2: 6: 4: -] rows.
Cast off rem 43 [45: 47: 49: 51] sts.

MAKING UP
Press as described on the information page.
Mark points along side seam edges 28 [29.5: 31: 32.5: 34] cm either side of shoulder markers (to denote base of armhole opening). See information page for finishing instructions, setting in sleeves using the straight cast-off method.

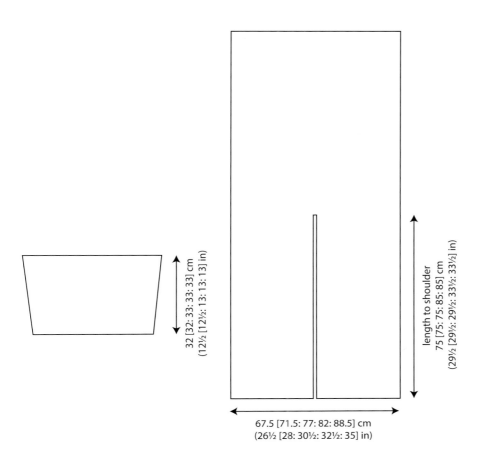

32 [32: 33: 33: 33] cm
(12½ [12½: 13: 13: 13] in)

length to shoulder
75 [75: 75: 85: 85] cm
(29½ [29½: 29½: 33½: 33½] in)

67.5 [71.5: 77: 82: 88.5] cm
(26½ [28: 30½: 32½: 35] in)

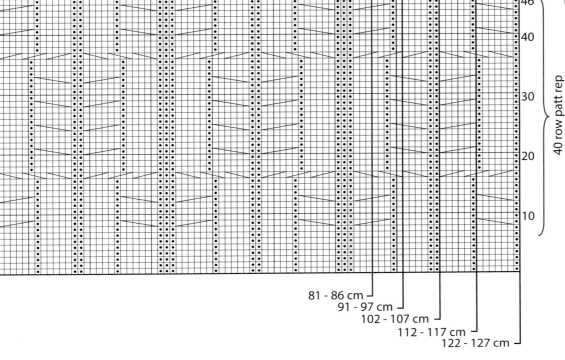

81 - 86 cm
91 - 97 cm
102 - 107 cm
112 - 117 cm
122 - 127 cm

40 row patt rep

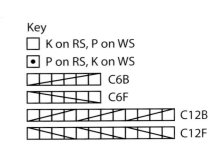

Key
☐ K on RS, P on WS
⊡ P on RS, K on WS
C6B
C6F
C12B
C12F

Sleeve Chart

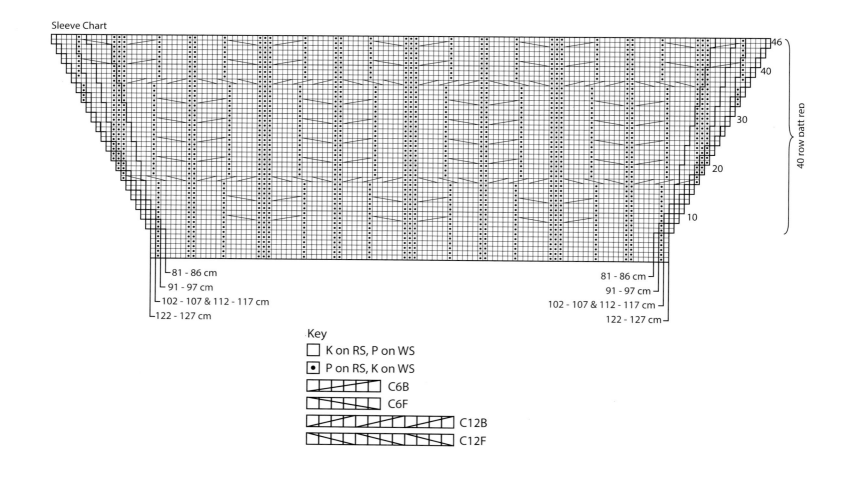

81 - 86 cm
91 - 97 cm
102 - 107 & 112 - 117 cm
122 - 127 cm

81 - 86 cm
91 - 97 cm
102 - 107 & 112 - 117 cm
122 - 127 cm

46
40
30
20
10

40 row patt rep

Key

☐ K on RS, P on WS

⊡ P on RS, K on WS

▦ C6B

▦ C6F

▦ C12B

▦ C12F

DUSKY

Martin Storey

Main image page **54, 55, 73**

● ● ●

YARN

Kidsilk Haze and Felted Tweed

| A | ★KSH | Pearl | 590 | 4 | x 25gm |
| B | FTwd | Granite | 191 | 6 | x 50gm |

★Kidsilk Haze is used DOUBLE throughout

NEEDLES

1 pair 3¾mm (no 9) (US 5) needles

TENSION

21 sts and 42 rows to 10 cm measured over g st using 3¾mm (US 5) needles and Felted Tweed.

FINISHED SIZE

Completed wrap is 43 cm (17 in) wide and 210 cm (82½ in) long.

WRAP

First section

Using 3¾mm (US 5) needles and yarn B cast on 127 sts **loosely**.

Joining in yarn A DOUBLE when required, now work in patt as folls:

Row 1 (RS): Using yarn B, K1, ★yfrn, P5, P3tog, P5, yon, K1, rep from ★ to end.

Row 2: Using yarn A DOUBLE purl.

Row 3: Using yarn A DOUBLE, K1, ★yfrn, P5, P3tog, P5, yon, K1, rep from ★ to end.

Rows 4 to 11: As rows 2 and 3, 4 times.

Row 12: Using yarn B purl.

Rep last 12 rows 5 times more, and then rows 1 to 6 again, ending with RS facing for next row.

Break off yarn B and cont using yarn A DOUBLE as folls:

Row 79 (RS): K1, ★yfwd, sl 1, K1, psso, yfrn, P3, P3tog, P3, yon, K2tog, yfwd, K1, rep from ★ to end.

Row 80 and every foll alt row: Purl.

Row 81: K1, ★yfwd, K1, sl 1, K1, psso, yfrn, P2, P3tog, P2, yon, K2tog, K1, yfwd, K1, rep from ★ to end.

Row 83: K1, ★yfwd, K2, sl 1, K1, psso, yfrn, P1, P3tog, P1, yon, K2tog, K2, yfwd, K1, rep from ★ to end.

Row 85: K1, ★yfwd, K3, sl 1, K1, psso, yfrn, P3tog, yon, K2tog, K3, yfwd, K1, rep from ★ to end.

Row 87: K1, ★K3, K2tog, yfwd, K3, yfwd, sl 1, K1, psso, K4, rep from ★ to end.

Row 89: K1, ★K2, K2tog, yfwd, K5, yfwd, sl 1, K1, psso, K3, rep from ★ to end.

Row 91: K1, ★K1, K2tog, yfwd, K7, yfwd, sl 1, K1, psso, K2, rep from ★ to end.

Row 93: K1, ★K2tog, yfwd, K9, yfwd, sl 1, K1, psso, K1, rep from ★ to end.

Row 95: K2tog, yfwd, ★K11, slip next 2 sts as though to K2tog, K1, then pass 2 slipped sts over, rep from ★ to last 13 sts, K11, yfwd, sl 1, K1, psso. 111 sts.

Row 96: Purl.

This completes lacy border.

Break off yarn A DOUBLE and join in yarn B.

Row 97 (RS): K5, (K2tog, K3) 20 times, K2tog, K4. 90 sts.

Now work in g st until first section meas 105 cm from cast-on edge, ending with RS facing for next row.★★

Break yarn and leave sts on a holder.

Second section

Work as given for first section to ★★.

Break yarn, leaving a long end.

Join sections

Carefully graft together last row of both sections to form completed wrap.

MAKING UP

Press as described on the information page.

SIZE

To fit bust

81-86 91-97 102-107 112-117 122-127 cm
32-34 36-38 40-42 44-46 48-50 in

Actual bust measurement of garment

90 101 110 121 130 cm
35½ 40 43½ 47½ 51 in

YARN

Alpaca Merino DK

12 14 15 16 18 x 25gm

(photographed in Glenfield 112)

NEEDLES

1 pair 4mm (no 8) (US 6) needles
1 pair 4½mm (no 7) (US 7) needles

TENSION

22 sts and 30 rows to 10 cm measured over st st,
20 sts and 42 rows to 10 cm measured over rib,
both using 4½mm (US 7) needles.

SPECIAL ABBREVIATION

K1 below = K into next st one row below and at
same time slipping off st above.

BACK

Using 4½mm (US 7) needles cast on 91 [101: 111:
121: 131] sts.
Row 1 (RS): Knit.
Row 2: Sl 1, ★K1 below (see special abbreviation),
P1, rep from ★ to last 2 sts, K1 below (see special
abbreviation), K1.
Row 3: Sl 1, ★P1, K1 below (see special
abbreviation), rep from ★ to last 2 sts, P1, K1.

Rows 2 and 3 form rib.
Cont in rib for a further 14 rows, ending with **WS**
facing for next row.
Row 18 (WS): P6 [5: 5: 5: 4], inc purlwise in
next st, (P10 [9: 10: 9: 10], inc purlwise in next st)
7 [9: 9: 11: 11] times, P7 [5: 6: 5: 5].
99 [111: 121: 133: 143] sts.
Beg with a K row, now work in st st throughout
as folls:
Cont straight until back meas 35 [35.5: 36: 36.5:
37] cm, ending with RS facing for next row.
Shape armholes
Cast off 3 [4: 5: 6: 7] sts at beg of next 2 rows.
93 [103: 111: 121: 129] sts.
Dec 1 st at each end of next 3 [3: 5: 5: 7] rows,
then on foll 2 [4: 3: 5: 3] alt rows.
83 [89: 95: 101: 109] sts.
Cont straight until armhole meas 20 [21.5: 23:
24.5: 26] cm, ending with RS facing for next row.
Shape shoulders
Cast off 4 [5: 6: 6: 7] sts at beg of next 2 [4: 8: 2: 4]
rows, then 5 [6: –: 7: 8] sts at beg of foll 6 [4: –: 6:
4] rows.
Break yarn and leave rem 45 [45: 47: 47: 49] sts on
a holder (for neckband).

FRONT

Work as given for back until 10 [10: 12: 12: 14]
rows less have been worked than on back to beg
of shoulder shaping, ending with RS facing for
next row.
Shape front neck
Next row (RS): K29 [32: 35: 38: 42] and turn,
leaving rem sts on a holder.
Work each side of neck separately.
Dec 1 st at neck edge of next 8 rows, then on foll
0 [0: 1: 1: 2] alt rows. 21 [24: 26: 29: 32] sts.
Work 1 row, ending with RS facing for next row.
Shape shoulder
Cast off 4 [5: 6: 6: 7] sts at beg of next and foll
0 [1: 2: 0: 1] alt rows, then 5 [6: –: 7: 8] sts at beg
of foll 2 [1: –: 2: 1] alt rows **and at same time**
dec 1 st at neck edge of next and foll alt row.
Work 1 row.
Cast off rem 5 [6: 6: 7: 8] sts.
With RS facing, slip centre 25 sts onto a holder,
rejoin yarn and K to end.
Complete to match first side, reversing shapings.

SLEEVES

Using 4½mm (US 7) needles cast on 41 [43: 45:
45: 47] sts.
Work rows 1 to 3 as given for back.
Working in rib as now set throughout, cont as
folls:
Inc 1 st at each end of 12th [12th: 10th: 10th: 8th]
and every foll 12th [12th: 10th: 10th: 8th] row to
53 [69: 53: 77: 57] sts, then on every foll 14th [–:
12th: –: 10th] row until there are 65 [–: 73: –: 81]
sts, taking inc sts into rib.
Cont straight until sleeve meas 42 [42: 43: 43: 43] cm,
ending with RS facing for next row.
Shape top
Keeping rib correct, cast off 3 [4: 5: 6: 7] sts at beg
of next 2 rows. 59 [61: 63: 65: 67] sts.
Dec 1 st at each end of next 3 rows, then on foll
alt row, then on 9 foll 4th rows.
33 [35: 37: 39: 41] sts.
Work 1 row, ending with RS facing for next row.
Dec 1 st at each end of next and every foll alt row
until 23 sts rem, then on foll 5 rows, ending with
RS facing for next row.
Cast off rem 13 sts.

MAKING UP

Press as described on the information page.
Join right shoulder seam using back stitch, or
mattress stitch if preferred.
Neckband
With RS facing and using 4mm (US 6) needles,
pick up and knit 15 [15: 17: 17: 19] sts down left
side of front neck, K across 25 sts on front holder,
pick up and knit 15 [15: 17: 17: 19] sts up right side
of front neck, then K across 45 [45: 47: 47: 49] sts
on back holder. 100 [100: 106: 106: 112] sts.
Work in g st for 4 rows, ending with **WS** facing
for next row.
Cast off knitwise (on **WS**).
Cuff ties (make 2)
Using 4mm (US 6) needles cast on 9 sts.
Work in g st until tie meas 44 [45: 46: 46: 47] cm,
ending with **WS** facing for next row.
Cast off knitwise (on **WS**).
See information page for finishing instructions,
setting in sleeves using the set-in method. Sew
centre of tie to sleeve seam, positioning tie approx
12 cm up from cast-on edge as in photograph.

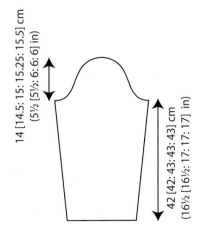

14 [14.5: 15: 15.25: 15.5] cm
(5½ [5½: 6: 6: 6] in)

42 [42: 43: 43: 43] cm
(16½ [16½: 17: 17: 17] in)

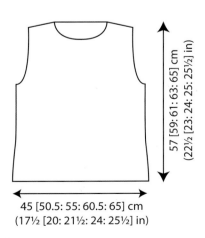

57 [59: 61: 63: 65] cm
(22½ [23: 24: 25: 25½] in)

45 [50.5: 55: 60.5: 65] cm
(17½ [20: 21½: 24: 25½] in)

BUTTRICK

Martin Storey

Main image page **27**

● ● ●

SIZE

To fit bust

81-86	91-97	102-107	112-117	122-127	cm
32-34	36-38	40-42	44-46	48-50	in

Actual bust measurement of garment

113	123	133	143	153	cm
44½	48½	52½	56½	60	in

YARN

Hemp Tweed

15	17	18	20	21	x 50gm

(photographed in Almond 141)

NEEDLES

1 pair 4mm (no 8) (US 6) needles
1 pair 4½mm (no 7) (US 7) needles
Cable needle

TENSION

32 sts and 27 rows to 10 cm measured over cable patt, 18 sts and 40 rows to 10 cm measured over sleeve patt, both using 4½mm (US 7) needles.

SPECIAL ABBREVIATIONS

C6B = slip next 3 sts onto cable needle and leave at back of work, K3, then K3 from cable needle; **K1 below** = K into next st one row below and at same time slipping off st above; **Tw3** = slip next 2 sts onto cable needle and leave at back of work, K1, slip centre st of this group of 3 sts back onto left needle and K this st, then K1 from cable needle.

BACK

Using 4mm (US 6) needles cast on 130 [142: 154: 166: 178] sts.

Row 1 (RS): K2, *P2, K2, rep from * to end.

Row 2: P2, *K2, P2, rep from * to end.

These 2 rows form rib.

Work in rib for a further 7 rows, ending with **WS** facing for next row.

Row 10 (WS): Rib 2 [3: 4: 5: 6], (rib 1, M1, rib 3, M1, rib 1) 25 [27: 29: 31: 33] times, rib 3 [4: 5: 6: 7]. 180 [196: 212: 228: 244] sts.

Change to 4½mm (US 7) needles.

Beg and ending rows as indicated and repeating the 20 row patt repeat throughout, cont in patt from chart as folls:

Cont straight until back meas 34 [34.5: 35: 35.5: 36] cm, ending with RS facing for next row.

Shape raglan armholes

Keeping patt correct, cast off 5 sts at beg of next 2 rows. 170 [186: 202: 218: 234] sts.

Size 81-86 cm only

Next row (RS): K2, sl 1, K1, psso, patt to last 4 sts, K2tog, K2.

Next row: P3, patt to last 3 sts, P3.

Rep last 2 rows once more. 166 sts.

Sizes 91-97, 102-107, 112-117 and 122-127 cm only

Next row (RS): K2, sl 1, K2tog, psso, patt to last

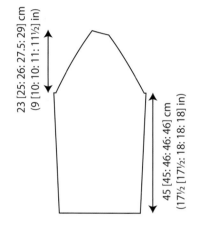

23 [25: 26: 27.5: 29] cm
(9 [10: 10: 11: 11½] in)

45 [45: 46: 46: 46] cm
(17½ [17½: 18: 18: 18] in)

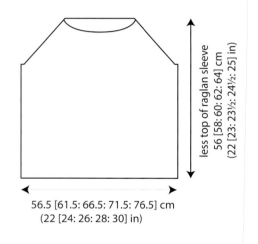

less top of raglan sleeve
56 [58: 60: 62: 64] cm
(22 [23: 23½: 24½: 25] in)

56.5 [61.5: 66.5: 71.5: 76.5] cm
(22 [24: 26: 28: 30] in)

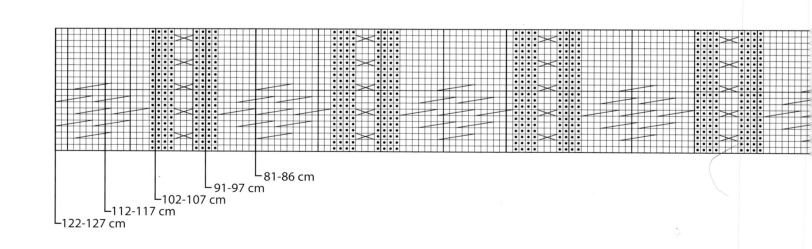

81-86 cm

91-97 cm

102-107 cm

112-117 cm

122-127 cm

5 sts, K3tog, K2.
Next row: P2, P3tog, patt to last 5 sts, P3tog tbl, P2.
Rep last 2 rows – [0: 1: 3: 5] times more.
– [178: 186: 186: 186] sts.
Sizes 102-107 and 112-117 cm only
Next row (RS): K2, sl 1, K2tog, psso, patt to last 5 sts, K3tog, K2.
Next row: P2, P2tog, patt to last 4 sts, P2tog tbl, P2. – [-: 180: 180: -] sts.
All sizes
Next row (RS): K2, sl 1, K1, psso, patt to last 4 sts, K2tog, K2.
Next row: P2, P2tog, patt to last 4 sts, P2tog tbl, P2.
Rep last 2 rows 26 [29: 29: 29: 30] times more, ending with RS facing for next row.
58 [58: 60: 60: 62] sts.
Break yarn and leave sts on a holder.

FRONT
Work as given for back until 90 [90: 96: 96: 102] sts rem in raglan armhole shaping, ending with RS facing for next row.
Shape front neck
Next row (RS): K2, sl 1, K1, psso, patt 16 [16: 19: 19: 22] sts and turn, leaving rem sts on a holder.
19 [19: 22: 22: 25] sts.
Work each side of neck separately.
Keeping patt correct, dec 1 st at raglan armhole edge of next 7 [7: 9: 9: 11] rows, ending with RS facing for next row, **and at same time** dec 1 st at neck edge of next 7 [7: 8: 8: 8] rows, then on foll 0 [0: 0: 0: 1] alt row. 5 sts.
Next row (RS): K2, sl 1, K2tog, psso. 3 sts.
Next row: P2tog tbl, P1.
Next row: K2tog and fasten off.
With RS facing, slip centre 50 sts onto a holder, rejoin yarn and patt to last 4 sts, K2tog, K2.
19 [19: 22: 22: 25] sts.
Complete to match first side, reversing shapings.

SLEEVES
Using 4mm (US 6) needles cast on 43 [45: 47: 47: 49] sts.

Row 1 (RS): K1, *P1, K1, rep from * to end.
Row 2: P1, *K1, P1, rep from * to end.
These 2 rows form rib.
Work in rib for a further 18 rows, ending with RS facing for next row.
Change to 4½mm (US 7) needles.
Now work in sleeve patt as folls:
Row 1 (RS): Knit.
Row 2: P1, *K1 below (see special abbreviations), P1, rep from * to end.
These 2 rows form sleeve patt.
Inc 1 st at each end of 7th [7th: 5th: 5th: 5th] and every foll 10th [10th: 8th: 8th: 8th] row to 59 [61: 55: 75: 77] sts, then on every foll 12th [12th: 10th: 10th: 10th] row until there are 67 [69: 75: 79: 81] sts, taking inc sts into patt.
Cont straight until sleeve meas 45 [45: 46: 46: 46] cm, ending with RS facing for next row.
Shape raglan
Keeping patt correct, cast off 4 sts at beg of next 2 rows. 59 [61: 67: 71: 73] sts.
Work 4 rows, ending with RS facing for next row.
Next row (RS): Patt 4 sts, sl 1, K2tog, psso, patt to last 7 sts, K3tog, patt 4 sts. 55 [57: 63: 67: 69] sts.
Working all decreases as set by last row, dec **2** sts at each end of 8th and 4 [7: 4: 4: 7] foll 8th rows, then on 5 [2: 7: 8: 5] foll 6th rows.
15 [17: 15: 15: 17] sts.
Work 3 rows, ending with RS facing for next row.
Left sleeve only
Work 1 row, then cast off 4 [5: 4: 4: 5] sts at beg of foll row. 11 [12: 11: 11: 12] sts.
Dec 2 sts at beg of next row, then cast off 3 [4: 3: 3: 4] sts at beg of foll row. 6 sts.
Dec 1 st at end of next row and at same edge on foll 3 rows. 2 sts.
Right sleeve only
Cast off 3 [4: 3: 3: 4] sts at beg of next and foll alt row **and at same time** dec 2 sts at end of 3rd row. 7 sts.
Dec 1 st at end of next row and at same edge on foll 4 rows. 2 sts.
Both sleeves
Next row (RS): K2tog and fasten off.

MAKING UP
Press as described on the information page.
Join both front and right back raglan seams using back stitch, or mattress stitch if preferred. (**Note:** Due to difference in row tensions, there will be 28 [30: 32: 34: 36] more rows in sleeve raglan edges than body raglan edges but edges should be same length.)
Neckband
With RS facing and using 4mm (US 6) needles, pick up and knit 12 [12: 13: 13: 13] sts from top of left sleeve, 9 [9: 11: 11: 13] sts down left side of front neck, K across 50 sts on front holder as folls: K2tog, (K1, K2tog) 16 times, pick up and knit 9 [9: 11: 11: 13] sts up right side of front neck, and 12 [12: 13: 13: 13] sts from top of right sleeve, then K across 58 [58: 60: 60: 62] sts on back holder as folls: K1 [1: 2: 2: 0], K2tog, (K1, K2tog) 18 [18: 18: 18: 20] times, K1 [1: 2: 2: 0].
114 [114: 122: 122: 126] sts.
Beg with row 2, work in rib as given for back for 7 rows, ending with RS facing for next row.
Cast off in rib.
See information page for finishing instructions.

Key

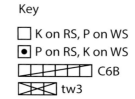

☐ K on RS, P on WS
⊡ P on RS, K on WS
C6B
tw3

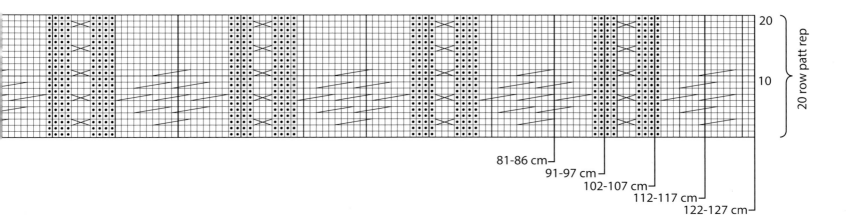

20

10

20 row patt rep

81-86 cm
91-97 cm
102-107 cm
112-117 cm
122-127 cm

FUMBER

Marie Wallin

Main image page **24, 25**

● ● ● ●

SIZE

To fit bust

81–86 91–97 102–107 112–117 122–127 cm
32–34 36–38 40–42 44–46 48–50 in

Actual bust measurement of garment

88 98 109 118 128 cm
34½ 38½ 43 46½ 50½ in

YARN

Felted Tweed

A	Ancient 172					
	6	7	7	8	9	x 50gm
B	Stone 190					
	1	1	1	1	1	x 50gm
C	Clay 177					
	1	1	1	1	1	x 50gm

NEEDLES

2¾mm (no 12) (US 2) circular needle no more
than 80 cm long

3mm (no 11) (US 2/3) circular needle no more
than 80 cm long

3¼mm (no 10) (US 3) circular needle no more
than 80 cm long

Set of 4 double-pointed 2¾mm (no 12) (US 2)
needles

Set of 4 double-pointed 3mm (no 11) (US 2/3)
needles

Set of 4 double-pointed 3¼mm (no 10) (US 3)
needles

TENSION

25 sts and 36 rounds to 10 cm measured over
plain st st using 3mm (US 2/3) needles. 25 sts and
29 rounds to 10 cm measured over patterned st st
using 3¼mm (US 3) needles.

BODY (worked in one piece to armholes)
Using 2¾mm (US 2) circular needle and yarn A
cast on 220 [244: 272: 296: 320] sts **loosely**.
Taking care not to twist cast-on edge, work in
rounds as folls:

Round 1 (RS): ★K1, P1, rep from ★ to end.
This round forms rib.
Place marker on first st of last round – this is
centre back st.
Cont in rib until work meas 6 cm.
Change to 3mm (US 2/3) circular needle.
Work in st st (K every round) until body meas
32 [32.5: 33: 33.5: 34] cm.
Do NOT break yarn, but set this ball of yarn to
one side and leave sts on a holder (for yoke).

SLEEVES

Using 2¾mm (US 2) double-pointed needles and
yarn A cast on 48 [50: 52: 52: 56] sts **loosely**.
Taking care not to twist cast-on edge, distribute sts
over 3 of the 4 needles and, using 4th needle, work
in rounds as folls:
Round 1 (RS): ★K1, P1, rep from ★ to end.
This round forms rib.
Place marker on first st of last round – this st
denotes sleeve "seam".
Cont in rib until sleeve meas 6 cm.
Change to 3mm (US 2/3) double-pointed needles.
Now work in rounds of st st (K every round) as
folls:
Work 5 [5: 5: 3: 3] rounds.
Next round: K2, M1, K to last st, M1, K1.
Working all sleeve increases as set by last round,
inc 1 st at each end of 6th [6th: 6th: 4th: 4th] and
every foll 6th [6th: 6th: 4th: 4th] round to 58 [76:
82: 62: 66] sts, then on every foll 8th [8th: 8th: 6th:
6th] round until there are 80 [86: 90: 96: 100] sts.
Cont straight until sleeve meas 44 [44: 45: 45: 45] cm.
Next round: K5 and slip these 5 sts onto a holder,
K to last 4 sts and break yarn. Slip rem 4 sts onto
same holder as first 5 sts, then leave rem 71 [77: 81:
87: 91] sts on another holder (for yoke).

YOKE

Using 3mm (US 2/3) circular needle and ball of
yarn A set to one side with body, join body and
sleeves as folls:
Next round (RS): K first 51 [57: 64: 70: 76] sts
of body, place marker on needle, slip next 9 sts of
body onto a holder (for left underarm seam) and,
in their place, K across 71 [77: 81: 87: 91] sts of left
sleeve, place second marker on needle, K next
101 [113: 127: 139: 151] sts of body, place third
marker on needle, slip next 9 sts of body onto a
holder (for right underarm seam) and, in their
place, K across 71 [77: 81: 87: 91] sts of right sleeve,
place fourth marker on needle, K rem 50 [56: 63:
69: 75] sts of body. 344 [380: 416: 452: 484] sts.

key

□ A

⊡ B

⊠ C

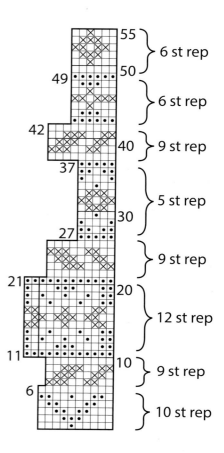

55
6 st rep
49   50
6 st rep
42   40
9 st rep
37
5 st rep
30
27   9 st rep
21   20
12 st rep
11   10
9 st rep
6
10 st rep

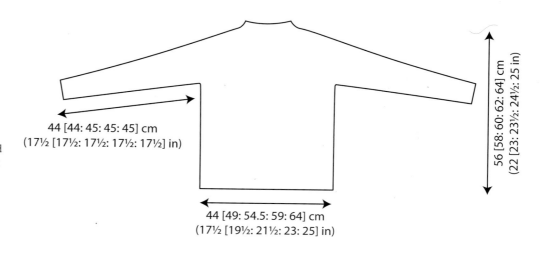

44 [44: 45: 45: 45] cm
(17½ [17½: 17½: 17½: 17½] in)

44 [49: 54.5: 59: 64] cm
(17½ [19½: 21½: 23: 25] in)

56 [58: 60: 62: 64] cm
(22 [23: 23½: 24½: 25 in)

Working in rounds of st st throughout (K every round), cont as folls:
Work 1 round.
Next round: ★K to within 3 sts of marker, K2tog, K2 (marker is between these 2 sts), sl 1, K1, psso, rep from ★ 3 times more, K to end.
336 [372: 408: 444: 476] sts.
Rep last 2 rounds 5 [8: 11: 13: 16] times more.
296 [308: 320: 340: 348] sts.
Next round: K25 [17: 320: 340: 19], (K2tog) 1 [1: 0: 0: 1] times, (K47 [37: –: –: 42], K2tog) 5 [7: 0: 0: 7] times, K24 [16: 0: 0: 19].
290 [300: 320: 340: 340] sts.
Change to 3¼mm (US 3) circular needle.
(**Note**: As the number of sts decreases whilst working yoke, change to double-pointed needles.)
Using the **fairisle** technique as described on the information page, cont in patt from chart, which is worked entirely in st st (K every round), as folls:
Repeating the 10 st patt rep 29 [30: 32: 34: 34] times around each round, work chart rounds 1 to 5.
Round 6: Using yarn A, K4, K2tog, (K8, K2tog) 28 [29: 31: 33: 33] times, K4.
261 [270: 288: 306: 306] sts.
Repeating the 9 st patt rep 29 [30: 32: 34: 34] times around each round, work chart rounds 7 to 10.

Round 11: Using yarn B, K10 [4: 3: 9: 9], K2tog, (K10 [7: 6: 5: 5], K2tog) 20 [29: 35: 41: 41] times, K9 [3: 3: 8: 8]. 240 [240: 252: 264: 264] sts.
Repeating the 12 st patt rep 20 [20: 21: 22: 22] times around each round, work chart rounds 12 to 20.
Round 21: Using yarn B, K4 [4: 8: 1: 1], K2tog, (K8 [8: 7: 7: 7], K2tog) 23 [23: 26: 29: 29] times, K4 [4: 8: 0: 0]. 216 [216: 225: 234: 234] sts.
Repeating the 9 st patt rep 24 [24: 25: 26: 26] times around each round, work chart rounds 22 to 26.
Round 27: Using yarn B, K7 [7: 4: 1: 1], K2tog, (K6 [6: 7: 8: 8], K2tog) 25 [25: 24: 23: 23] times, K7 [7: 3: 1: 1]. 190 [190: 200: 210: 210] sts.
Repeating the 5 st patt rep 38 [38: 40: 42: 42] times around each round, work chart rounds 28 to 36.
Round 37: Using yarn B, K13 [13: 1: 3: 3], K2tog, (K4 [4: 5: 5: 5], K2tog) 27 [27: 28: 29: 29] times, K13 [13: 1: 2: 2]. 162 [162: 171: 180: 180] sts.
Repeating the 9 st patt rep 18 [18: 19: 20: 20] times around each round, work chart rounds 38 to 41.
Round 42: Using yarn A, K8 [8: 5: 2: 2], K2tog, (K3, K2tog) 29 [29: 32: 35: 35] times, K7 [7: 4: 1: 1]. 132 [132: 138: 144: 144] sts.

Repeating the 6 st patt rep 22 [22: 23: 24: 24] times around each round, work chart rounds 43 to 48.
Round 49: Using yarn B, K7 [7: 10: 13: 13], K2tog, (K2, K2tog) 29 times, K7 [7: 10: 13: 13]. 102 [102: 108: 114: 114] sts.
Repeating the 6 st patt rep 17 [17: 18: 19: 19] times around each round, work chart rounds 50 to 55.
Break off yarns B and C and cont using yarn A **only** as folls:
Work 1 round.
Round 57: K5 [5: 4: 7: 7], K2tog, (K8 [8: 9: 9: 9], K2tog) 9 times, K5 [5: 3: 6: 6]. 92 [92: 98: 104: 104] sts.
Work 2 rounds.
Change to 2¾mm (US 2) double-pointed needles.
Work in rib as given for lower edge of body for 2 cm.
Cast off in rib.

MAKING UP
Press as described on the information page.
Join sets of 9 underarm sts by grafting sets of sts together.
See information page for finishing instructions.

GLOAMING
Lisa Richardson
Main image page **60, 61, 79**
●●

SIZE
To fit bust
81-86 91-97 102-107 112-117 122-127 cm
32-34 36-38 40-42 44-46 48-50 in
Actual bust measurement of garment
113   123   133   143   153   cm
44½   48½   52½   56½   60   in

YARN
Kidsilk Haze and Fine Lace
A KSH Liqueur 595

| 8 | 8 | 9 | 9 | 10 | x 25gm |

B Lace Dark Burgundy 951

| 4 | 4 | 5 | 5 | 5 | x 50gm |

NEEDLES
1 pair 3mm (no 11) (US 2/3) needles
1 pair 3¼mm (no 10) (US 3) needles
3mm (no 11) (US 2/3) circular needle at least 120 cm long

BUTTONS – 6 x G427224190 by Groves & Banks. Please see information page for contact details.

TENSION
24 sts and 33 rows to 10 cm measured over st st using 3¼mm (US 3) needles and one strand of each of yarns A and B held together.

BACK
Using 3mm (US 2/3) needles and one strand each of yarns A and B held together cast on 134 [146: 158: 170: 182] sts.
Row 1 (RS): K2, ★P2, K2, rep from ★ to end.
Row 2: P2, ★K2, P2, rep from ★ to end.
These 2 rows form rib.
Work in rib for a further 12 rows, inc 1 st at end of last row and ending with RS facing for next row. 135 [147: 159: 171: 183] sts.
Change to 3¼mm (US 3) needles.

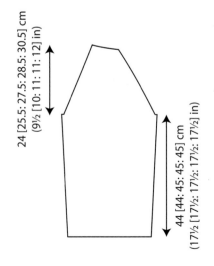

24 [25.5: 27.5: 28.5: 30.5] cm
(9½ [10: 11: 11: 12] in)

44 [44: 45: 45: 45] cm
(17½ [17½: 17½: 17½: 17½] in)

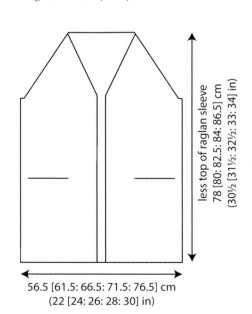

less top of raglan sleeve
78 [80: 82.5: 84: 86.5] cm
(30½ [31½: 32½: 33: 34] in)

56.5 [61.5: 66.5: 71.5: 76.5] cm
(22 [24: 26: 28: 30] in)

Beg with a K row, work in st st throughout as folls:
Cont straight until back meas 54 [54.5: 55: 55.5: 56] cm, ending with RS facing for next row.
Shape raglan armholes
Cast off 3 sts at beg of next 2 rows.
129 [141: 153: 165: 177] sts.
Next row (RS): K3, sl 1, K1, psso, K to last 5 sts, K2tog, K3.
Next row: P3, P2tog, P to last 5 sts, P2tog tbl, P3.
125 [137: 149: 161: 173] sts.
Working all raglan armhole decreases as set by last 2 rows, dec 1 st at each end of next 23 [31: 35: 43: 47] rows, then on foll 26 [24: 25: 23: 24] alt rows.
27 [27: 29: 29: 31] sts.
Work 1 row, ending with RS facing for next row.
Break yarn and leave rem sts on a holder.

POCKET LININGS (make 2)
Using 3¼mm (US 3) needles and one strand each of yarns A and B held together cast on 38 [38: 40: 40: 42] sts.
Beg with a K row, work in st st for 66 rows, ending with RS facing for next row.
Break yarn and leave sts on a holder.

LEFT FRONT
Using 3mm (US 2/3) needles and one strand each of yarns A and B held together cast on 67 [75: 79: 87: 91] sts.
Row 1 (RS): K2, *P2, K2, rep from * to last st, K1.
Row 2: K1, P2, *K2, P2, rep from * to end.
These 2 rows form rib.
Work in rib for a further 12 rows, dec 0 [2: 0: 2: 0] sts evenly across last row and ending with RS facing for next row. 67 [73: 79: 85: 91] sts.
Change to 3¼mm (US 3) needles.
Beg with a K row, work in st st throughout as folls:
Work 66 rows, ending with RS facing for next row.
Place pocket
Next row (RS): K10 [12: 13: 15: 16], slip next 38 [38: 40: 40: 42] sts onto a holder (for pocket top) and, in their place, K across 38 [38: 40: 40: 42] sts of first pocket lining, K19 [23: 26: 30: 33].
Cont straight until left front matches back to beg of raglan armhole shaping, ending with RS facing for next row.
Shape raglan armhole
Cast off 3 sts at beg of next row.
64 [70: 76: 82: 88] sts.
Work 1 row.
Working all raglan armhole decreases as set by back, dec 1 st at raglan armhole edge of next 4 rows, ending with RS facing for next row.
60 [66: 72: 78: 84] sts.
Shape front slope
Dec 1 st at raglan armhole edge of next 37 [45: 49: 57: 61] rows, then on foll 4 [2: 3: 1: 1] alt rows **and at same time** dec 1 st at front slope edge of next and foll 5 [3: 2: 0: 0] alt rows, then on 8 [10: 12: 14: 15] foll 4th rows. 5 [5: 5: 5: 6] sts.
Work 1 row, ending with RS facing for next row.
Sizes 81-86, 91-97, 102-107 and 112-117 cm only
Next row (RS): K2, sl 1, K2tog, psso.

Size 122-127 cm only
Next row (RS): K3, sl 1, K2tog, psso.
Next row: P4.
Next row: K2, sl 1, K1, psso.
All sizes
Next row (WS): P3.
Next row: K1, sl 1, K1, psso.
Next row: P2.
Next row: K2tog and fasten off.

RIGHT FRONT
Using 3mm (US 2/3) needles and one strand each of yarns A and B held together cast on 67 [75: 79: 87: 91] sts.
Row 1 (RS): K3, *P2, K2, rep from * to end.
Row 2: P2, *K2, P2, rep from * to last st, K1.
These 2 rows form rib.
Work in rib for a further 12 rows, dec 0 [2: 0: 2: 0] sts evenly across last row and ending with RS facing for next row. 67 [73: 79: 85: 91] sts.
Change to 3¼mm (US 3) needles.
Beg with a K row, work in st st throughout as folls:
Work 66 rows, ending with RS facing for next row.
Place pocket
Next row (RS): K19 [23: 26: 30: 33], slip next 38 [38: 40: 40: 42] sts onto a holder (for pocket top) and, in their place, K across 38 [38: 40: 40: 42] sts of second pocket lining, K10 [12: 13: 15: 16].
Complete to match left front, reversing shapings.

LEFT SLEEVE
Using 3mm (US 2/3) needles and one strand each of yarns A and B held together cast on 42 [46: 46: 46: 50] sts.
Work in rib as given for back for 13 rows, ending with **WS** facing for next row.
Row 14 (WS): Rib 5 [2: 7: 7: 4], M1, (rib 2 [3: 2: 2: 3], M1) 16 [14: 16: 16: 14] times, rib 5 [2: 7: 7: 4]. 59 [61: 63: 63: 65] sts.
Change to 3¼mm (US 3) needles.
Beg with a K row, work in st st throughout as folls:
Inc 1 st at each end of 5th [3rd: 3rd: 3rd: 3rd] and every foll 6th [4th: 4th: 4th: 4th] row to 87 [65: 77: 95: 109] sts, then on every foll 8th [6th: 6th: 6th: 6th] row until there are 95 [101: 107: 113: 119] sts.
Cont straight until sleeve meas 44 [44: 45: 45: 45] cm, ending with RS facing for next row.
Shape raglan
Cast off 3 sts at beg of next 2 rows.
89 [95: 101: 107: 113] sts.
Working all raglan decreases in same way as raglan armhole decreases, dec 1 st at each end of next and 7 [6: 6: 5: 5] foll 4th rows. 73 [81: 87: 95: 101] sts.
Work 1 row, ending with RS facing for next row.**
Dec 1 st at beg of next and foll 11 [15: 18: 22: 25] alt rows **and at same time** dec 1 st at end of 3rd and 3 foll 4th rows, then on foll 4 [8: 11: 15: 18] alt rows. 53 sts.
Work 1 row, ending with RS facing for next row.
Dec 1 st at each end of next row, then cast off 4 sts at beg of foll row. 47 sts.
Dec 1 st at beg of next row, then cast off 3 sts at

beg of foll row.
Rep last 2 rows 10 times more.
Cast off rem 3 sts.

RIGHT SLEEVE
Work as given for left sleeve to **.
Dec 1 st at end of next and foll 11 [15: 18: 22: 25] alt rows **and at same time** dec 1 st at beg of 3rd and 3 foll 4th rows, then on foll 4 [8: 11: 15: 18] alt rows. 53 sts.
Work 1 row, ending with RS facing for next row.
Cast off 4 sts at beg and dec 1 st at end of next row. 48 sts.
Work 1 row.
Rep last 2 rows once more. 43 sts.
Cast off 3 sts at beg and dec 1 st at end of next row. 39 sts.
Work 1 row.
Rep last 2 rows 9 times more.
Cast off rem 3 sts.

MAKING UP
Press as described on the information page.
Join all raglan seams using back stitch, or mattress stitch if preferred.
Front band
With RS facing, using 3mm (US 2/3) circular needle and one strand each of yarns A and B held together, beg and ending at front cast-on edges, pick up and knit 144 [146: 148: 148: 150] sts evenly up right front opening edge to beg of front slope shaping, 50 [54: 59: 63: 70] sts up right front slope, and 39 sts from top of right sleeve, K across 27 [27: 29: 29: 31] sts on back holder dec 1 st at centre, pick up and knit 39 sts from top of left sleeve, 50 [54: 59: 63: 70] sts down left front slope to beg of front slope shaping, and 144 [146: 148: 148: 150] sts evenly down left front opening edge. 492 [504: 520: 528: 548] sts.
Row 1 (WS): K1, P2, *K2, P2, rep from * to last st, K1.
Row 2: K3, *P2, K2, rep from * to last st, K1.
These 2 rows form rib.
Work in rib for 1 row more, ending with RS facing for next row.
Row 4 (RS): Rib 5 [3: 4: 4: 2], *work 2 tog, yrn (to make a buttonhole), rib 25 [26: 26: 26: 27], rep from * 4 times more, work 2 tog, yrn (to make 6th buttonhole), rib to end.
Work in rib for a further 5 rows, ending with RS facing for next row.
Cast off in rib.
Pocket tops (both alike)
Slip 38 [38: 40: 40: 42] sts on pocket holder onto 3mm (US 2/3) needles and rejoin one strand each of yarns A and B held together with RS facing.
Row 1 (RS): K10 [10: 5: 5: 10], M1, (K18 [18: 10: 10: 22], M1) 1 [1: 3: 3: 1] times, K10 [10: 5: 5: 10]. 40 [40: 44: 44: 44] sts.
Beg with row 1, work in rib as given for front band for 13 rows, ending with RS facing for next row.
Cast off in rib.
See information page for finishing instructions.

EVENING

Martin Storey

Main image page **53, 70, 75**

● ● ●

SIZE

To fit bust

81-86 91-97 102-107 112-117 122-127 cm
32-34 36-38 40-42 44-46 48-50 in

Actual body measurement of garment

112 122 133 141 152 cm
44 48 52½ 55½ 60 in

YARN

Kid Classic

6 6 7 7 8 x 50gm

(photographed in Henna 891)

NEEDLES

1 pair 4mm (no 8) (US 6) needles
1 pair 5mm (no 6) (US 8) needles
2 cable needles

BEADS – approx 64 [64: 68: 68: 72] beads (ref Debbie Abrahams size 6, colour Bronze 601)

TENSION

19 sts and 25 rows to 10 cm measured over st st using 5mm (US 8) needles. Beaded patt panel (27 sts) meas 9.5 cm.

SPECIAL ABBREVIATIONS

bead 1 = place a bead by taking yarn to RS of work and slipping bead up next to st just worked, slip next st purlwise from left needle to right needle and take yarn back to WS of work, leaving bead sitting in front of slipped st on RS; **Cr5** = slip next st onto first cable needle and leave at front of work, slip next 3 sts onto second cable needle and leave at back of work, K1, then K3 from second cable needle, then K1 from first cable needle.

Beading note: Before starting to knit front of garment, thread beads onto yarn. To do this, thread a fine sewing needle (one that will easily pass through the beads) with sewing thread. Knot ends of thread and then pass end of yarn through

this loop. Thread a bead onto sewing thread and then gently slide it along and onto knitting yarn. Continue in this way until required number of beads are on yarn.

BACK

Using 4mm (US 6) needles cast on 106 [118: 126: 134: 146] sts.
Row 1 (RS): K2, *P2, K2, rep from * to end.
Row 2: P2, *K2, P2, rep from * to end.
These 2 rows form rib.
Work in rib for a further 8 rows, dec 0 [1: 0: 0: 1] st at each end of last row and ending with RS facing for next row.
106 [116: 126: 134: 144] sts.
Change to 5mm (US 8) needles.
Beg with a K row, work in st st throughout as folls:
Cont straight until back meas 15 [15.5: 16: 16.5: 17] cm, ending with RS facing for next row.
Shape raglan armholes
Cast off 3 sts at beg of next 2 rows.
100 [110: 120: 128: 138] sts.
Next row (RS): K2, sl 1, K1, psso, K to last 4 sts, K2tog, K2.
Working all raglan armhole decreases as set by last row, dec 1 st at each end of 2nd and foll 11 [19: 25: 31: 37] alt rows, then on 20 [17: 15: 13: 11] foll 4th rows. 34 [34: 36: 36: 38] sts.
Work 3 rows, ending with RS facing for next row.
Break yarn and leave rem sts on a holder (for neckband).

FRONT

Using 4mm (US 6) needles cast on 106 [118: 126: 134: 146] sts.
Work in rib as given for back for 9 rows, ending with **WS** facing for next row.
Row 10 (WS): (P2tog) 0 [1: 0: 0: 1] times, rib 44 [48: 54: 58: 62], (rib 1, M1, rib 1) 9 times, rib 44 [48: 54: 58: 62], (P2tog) 0 [1: 0: 0: 1] times.
115 [125: 135: 143: 153] sts.
Change to 5mm (US 8) needles.
Now work in patt as folls:
Row 1 (RS): K44 [49: 54: 58: 63], P2, (K5, P1) 3 times, K5, P2, K44 [49: 54: 58: 63].
Row 2: P44 [49: 54: 58: 63], K2, (P5, K1) 3 times, P5, K2, P44 [49: 54: 58: 63].
Row 3: K44 [49: 54: 58: 63], P2, *slip next st keeping yarn at back (**WS**) of work, K3, slip next st keeping yarn at **WS** of work, P1, rep from * 3 times more, P1, K44 [49: 54: 58: 63].
Row 4: P44 [49: 54: 58: 63], K2, *slip next st keeping yarn at front (**WS**) of work, P3, slip next st keeping yarn at **WS** of work, K1, rep from * 3 times more, K1, P44 [49: 54: 58: 63].
Row 5: K44 [49: 54: 58: 63], P2, (Cr5, P1) 4

times, P1, K44 [49: 54: 58: 63].
Row 6: As row 2.
Row 7: As row 1.
Row 8: P44 [49: 54: 58: 63], K2, (P2, bead 1, P2, K1) 4 times, K1, P44 [49: 54: 58: 63].
These 8 rows form patt.
Cont in patt until front matches back to beg of raglan armhole shaping, ending with RS facing for next row.
Shape raglan armholes
Keeping patt correct, cast off 3 sts at beg of next 2 rows. 109 [119: 129: 137: 147] sts.
Working all raglan armhole decreases as set by back, dec 1 st at each end of next and foll 12 [20: 26: 32: 38] alt rows, then on 16 [13: 11: 9: 6] foll 4th rows. 51 [51: 53: 53: 57] sts.
Work 3 [3: 1: 1: 3] rows, ending with RS facing for next row.
Shape front neck
Next row (RS): (K2, sl 1, K1, psso) 1 [1: 0: 0: 1] times, patt 9 [9: 14: 14: 12] sts and turn, leaving rem sts on a holder. 12 [12: 14: 14: 15] sts.
Work each side of neck separately.
Keeping patt and raglan armhole decreases correct as set, dec 1 st at neck edge of next 7 [7: 8: 8: 8] rows, then on foll 0 [0: 0: 0: 1] alt row **and at same time** dec 1 st at raglan armhole edge of 4th [4th: 2nd: 2nd: 4th] and 0 [0: 1: 1: 1] foll 4th row.
4 sts.
Work 0 [0: 1: 1: 1] row, ending with RS facing for next row.
Next row (RS): K1, sl 1, K2tog, psso. 2 sts.
Work 1 row.
Next row: K2tog and fasten off.
With RS facing, slip centre 25 sts onto a holder, rejoin yarn and patt to last 4 [4: 0: 0: 4] sts, (K2tog, K2) 1 [1: 0: 0: 1] times. 12 [12: 14: 14: 15] sts.
Complete to match first side, reversing shapings.

SLEEVES

Using 4mm (US 6) needles cast on 78 [78: 82: 82: 86] sts.
Work in rib as given for back for 10 rows, dec 2 [0: 2: 0: 2] sts evenly across last row and ending with RS facing for next row. 76 [78: 80: 82: 84] sts.
Change to 5mm (US 8) needles.
Beg with a K row, complete sleeve in st st throughout as folls:
Shape raglan
Cast off 3 sts at beg of next 2 rows.
70 [72: 74: 76: 78] sts.
Working all raglan deceases in same way as raglan armhole decreases, dec 1 st at each end of next and 12 foll 6th rows, then on every foll 4th row until 30 sts rem.
Work 1 row, ending with RS facing for next row.

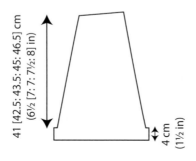

41 [42.5: 43.5: 45: 46.5] cm
(6½ [7: 7: 7½: 8] in)

4 cm
(1½ in)

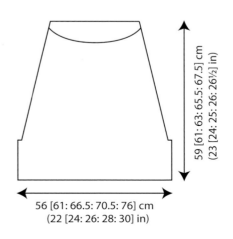

59 [61: 65.5: 67.5] cm
(23 [24: 25: 26: 26½] in)

56 [61: 66.5: 70.5: 76] cm
(22 [24: 26: 28: 30] in)

Left sleeve only

Work 1 row, ending with **WS** facing for next row.
Cast off 7 sts at beg of next and foll 2 alt rows **and at same time** dec 1 st at beg of 2nd row.

Right sleeve only

Cast off 7 sts at beg of next and foll 2 alt rows **and at same time** dec 1 st at end of 3rd row.
Work 1 row.

Both sleeves

Cast off rem 8 sts.

MAKING UP

Press as described on the information page.
Join both front and right back raglan seams using back stitch, or mattress stitch if preferred.

Neckband

With RS facing and using 4mm (US 6) needles, pick up and knit 29 sts from top of left sleeve, and 9 [9: 10: 10: 13] sts down left side of front neck, K across 25 sts on front holder as folls: (K1, K2tog) 8 times, K1, pick up and knit 9 [9: 10: 10: 13] sts up right side of front neck, and 28 sts from top of right sleeve, then K across 34 [34: 36: 36: 38] sts on back holder. 126 [126: 130: 130: 138] sts.
Beg with row 2, work in rib as given for back for 7 rows, ending with RS facing for next row.
Cast off in rib.
See information page for finishing instructions.

COWLAM

Lisa Richardson

Main image page **30, 31**

● ● ●

SIZE

To fit bust

81-86	91-97	102-107	112-117	122-127	cm
32-34	36-38	40-42	44-46	48-50	in

Actual bust measurement of garment

95	104	115	124	135	cm
37½	41	45½	49	53	in

YARN

Hemp Tweed

11	12	14	15	16	x 50gm

(photographed in Pumice 138)

NEEDLES

1 pair 4mm (no 8) (US 6) needles
1 pair 4½mm (no 7) (US 7) needles
4mm (no 8) (US 6) circular needle no more than 40 cm long
Cable needle

TENSION

22 sts and 26 rows to 10 cm measured over patt using 4½mm (US 7) needles.

SPECIAL ABBREVIATIONS

C4B = slip next 2 sts onto cable needle and leave at back of work, K2, then K2 from cable needle; **C4F** = slip next 2 sts onto cable needle and leave at front of work, K2, then K2 from cable needle.

BACK

Using 4mm (US 6) needles cast on 98 [110: 122: 130: 142] sts.
Row 1 (RS): K2, *P2, K2, rep from * to end.
Row 2: P2, *K2, P2, rep from * to end.
These 2 rows form rib.
Work in rib for a further 12 rows, inc 1 [0: 0: 1: 1] st at each end of last row and ending with RS facing for next row. 100 [110: 122: 132: 144] sts.
Change to 4½mm (US 7) needles.
Beg and ending rows as indicated and repeating the 16 row patt repeat throughout, cont in patt from chart as folls:
Work 6 [6: 6: 10: 10] rows, ending with RS facing for next row.
Keeping patt correct, dec 1 st at each end of next and foll 8th [10th: 10th: 12th: 14th] row. 96 [106: 118: 128: 140] sts.
Work 13 rows, ending with RS facing for next row.
Inc 1 st at each end of next and 3 foll 8th [8th: 8th: 6th: 6th] rows, taking inc sts into patt. 104 [114: 126: 136: 148] sts.
Cont straight until back meas 30 [30.5: 31: 31.5: 32] cm, ending with RS facing for next row.

Shape armholes

Keeping patt correct, cast off 4 [5: 6: 7: 8] sts at beg of next 2 rows. 96 [104: 114: 122: 132] sts.
Dec 1 st at each end of next 5 [5: 7: 7: 9] rows, then on foll 3 [5: 5: 6: 5] alt rows. 80 [84: 90: 96: 104] sts.

Cont straight until armhole meas 20 [21.5: 23: 24.5: 26] cm, ending with RS facing for next row.

Shape shoulders and back neck

Next row (RS): Cast off 5 [6: 6: 7: 8] sts, patt until there are 21 [22: 24: 26: 28] sts on right needle and turn, leaving rem sts on a holder.
Work each side of neck separately.
Keeping patt correct, dec 1 st at neck edge of next 4 rows **and at same time** cast off 5 [6: 6: 7: 8] sts at beg of 2nd row, then 6 [6: 7: 7: 8] sts at beg of foll alt row.
Work 1 row.
Cast off rem 6 [6: 7: 8: 8] sts.
With RS facing, slip centre 28 [28: 30: 30: 32] sts onto a holder, rejoin yarn and patt to end.
Complete to match first side, reversing shapings.

FRONT

Work as given for back until 10 [10: 12: 12: 14] rows less have been worked than on back to beg of shoulder shaping, ending with RS facing for next row.

Shape front neck

Next row (RS): Patt 29 [31: 34: 37: 41] sts and turn, leaving rem sts on a holder.
Work each side of neck separately.
Keeping patt correct, dec 1 st at neck edge of next 4 rows, then on foll 2 [2: 3: 3: 4] alt rows. 23 [25: 27: 30: 33] sts.
Work 1 row, ending with RS facing for next row.

Shape shoulder

Cast off 5 [6: 6: 7: 8] sts at beg of next and foll 1 [2: 1: 2: 2] alt rows, then 6 [-: 7: -: -] sts at beg of foll 1 [-: 1: -: -] alt row **and at same time** dec 1 st at neck edge of 2nd row.

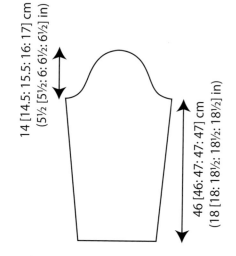

14 [14.5: 15.5: 16: 17] cm
(5½ [5½: 6: 6½: 6½] in)

46 [46: 47: 47: 47] cm
(18 [18: 18½: 18½: 18½] in)

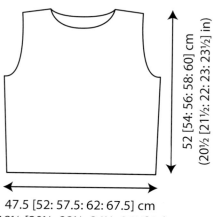

52 [54: 56: 58: 60] cm
(20½ [21½: 22: 23: 23½] in)

47.5 [52: 57.5: 62: 67.5] cm
(18½ [20½: 22½: 24½: 26½] in)

120

Work 1 row.

Cast off rem 6 [6: 7: 8: 8] sts.

With RS facing, slip centre 22 sts onto a holder, rejoin yarn and patt to end.

Complete to match first side, reversing shapings.

SLEEVES

Using 4mm (US 6) needles cast on 38 [40: 42: 42: 44] sts.

Row 1 (RS): P0 [1: 0: 0: 1], K2, *P2, K2, rep from * to last 0 [1: 0: 0: 1] st, P0 [1: 0: 0: 1].

Row 2: K0 [1: 0: 0: 1], P2, *K2, P2, rep from * to last 0 [1: 0: 0: 1] st, K0 [1: 0: 0: 1].

These 2 rows form rib.

Cont in rib, inc 1 st at each end of 9th and 0 [0: 1: 5: 5] foll 4th rows, then on foll 3 [3: 2: 0: 0] foll 6th rows, taking inc sts into rib. 46 [48: 50: 54: 56] sts.

Work 3 [3: 5: 1: 1] rows, ending with RS facing for next row.

Change to 4½mm (US 7) needles.

Beg and ending rows as indicated and repeating the 16 row patt repeat throughout, cont in patt from chart as folls:

Inc 1 st at each end of 3rd [3rd: next: 3rd: 3rd] and every foll 6th [6th: 6th: 4th: 4th] row to 64 [74: 78: 58: 66] sts, then on every foll 8th [-: -: 6th: 6th] row until there are 70 [-: -: 82: 86] sts, taking inc sts into patt.

Cont straight until sleeve meas 46 [46: 47: 47: 47] cm, ending with RS facing for next row.

Shape top

Keeping patt correct, cast off 4 [5: 6: 7: 8] sts at beg of next 2 rows. 62 [64: 66: 68: 70] sts.

Dec 1 st at each end of next 3 rows, then on foll 3 alt rows, then on 2 foll 4th rows.

46 [48: 50: 52: 54] sts.

Work 1 row, ending with RS facing for next row.

Dec 1 st at each end of next and every foll alt row until 36 sts rem, then on foll 7 rows, ending with RS facing for next row.

Cast off rem 22 sts.

MAKING UP

Press as described on the information page.

Join both shoulder seams using back stitch, or mattress stitch if preferred.

Collar

With RS facing and using 4mm (US 6) circular needle, pick up and knit 15 [15: 17: 17: 19] sts down left side of front neck, K across 22 sts on front holder, pick up and knit 15 [15: 17: 17: 19] sts up right side of front neck, and 5 sts down right side of back neck, K across 28 [28: 30: 30: 32] sts on back holder, then pick up and knit 5 sts up left side of back neck. 90 [90: 96: 96: 102] sts.

Round 1 (RS): *K1, P1, rep from * to end.

Rep last round 9 times more.

Round 11: *K1, inc purlwise in next st, rep from * to end. 135 [135: 144: 144: 153] sts.

Round 12: *K1, P2, rep from * to end.

Rep last round 9 times more.

Round 22: *Inc in next st, P2, rep from * to end. 180 [180: 192: 192: 204] sts.

Round 23: *K2, P2, rep from * to end.

Rep last round until collar meas 22 cm from pick-up round.

Cast off in rib.

See information page for finishing instructions, setting in sleeves using the set-in method.

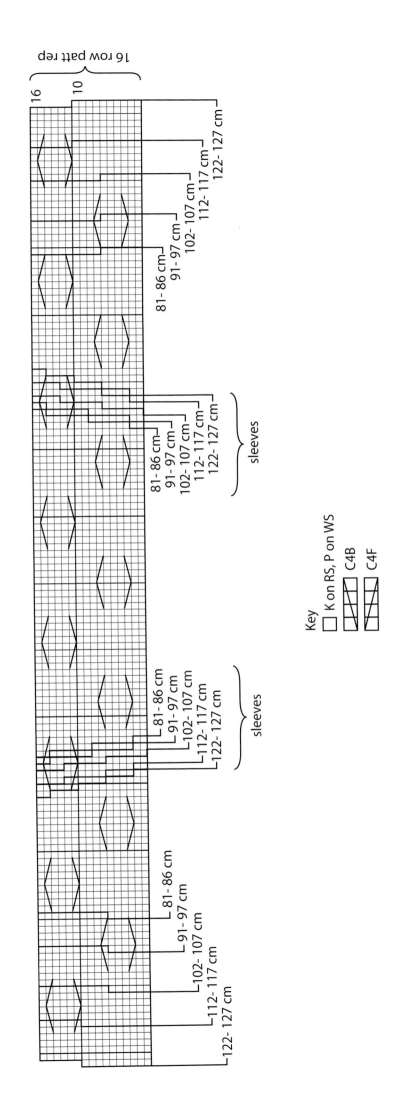

Key

☐ K on RS, P on WS

C4B

C4F

DAYBREAK

Marie Wallin

Main image page **91**

SIZE

To fit bust

81-86	91-97	102-107	112-117	122-127	cm
32-34	36-38	40-42	44-46	48-50	in

Actual bust measurement of garment

89	100	111	121	132	cm
35	39½	43½	47½	52	in

YARN

Kid Classic

9	10	10	11	13	x 50gm

(photographed in Canard 871)

NEEDLES

1 pair 3½mm (no 10/9) (US 4) needles
1 pair 4mm (no 8) (US 6) needles

TENSION

30 sts and 27 rows to 10 cm measured over patt
using 4mm (US 6) needles.

SPECIAL ABBREVIATIONS

Tw2 = K into back of 2nd st on left needle, K
first st and slip both sts off left needle together.

BACK

Using 3½mm (US 4) needles cast on 134 [150:
166: 182: 198] sts.
Row 1 (RS): P2, ★K2, P2, rep from ★ to end.
Row 2: K2, ★P2, K2, rep from ★ to end.
These 2 rows form rib patt.
Work in rib patt for a further 10 rows, ending
with RS facing for next row.
Change to 4mm (US 6) needles.
Cont in rib patt until back meas 9 [10: 11: 13: 14]
cm, ending with RS facing for next row.
Beg and ending rows as indicated, working chart
rows 1 to 96 **once only** and then repeating chart
rows 97 to 100 **throughout**, cont in patt from
chart for body as folls:
Cont straight until back meas 38 [38.5: 39: 39.5:
40] cm, ending with RS facing for next row.

Shape armholes

Keeping patt correct, cast off 5 [6: 7: 8: 9] sts at beg
of next 2 rows. 124 [138: 152: 166: 180] sts.
Dec 1 st at each end of next 5 [7: 9: 11: 13] rows,
then on foll 3 [4: 5: 6: 6] alt rows.
108 [116: 124: 132: 142] sts.
Cont straight until armhole meas 18 [19.5: 21:
22.5: 24] cm, ending with RS facing for next row.
Shape back neck and shoulders
Next row (RS): Cast off 6 [7: 8: 9: 10] sts, patt
until there are 25 [28: 30: 33: 36] sts on right
needle and turn, leaving rem sts on a holder.
Work each side of neck separately.
Dec 1 st at neck edge of next 4 rows **and at
same time** cast off 7 [8: 8: 9: 10] sts at beg of 2nd
row, then 7 [8: 9: 10: 11] sts at beg of foll alt row.
Work 1 row.
Cast off rem 7 [8: 9: 10: 11] sts.
With RS facing, slip centre 46 [46: 48: 48: 50] sts
onto a holder, rejoin yarn and patt to end.
Complete to match first side, reversing shapings.

FRONT

Work as given for back until 10 [10: 12: 12: 14]
rows less have been worked than on back to beg
of shoulder shaping, ending with RS facing for
next row.
Shape front neck
Next row (RS): Patt 36 [40: 44: 48: 53] sts and
turn, leaving rem sts on a holder.
Work each side of neck separately.
Keeping patt correct, dec 1 st at neck edge of next
6 rows, then on foll 1 [1: 2: 2: 3] alt rows.
29 [33: 36: 40: 44] sts.
Work 1 row, ending with RS facing for next row.
Shape shoulder
Cast off 6 [7: 8: 9: 10] sts at beg of next and foll
0 [0: 1: 1: 1] alt rows, then 7 [8: 9: 10: 11] sts at beg
of foll 2 [2: 1: 1: 1] alt rows **and at same time**
dec 1 st at neck edge of next and foll alt row.
Work 1 row.
Cast off rem 7 [8: 9: 10: 11] sts.
With RS facing, slip centre 36 sts onto a holder,
rejoin yarn and patt to end.
Complete to match first side, reversing shapings.

SLEEVES

Using 3½mm (US 4) needles cast on 54 [58: 60:
64: 66] sts.
Beg and ending rows as indicated, working chart
rows 1 to 40 **once only** and then repeating chart
rows 41 and 42 **throughout**, cont in patt from
chart for sleeve as folls:
Work 10 rows, ending with RS facing for next
row.
Change to 4mm (US 6) needles.
Cont in patt, shaping sides by inc 1 st at each end
of next and every foll 4th [4th: 4th: 4th: alt] row
to 98 [102: 108: 112: 70] sts, then on every foll 6th
[6th: 6th: 6th: 4th] row until there are 102 [106:
110: 114: 118] sts, taking inc sts into patt.
Cont straight until sleeve meas 44 [44: 45: 45: 45]
cm, ending with RS facing for next row.
Shape top
Keeping patt correct, cast off 5 [6: 7: 8: 9] sts at beg
of next 2 rows. 92 [94: 96: 98: 100] sts.
Dec 1 st at each end of next 9 rows, then on every
foll alt row until 68 sts rem, then on foll 7 rows,
ending with RS facing for next row. 54 sts.
Cast off 4 sts at beg of next 8 rows.
Cast off rem 22 sts.

MAKING UP

Press as described on the information page.
Join right shoulder seam using back stitch, or
mattress stitch if preferred.
Neckband
With RS facing and using 3½mm (US 4) needles,
pick up and knit 13 [13: 15: 15: 17] sts down left
side of front neck, K across 36 sts on front holder
as folls: K3, (K2tog, K2) 8 times, K1, pick up and
knit 13 [13: 15: 15: 17] sts up right side of front
neck, and 5 sts down right side of back neck, K
across 46 [46: 48: 48: 50] sts on back holder as folls:
K0 [0: 1: 1: 2], (K2tog, K2) 11 times, K2tog, K0 [0:
1: 1: 2], then pick up and knit 5 sts up left side of
back neck. 98 [98: 104: 104: 110] sts.
Cast off knitwise (on **WS**).
See information page for finishing instructions,
setting in sleeves using the set-in method.

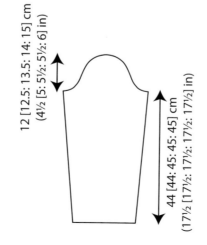

12 [12.5: 13.5: 14: 15] cm
(4½ [5: 5½: 5½: 6] in)

44 [44: 45: 45: 45] cm
(17½ [17½: 17½: 17½: 17½] in)

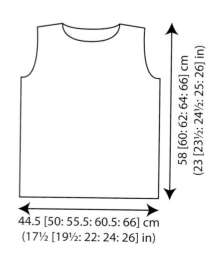

58 [60: 62: 64: 66] cm
(23 [23½: 24½: 25: 26] in)

44.5 [50: 55.5: 60.5: 66] cm
(17½ [19½: 22: 24: 26] in)

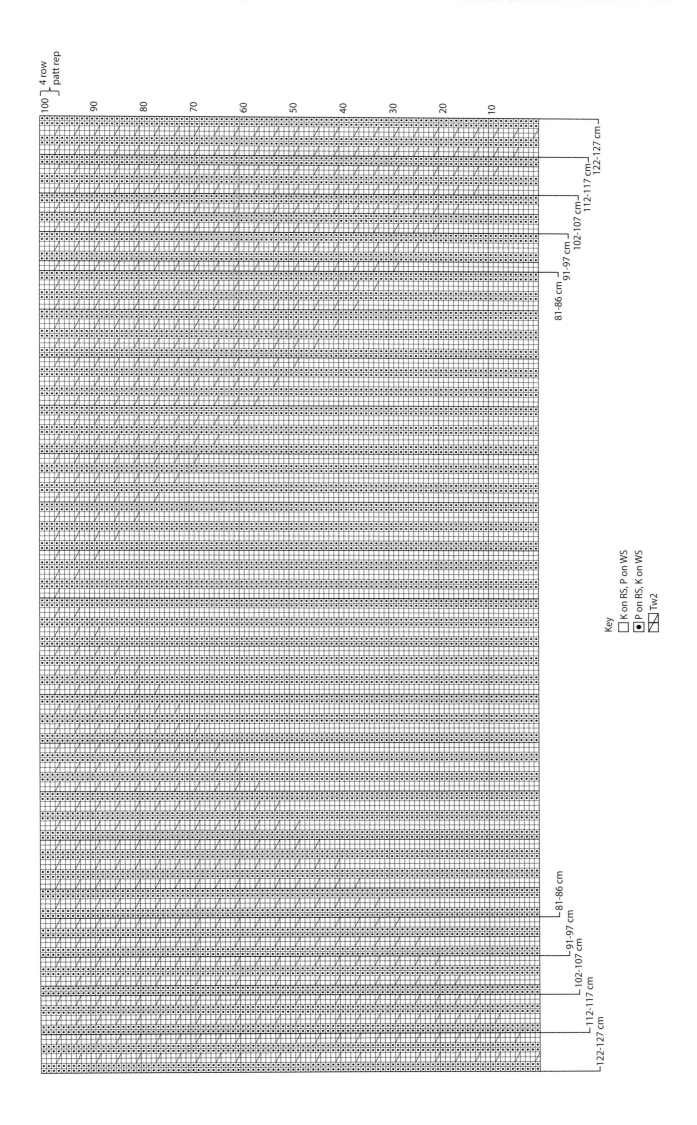

Key
□ K on RS, P on WS
● P on RS, K on WS
◪ Tw2

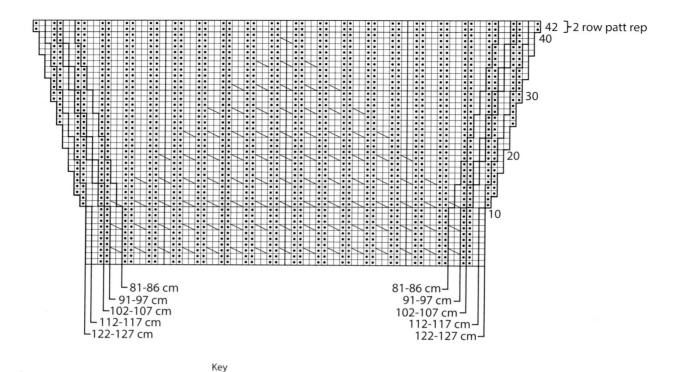

81-86 cm
91-97 cm
102-107 cm
112-117 cm
122-127 cm

81-86 cm
91-97 cm
102-107 cm
112-117 cm
122-127 cm

42 } 2 row patt rep
40
30
20
10

Key
☐ K on RS, P on WS
⊡ P on RS, K on WS
◩ Tw2

OXTON
Sarah Hatton
Main image page **4, 9**
● ● ●

SIZE
To fit bust

| 81-86 | 91-97 | 102-107 | 112-117 | 122-127 | cm |
| 32-34 | 36-38 | 40-42 | 44-46 | 48-50 | in |

Actual bust measurement of garment

| 106 | 115 | 127 | 136 | 146 | cm |
| 41½ | 45½ | 50 | 53½ | 57½ | in |

YARN
Kid Classic

| 8 | 9 | 10 | 10 | 11 | x 50gm |

(photographed in Henna 891)

NEEDLES
1 pair 4mm (no 8) (US 6) needles
1 pair 4½mm (no 7) (US 7) needles

TENSION
21 sts and 28 rows to 10 cm measured over patt,
20 sts and 28 rows to 10 cm measured over st st,
both using 4½mm (US 7) needles.

Pattern note: When working patt from chart,
take care to ensure each dec of patt is matched by
an inc. If there are insufficient sts to work both,
work end sts of rows in double moss st.

BACK
Using 4mm (US 6) needles cast on 110 [122: 134:
142: 154] sts.
Row 1 (RS): K2, *P2, K2, rep from * to end.
Row 2: P2, *K2, P2, rep from * to end.
These 2 rows form rib.
Work in rib for a further 10 rows, inc [dec: dec:
inc: dec] 1 st at end of last row and ending with
RS facing for next row.
111 [121: 133: 143: 153] sts.
Change to 4½mm (US 7) needles.
Beg and ending rows as indicated, repeating the
26 st patt repeat 4 times across each row, working
chart rows 1 and 2 **once only** and then repeating
chart rows 3 to 38 **throughout**, cont in patt from
chart as folls:
Cont straight until back meas 42 [42.5: 43: 43.5:
44] cm, ending with RS facing for next row.

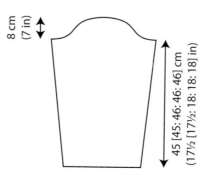

8 cm
(7 in)

45 [45: 46: 46: 46] cm
(17½ [17½: 18: 18: 18] in)

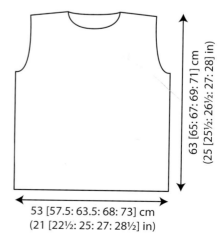

63 [65: 67: 69: 71] cm
(25 [25½: 26½: 27: 28] in)

53 [57.5: 63.5: 68: 73] cm
(21 [22½: 25: 27: 28½] in)

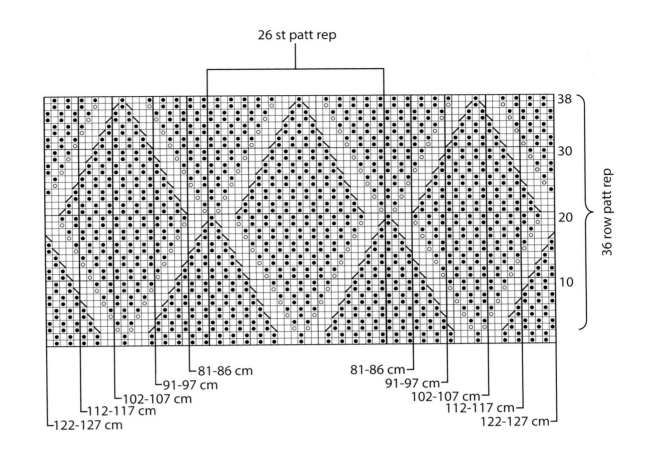

Key

☐ K on RS, P on WS

▣ P on RS, K on WS

◩ yfwd

◪ K2tog

◿ sl 1, K1, psso

26 st patt rep

38
30
20
10

36 row patt rep

81-86 cm
91-97 cm
102-107 cm
112-117 cm
122-127 cm

81-86 cm
91-97 cm
102-107 cm
112-117 cm
122-127 cm

Shape armholes

Keeping patt correct, cast off 5 sts at beg of next 2 rows. 101 [111: 123: 133: 143] sts.

Dec 1 st at each end of next and foll 5 alt rows. 89 [99: 111: 121: 131] sts.

Cont straight until armhole meas 20 [21.5: 23: 24.5: 26] cm, ending with RS facing for next row.

Shape shoulders and back neck

Next row (RS): Cast off 11 [14: 16: 19: 21] sts, patt until there are 15 [17: 20: 22: 24] sts on right needle and turn, leaving rem sts on a holder.

Work each side of neck separately.

Cast off 3 sts at beg of next row.

Cast off rem 12 [14: 17: 19: 21] sts.

With RS facing, slip centre 37 [37: 39: 39: 41] sts onto a holder, rejoin yarn and patt to end.

Complete to match first side, reversing shapings.

FRONT

Work as given for back until 14 [14: 16: 16: 18] rows less have been worked than on back to beg of shoulder shaping, ending with RS facing for next row.

Shape front neck

Next row (RS): Patt 32 [37: 43: 48: 53] sts and turn, leaving rem sts on a holder.

Work each side of neck separately.

Keeping patt correct, dec 1 st at neck edge of next 6 rows, then on foll 3 [3: 4: 4: 5] alt rows. 23 [28: 33: 38: 42] sts.

Work 1 row, ending with RS facing for next row.

Shape shoulder

Cast off 11 [14: 16: 19: 21] sts at beg of next row.

Work 1 row.

Cast off rem 12 [14: 17: 19: 21] sts.

With RS facing, slip centre 25 sts onto a holder, rejoin yarn and patt to end.

Complete to match first side, reversing shapings.

SLEEVES

Using 4mm (US 6) needles cast on 38 [40: 42: 42: 44] sts.

Row 1 (RS): P0 [1: 0: 0: 1], K2, ★P2, K2, rep from ★ to last 0 [1: 0: 0: 1] st, P0 [1: 0: 0: 1].

Row 2: K0 [1: 0: 0: 1], P2, ★K2, P2, rep from ★ to last 0 [1: 0: 0: 1] st, K0 [1: 0: 0: 1].

These 2 rows form rib.

Work in rib for a further 12 rows, ending with RS facing for next row.

Change to 4½mm (US 7) needles.

Beg with a K row, cont in st st throughout as folls:

Inc 1 st at each end of 3rd [3rd: 3rd: 3rd: next] and every foll 4th [4th: 4th: 4th: alt] row to 42 [56: 68: 86: 48] sts, then on every foll 6th [6th: 6th: 6th: 4th] row until there are 72 [78: 84: 90: 96] sts.

Cont straight until sleeve meas 45 [45: 46: 46: 46] cm, ending with RS facing for next row.

Shape top

Cast off 5 sts at beg of next 2 rows. 62 [68: 74: 80: 86] sts.

Dec 1 st at each end of next and foll 4 alt rows, then on foll row, ending with RS facing for next

row. 50 [56: 62: 68: 74] sts.

Cast off 3 [3: 4: 4: 5] sts at beg of next 6 [2: 8: 4: 10] rows, then 4 [4: 5: 5: -] sts at beg of foll 4 [8: 2: 6: -] rows.

Cast off rem 16 [18: 20: 22: 24] sts.

MAKING UP

Press as described on the information page.

Join right shoulder seam using back stitch, or mattress stitch if preferred.

Collar

With RS facing and using 4mm (US 6) needles, pick up and knit 15 [15: 18: 18: 19] sts down left side of front neck, K across 25 sts on front holder, pick up and knit 15 [15: 18: 18: 19] sts up right side of front neck, and 3 sts down right side of back neck, K across 37 [37: 39: 39: 41] sts on back holder, then pick up and knit 3 sts up left side of back neck. 98 [98: 106: 106: 110] sts.

Beg with row 1, work in rib as given for back until collar meas 10 cm from pick-up row.

Change to 4½mm (US 7) needles.

Cont in rib until collar meas 20 cm from pick-up row, ending with **WS** of body (RS of collar) facing for next row.

Cast off in rib.

See information page for finishing instructions, setting in sleeves using the shallow set-in method and reversing collar seam for last 11 cm (for turn-back).

DIMMET

Lisa Richardson
Main image page **84, 85, 87**

SIZE
To fit bust
81-86 91-97 102-107 112-117 122-127 cm
32-34 36-38 40-42 44-46 48-50 in
Actual bust measurement of garment
90 100 110 121 130 cm
35½ 39½ 43½ 47½ 51 in

YARN
Kidsilk Haze
3 4 4 5 5 x 25gm
(photographed in Mulberry 679)

NEEDLES
1 pair 2¾mm (no 12) (US 2) needles
1 pair 3¼mm (no 10) (US 3) needles

TENSION
25 sts and 34 rows to 10 cm measured over st st
using 3¼mm (US 3) needles.

BACK
Using 2¾mm (US 2) needles cast on 113 [125:
137: 151: 163] sts **loosely**.
Work in g st for 6 rows, ending with RS facing for
next row.
Change to 3¼mm (US 3) needles.
Beg with a K row, work in st st throughout as folls:
Cont straight until back meas 7 [8: 9: 11: 12] cm,
ending with RS facing for next row.
Next row (RS): K2, sl 1, K1, psso, K to last 4 sts,
K2tog, K2.
Working all side seam decreases as set by last row,
dec 1 st at each end of 8th and 3 foll 8th rows.
103 [115: 127: 141: 153] sts.
Work 13 [13: 13: 11: 11] rows, ending with RS
facing for next row.
Next row (RS): K3, M1, K to last 3 sts, M1, K3.
Working all side seam increases as set by last row,
inc 1 st at each end of 6th and 3 foll 6th rows.
113 [125: 137: 151: 163] sts.
Cont straight until back meas 32 [32.5: 33: 33.5:

34] cm, ending with RS facing for next row.
Shape cap sleeves
Place markers at both ends of last row (to denote
base of armhole openings).
Next row (RS): Knit.
Next row: K3, P to last 3 sts, K3.
Last 2 rows set the sts – armhole edge 3 sts in g st
with all other sts still in st st.
Keeping sts correct as now set, cont as folls:
Next row (RS): K6, M1, K to last 6 sts, M1, K6.
Work 2 rows.
Next row (WS): K3, P3, M1P, P to last 6 sts, M1P,
P3, K3. 117 [129: 141: 155: 167] sts.
Work 2 rows.★★
Working all cap sleeve increases as set by last 6
rows, inc 1 st at each end of next and 16 [17: 19:
21: 22] foll 3rd rows. 151 [165: 181: 199: 213] sts.
Work 1 [2: 2: 2: 3] rows, ending with RS facing
for next row.
Shape shoulders
Cast off 3 [3: 4: 4: 5] sts at beg of next 20 [6: 24: 6:
24] rows, then 4 [4: -: 5: -] sts at beg of foll 4 [18: -:
18: -] rows. 75 [75: 85: 85: 93] sts.
Shape back neck
Next row (RS): Cast off 4 [4: 5: 5: 5] sts, K until
there are 17 [17: 20: 20: 23] sts on right needle and
turn, leaving rem sts on a holder.
Work each side of neck separately.
Dec 1 st at neck edge of next 5 rows, ending with
RS facing for next row, **and at same time** cast
off 4 [4: 5: 5: 6] sts at beg of 2nd and foll alt row.
Cast off rem 4 [4: 5: 5: 6] sts.
With RS facing, slip centre 33 [33: 35: 35: 37] sts
onto a holder (for neckband), rejoin yarn and K
to end.
Complete to match first side, reversing shapings.

FRONT
Work as given for back to ★★.
Working all cap sleeve increases as set by last 6
rows, inc 1 st at each end of next and 9 [10: 11: 13:
13] foll 3rd rows. 137 [151: 165: 183: 195] sts.
Work 0 [1: 0: 0: 0] rows, ending with RS facing
for next row.
Shape front neck
Next row (RS): K55 [62: 69: 78: 84] and turn,
leaving rem sts on a holder.
Work each side of neck separately.

Next row (WS): P2, P2tog, P to last 3 [6: 3: 3: 3]
sts, (M1P, P3) 0 [1: 0: 0: 0] times, K3.
Next row: (K6, M1) 1 [0: 1: 1: 1] times, K to last
4 sts, K2tog, K2. 54 [61: 68: 77: 83] sts.
Working all neck shaping as set by last 2 rows (and
all cap sleeve shaping as set), cont as folls:
Inc 1 st at cap sleeve edge of 3rd [2nd: 3rd: 3rd:
3rd] and 5 [5: 6: 6: 7] foll 3rd rows **and at same
time** dec 1 st at neck edge of next 2 rows, then on
foll alt row, then on 3 [3: 4: 4: 5] foll 4th rows.
54 [61: 68: 77: 83] sts.
Work 1 [2: 2: 2: 3] rows, ending with RS facing
for next row.
Shape shoulder
Cast off 3 [3: 4: 4: 5] sts at beg of next and foll
9 [2: 11: 2: 12] alt rows, then 4 [4: 5: 5: 6] sts at beg
of foll 5 [12: 3: 12: 2] alt rows.
Work 1 row.
Cast off rem 4 [4: 5: 5: 6] sts.
With RS facing, slip centre 27 sts onto a holder
(for neckband), rejoin yarn and K to end.
Next row (WS): K3, (P3, M1P) 0 [1: 0: 0: 0]
times, P to last 4 sts, P2tog tbl, P2.
Next row: K2, sl 1, K1, psso, K to last 6 [0: 6: 6: 6]
sts, (M1, K6) 1 [0: 1: 1: 1] times.
54 [61: 68: 77: 83] sts.
Complete to match first side, reversing shapings.

MAKING UP
Press as described on the information page.
Join right shoulder seam using back stitch, or
mattress stitch if preferred.
Neckband
With RS facing and using 2¾mm (US 2) needles,
pick up and knit 39 [39: 42: 42: 45] sts down left
side of front neck, K 27 sts on front holder, pick
up and knit 39 [39: 42: 42: 45] sts up right side of
front neck, and 5 sts down right side of back neck,
K 33 [33: 35: 35: 37] sts on back holder, then pick
up and knit 5 sts up left side of back neck.
148 [148: 156: 156: 164] sts.
Work in g st for 4 rows, ending with **WS** facing
for next row.
Cast off **very loosely** knitwise (on **WS**).
See information page for finishing instructions,
leaving side seams open above markers (for
armhole openings).

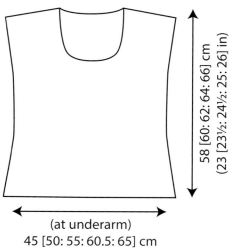

58 [60: 62: 64: 66] cm
(23 [23½: 24½: 25: 26] in)

(at underarm)
45 [50: 55: 60.5: 65] cm
(17½ [19½: 21½: 24: 25½] in)

BIELBY

Martin Storey

Main image page **35**

● ●

SIZE
To fit bust
81-86 91-97 102-107 112-117 122-127 cm
32-34 36-38 40-42 44-46 48-50 in
Actual bust measurement of garment
128 138 148 158 168 cm
50½ 54½ 58½ 62 66 in

YARN
Felted Tweed Aran
13 14 15 17 18 x 50gm
(photographed in Clay 777)

NEEDLES
1 pair 4½mm (no 7) (US 7) needles
1 pair 5mm (no 6) (US 8) needles
Cable needle

BUTTONS - 1 x BN1368 from Bedecked. Please
see information for contact details.

TENSION
16 sts and 29 rows to 10 cm measured over patt
using 5mm (US 8) needles.

SPECIAL ABBREVIATIONS
C12B = slip next 6 sts onto cable needle and leave
at back of work, K6, then K6 from cable needle.

BACK
Using 4½mm (US 7) needles cast on 102 [110:
118: 126: 134] sts.
Row 1 (RS): K2, ★P2, K2, rep from ★ to end.
Row 2: P2, ★K2, P2, rep from ★ to end.
These 2 rows form rib.
Work in rib for a further 6 rows, ending with RS
facing for next row.
Change to 5mm (US 8) needles.
Now work in patt as folls:
Row 1 (RS): K2, ★bring yarn to front (RS) of
work, slip next 2 sts purlwise, then take yarn back to
WS of work, leaving strand of yarn "sitting" in front

---

of slipped sts on RS of work, K2, rep from ★ to end.
Row 2: Purl.
These 2 rows form patt.
Cont in patt until back meas 58 [60: 62: 64: 66] cm,
ending with RS facing for next row.
Shape shoulders
Keeping patt correct, cast off 3 [3: 3: 4: 4] sts at beg
of next 18 [10: 2: 24: 16] rows, then 4 [4: 4: 5: 5] sts
at beg of foll 11 [19: 27: 5: 13] rows, ending with
WS facing for next row.
Cast off rem 4 [4: 4: 5: 5] sts, placing marker after
last cast-off st (to denote centre back neck).

POCKET LININGS (make 2)
Using 5mm (US 8) needles cast on 28 sts.
Beg with a K row, work in st st for 12 cm, ending
with RS facing for next row.
Break yarn and leave sts on a holder.

LEFT FRONT
Using 4½mm (US 7) needles cast on 51 [55: 59:
63: 67] sts.
Row 1 (RS): K2, ★P2, K2, rep from ★ to last st, K1.
Row 2: K1, P2, ★K2, P2, rep from ★ to end.
These 2 rows form rib.
Work in rib for a further 6 rows, ending with RS
facing for next row.
Change to 5mm (US 8) needles.
Now work in patt as folls:
Row 1 (RS): K2, ★bring yarn to front (RS) of
work, slip next 2 sts purlwise, then take yarn back
to WS of work, leaving strand of yarn "sitting" in
front of slipped sts on RS of work, K2, rep from
★ to last st, K1.
Row 2: K1, P to end.
These 2 rows form patt.
Cont in patt until left front meas 15 cm, ending
with RS facing for next row.
Place pocket
Next row (RS): Patt 9 [13: 13: 17: 17] sts, slip
next 28 sts onto a holder and, in their place, patt
across 28 sts of first pocket lining, patt 14 [14: 18:
18: 22] sts.
Cont straight until left front matches back to beg
of shoulder shaping, ending with RS facing for
next row.
Shape shoulder
Keeping patt correct, cast off 3 [3: 3: 4: 4] sts at beg
of next and foll 8 [4: 0: 11: 7] alt rows, then 4 [4: 4:
5: 5] sts at beg of foll 5 [9: 13: 2: 6] alt rows.
Work 1 row.
Cast off rem 4 [4: 4: 5: 5] sts.

RIGHT FRONT
Using 4½mm (US 7) needles cast on 51 [55: 59:
63: 67] sts.

Row 1 (RS): K3, ★P2, K2, rep from ★ to end.
Row 2: P2, ★K2, P2, rep from ★ to last st, K1.
These 2 rows form rib.
Work in rib for a further 6 rows, ending with RS
facing for next row.
Change to 5mm (US 8) needles.
Now work in patt as folls:
Row 1 (RS): K3, ★bring yarn to front (RS) of
work, slip next 2 sts purlwise, then take yarn back
to WS of work, leaving strand of yarn "sitting" in
front of slipped sts on RS of work, K2, rep from
★ to end.
Row 2: P to last st, K1.
These 2 rows form patt.
Cont in patt until right front meas 15 cm, ending
with RS facing for next row.
Place pocket
Next row (RS): Patt 14 [14: 18: 18: 22] sts, slip
next 28 sts onto a holder and, in their place, patt
across 28 sts of second pocket lining, patt 9 [13: 13:
17: 17] sts.
Complete to match left front, reversing shapings.

MAKING UP
Press as described on the information page.
Noting that front opening edges meet at marked
centre back neck point, join both shoulder seams
using back stitch, or mattress stitch if preferred.
Mark points along side seam edges 23 [24.5: 25:
26.5: 28] cm either side of shoulder seams (to
denote base of armhole opening).
Cuffs (both alike)
With RS facing and using 4½mm (US 7) needles,
pick up and knit 79 [83: 87: 91: 95] sts evenly
along armhole edge between markers.
Row 1 (WS): P1 tbl, ★K1 tbl, P1 tbl, rep from
★ to end.
Row 2: K1 tbl, ★P1 tbl, K1 tbl, rep from ★ to end.
These 2 rows form twisted rib.
Cont in twisted rib until cuff meas 11 cm **from
pick-up row**, ending with RS facing for next
row.
Cast off in twisted rib.
Pocket tops (both alike)
Slip 28 sts on pocket holder onto 4½mm (US 7)
needles and rejoin yarn with RS facing.
Row 1 (RS): K1, K1 tbl, P1 tbl, K1 tbl, M1,
(K1 tbl, P1 tbl) 5 times, M1, (P1 tbl, K1 tbl) 5
times, M1, K1 tbl, P1 tbl, K1 tbl, K1. 31 sts.
Row 2: K1, ★P1 tbl, K1 tbl, rep from ★ to last
2 sts, P1 tbl, K1.
Row 3: K1, ★K1 tbl, P1 tbl, rep from ★ to last
2 sts, K1 tbl, K1.
Rep last 2 rows once more, then row 2 again,
ending with RS facing for next row.
Cast off in twisted rib.

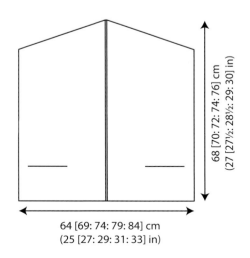

68 [70: 72: 74: 76] cm
(27 [27½: 28½: 29: 30] in)

64 [69: 74: 79: 84] cm
(25 [27: 29: 31: 33] in)

Front band
Using 4½mm (US 7) needles cast on 8 sts.
Row 1 (RS): Knit.
Row 2: K2, M1, (K1, M1) 5 times, K1. 14 sts.
Now work in patt as folls:
Row 1 (RS): K1, P1, K12.
Row 2: P12, K2.
Rows 3 and 4: As rows 1 and 2.
Row 5: K1, P1, C12B.

Row 6: As row 2.
Rows 7 and 8: As rows 1 and 2.
Last 8 rows form patt.
Cont in patt until band, when slightly stretched, fits up left front opening edge, then down right front opening edge to just above cast-on edge, ending after patt row 8 and with RS facing for next row.
Next row (RS): K1, (K2tog) 6 times, K1. 8 sts.

Work in g st for 2 rows, ending with **WS** facing for next row.
Cast off knitwise (on **WS**).
Neatly sew front band in place.
See information page for finishing instructions.
Using photograph as a guide, make button loop and attach button to fasten front opening edges.

FISHLAKE
Marie Wallin
Main image page **33, 34**
● ● ●

SIZE
To fit bust
81-86 91-97 102-107 112-117 122-127 cm
32-34 36-38 40-42 44-46 48-50 in
Actual bust measurement of garment
92   102   113   122   132   cm
36   40   44½   48   52   in

YARN
Felted Tweed

A Camel 157					
5	5	6	6	7	x 50gm
B Phantom 153					
3	3	3	4	4	x 50gm
C Cinnamon 175					
1	1	1	1	1	x 50gm

NEEDLES
1 pair 2¾mm (no 12) (US 2) needles
1 pair 3mm (no 11) (US 2/3) needles
1 pair 3¼mm (no 10) (US 3) needles

TENSION
25 sts and 36 rows to 10 cm measured over st st using 3mm (US 2/3) needles. 25 sts and 30 rows

to 10 cm measured over patt using 3¼mm (US 3) needles.

BACK
Using 2¾mm (US 2) needles and yarn B cast on 115 [127: 141: 153: 165] sts.
Row 1 (RS): K1, *P1, K1, rep from * to end.
Row 2: As row 1.
These 2 rows form moss st.
Work in moss st for a further 8 rows, ending with RS facing for next row.
Break off yarn B and join in yarn C.
Work in g st for 4 rows, ending with RS facing for next row.
Change to 3¼mm (US 3) needles.
Break off C and join in yarn A.
Next row (RS): Knit.
Noting that chart row 1 is a **WS** row, beg and ending rows as indicated, using the **fairisle** technique as described on the information page and repeating the 12 row patt repeat throughout, cont in patt from chart as folls:
Cont straight until back meas 36 [36.5: 37: 37.5: 38] cm, ending with RS facing for next row.
Shape raglan armholes
Keeping patt correct, cast off 3 sts at beg of next 2 rows. 109 [121: 135: 147: 159] sts.
Next row (RS): Using yarn A K2, sl 1, K1, psso, patt to last 4 sts, using yarn A K2tog, K2.
Next row: Using yarn A P2, P2tog, patt to last 4 sts, using yarn A P2tog tbl, P2.
Rep last 2 rows 8 [12: 15: 19: 22] times more. 73 [69: 71: 67: 67] sts.
Next row (RS): Using yarn A K2, sl 1, K1, psso, patt to last 4 sts, using yarn A K2tog, K2.
Next row: Using yarn A P3, patt to last 3 sts,

using yarn A P3.
Rep last 2 rows 16 [14: 14: 12: 11] times more, ending with RS facing for next row.
39 [39: 41: 41: 43] sts.
Break yarns and leave sts on a holder.

FRONT
Work as given for back until 51 [51: 55: 55: 59] sts rem in raglan armhole shaping.
Work 1 row, ending with RS facing for next row.
Shape front neck
Next row (RS): Using yarn A K2, sl 1, K1, psso, patt 7 [7: 9: 9: 11] sts and turn, leaving rem sts on a holder. 10 [10: 12: 12: 14] sts.
Work each side of neck separately.
Keeping raglan decreases and patt correct, dec 1 st at neck edge of next 4 rows, then on foll 0 [0: 1: 1: 2] alt rows **and at same time** dec 1 st at raglan armhole edge of 2nd and foll 1 [1: 2: 2: 3] alt rows. 4 sts.
Work 1 row, ending with RS facing for next row.
Next row (RS): Using yarn A K1, sl 1, K2tog, psso. 2 sts.
Next row: Using yarn A P2.
Next row: Using yarn A K2tog and fasten off.
With RS facing, slip centre 29 sts onto a holder, rejoin yarns and patt to last 4 sts, using yarn A K2tog, K2. 10 [10: 12: 12: 14] sts.
Complete to match first side, reversing shapings.

SLEEVES
Using 2¾mm (US 2) needles and yarn B cast on 45 [47: 51: 51: 53] sts.
Work in moss st as given for back for 10 rows, ending with RS facing for next row.
Break off yarn B and join in yarn C.

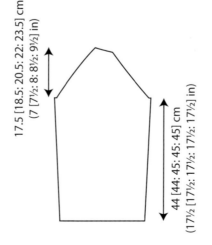

17.5 [18.5: 20.5: 22: 23.5] cm
(7 [7½: 8: 8½: 9½] in)

44 [44: 45: 45: 45] cm
(17½ [17½: 17½: 17½: 17½] in)

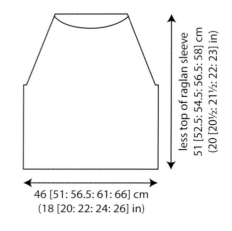

less top of raglan sleeve
51 [52.5: 54.5: 56.5: 58] cm
(20 [20½: 21½: 22: 23] in)

46 [51: 56.5: 61: 66] cm
(18 [20: 22: 24: 26] in)

Work in g st for 4 rows, ending with RS facing for next row.

Change to 3mm (US 2/3) needles.

Break off yarn C and join in yarn A.

Beg with a K row, work in st st, shaping sides by inc 1 st at each end of 3rd [3rd: 3rd: 3rd: next] and 2 [11: 15: 27: 2] foll 4th [4th: 4th: 4th: alt] rows, then on 17 [11: 9: 1: 29] foll 6th [6th: 6th: 6th: 4th] rows. 85 [93: 101: 109: 117] sts.

Work 4 [4: 4: 4: 0] rows, ending with **WS** facing for next row.

Change to 3¼mm (US 3) needles.

Noting that chart row 1 is a **WS** row and beg and ending rows as indicated, cont in patt from chart as folls:

Inc 1 st at each end of 2nd [2nd: 2nd: 2nd: 4th] and foll 6th [6th: 6th: 6th: 4th] row, taking inc sts into patt. 89 [97: 105: 113: 121] sts.

Work 13 rows, ending after chart row 9 and with RS facing for next row.

Break off yarn B.

Change to 3mm (US 2/3) needles.

Beg with a K row, complete sleeve in st st using yarn A **only** as folls:

Cont straight until sleeve meas 44 [44: 45: 45: 45] cm, ending with RS facing for next row.

Shape raglan

Cast off 3 sts at beg of next 2 rows.

83 [91: 99: 107: 115] sts.

Next row (RS): K2, sl 1, K1, psso, K to last 4 sts, K2tog, K2.

Next row: (P2, P2tog) 0 [0: 1: 1: 1] times, P to last 0 [0: 4: 4: 4] sts, (P2tog tbl, P2) 0 [0: 1: 1: 1] times.

Working all raglan decreases as set by last 2 rows, dec 1 st at each end of 3rd [next: next: next: next] and foll 0 [0: 0: 2: 6] rows, then on every foll alt row until 27 sts rem.

Work 1 row, ending with RS facing for next row.

Left sleeve only

Dec 1 st at each end of next row, then cast off 8 sts at beg of foll row. 17 sts.

Dec 1 st at beg of next row, then cast off 8 sts at beg of foll row.

Right sleeve only

Cast off 9 sts at beg and dec 1 st at end of next row. 17 sts.

Work 1 row.

Cast off 8 sts at beg and dec 1 st at end of next row.

Work 1 row.

Both sleeves

Cast off rem 8 sts.

MAKING UP

Press as described on the information page.

Join both front and right back raglan seams using back stitch, or mattress stitch if preferred. (**Note:** Due to difference in row tensions, there will be 10 [12: 12: 14: 14] more rows in sleeve raglan edges than body raglan edges but edges should be same length.)

Neckband

With RS facing, using 2¾mm (US 2) needles and yarn B, pick up and knit 23 sts from top of left sleeve, 7 [7: 9: 9: 11] sts down left side of front neck, K across 29 sts on front holder, pick up and knit 7 [7: 9: 9: 11] sts up right side of front neck, and 23 sts from top of right sleeve, then K across 39 [39: 41: 41: 43] sts on back holder dec 1 st at centre. 127 [127: 133: 133: 139] sts.

Work in moss st as given for back for 7 rows, ending with RS facing for next row.

Cast off in moss st.

See information page for finishing instructions.

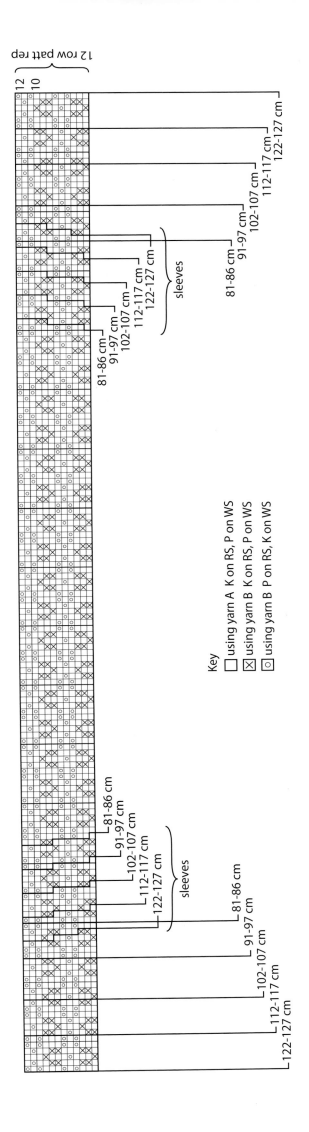

12 row patt rep

Key
☐ using yarn A K on RS, P on WS
☒ using yarn B K on RS, P on WS
⊙ using yarn B P on RS, K on WS

sleeves

81-86 cm
91-97 cm
102-107 cm
112-117 cm
122-127 cm

SIZE
To fit bust

81–97	97–112	112–127	cm
32–38	38–44	44–50	in

Actual bust measurement of garment

124	143	162	cm
49	56½	64	in

YARN
Kid Classic

14	16	19	x 50gm

(photographed in Bitter Sweet 866)

NEEDLES
1 pair 4½mm (no 7) (US 7) needles
1 pair 5mm (no 6) (US 8) needles
4½mm (no 7) (US 7) circular needle no more
than 60 cm long
5mm (no 6) (US 8) circular needle no more than
60 cm long
Cable needle

TENSION
22 sts and 25 rows to 10 cm measured over patt
using 5mm (US 8) needles.

SPECIAL ABBREVIATIONS
C4B = slip next 2 sts onto cable needle and leave
at back of work, K2, then K2 from cable needle;
C4F = slip next 2 sts onto cable needle and leave
at front of work, K2, then K2 from cable needle;
C9F = slip next 4 sts onto cable needle and leave
at front of work, K4, P1, then K4 from cable
needle.

BACK
Using 5mm (US 8) needles cast on 136 [157: 178] sts.
Beg and ending rows as indicated, working chart
rows 1 to 40 **once only** and then repeating chart
row 41 to 60 as required, and repeating the 21 st
patt rep 6 [7: 8] times across each row, cont in patt
from chart for body as folls:

Cont straight until back meas 69 [72: 75] cm,
ending with RS facing for next row.
Shape shoulders
Keeping patt correct, cast off 4 [5: 5] sts at beg of
next 14 [14: 2] rows, then – [-: 6] sts at beg of foll
– [-: 12] rows. 80 [87: 96] sts.
Shape back neck
Next row (RS): Cast off 4 [5: 6] sts, patt until
there are 19 [20: 22] sts on right needle and turn,
leaving rem sts on a holder.
Work each side of neck separately.
Dec 1 st at neck edge of next 4 rows **and at
same time** cast off 5 [5: 6] sts at beg of 2nd and
foll alt row.
Work 1 row.
Cast off rem 5 [6: 6] sts.
With RS facing, slip centre 34 [37: 40] sts onto a
holder, rejoin yarn and patt to end.
Complete to match first side, reversing shapings.

FRONT
Work as given for back until 2 [4: 6] rows less have
been worked than on back to beg of shoulder
shaping, ending with RS facing for next row.
Shape front neck
Next row (RS): Patt 57 [67: 77] sts and turn,
leaving rem sts on a holder.
Work each side of neck separately.
Keeping patt correct, dec 1 st at neck edge of next
1 [3: 5] rows, ending with RS facing for next row.
56 [64: 72] sts.
Shape shoulder
Cast off 4 [5: 5] sts at beg of next and foll 7 [9: 0]
alt rows, then 5 [-: 6] sts at beg of foll 2 [-: 9] alt
rows **and at same time** dec 1 st at neck edge of
next 5 [3: 1] rows, then on foll 3 [4: 5] alt rows,
then on foll 4th row.
Work 1 row.
Cast off rem 5 [6: 6] sts.
With RS facing, slip centre 22 [23: 24] sts onto a
holder, rejoin yarn and patt to end.
Complete to match first side, reversing shapings.

SLEEVES
Using 4½mm (US 7) needles cast on 50 [54: 58] sts.
Row 1 (RS): K2, *P2, K2, rep from * to end.
Row 2: P2, *K2, P2, rep from * to end.
These 2 rows form rib.
Cont in rib for a further 10 rows, inc 1 st at centre

of last row and ending with RS facing for next
row. 51 [55: 59] sts.
Change to 5mm (US 8) needles.
Beg and ending rows as indicated and repeating
the 20 row patt repeat throughout, cont in patt
from chart for sleeves as folls:
Inc 1 st at each end of 3rd [next: next] and every
foll 4th [alt: alt] row to 91 [71: 91] sts, then on
every foll 6th [4th: 4th] row until there are
93 [107: 119] sts, taking inc sts into patt.
Cont straight until sleeve meas 44 [45: 45] cm,
ending with RS facing for next row.
Shape top
Keeping patt correct, cast off 3 [4: 4] sts at beg of
next 2 [10: 2] rows, then 4 [5: 5] sts at beg of foll
14 [6: 14] rows.
Cast off rem 31 [37: 41] sts.

MAKING UP
Press as described on the information page.
Join right shoulder seam using back stitch, or
mattress stitch if preferred.
Neckband
With RS facing and using 4½mm (US 7) needles,
pick up and knit 19 [21: 23] sts down left side of
front neck, K across 22 [23: 24] sts on front holder
dec 1 st at centre, pick up and knit 19 [21: 23] sts
up right side of front neck, and 5 sts down right
side of back neck, K across 34 [37: 40] sts on back
holder dec 1 st at centre, then pick up and knit
5 sts up left side of back neck. 102 [110: 118] sts.
Beg with row 2, work in rib as given for sleeves
for 4 rows, ending with **WS** facing for next row.
Cast off in rib (on **WS**).
Join left shoulder and neckband seam. Mark points
along side seam edges 22 [25: 28] cm either side
of shoulder seams (to denote base of armhole
openings). See information page for finishing
instructions, setting in sleeves using the straight
cast-off method and joining side seams for just
15 cm below base of armholes, leaving rest of side
seams open.
Cowl
Using 5mm (US 8) circular needle cast on 168 sts.
Taking care not to twist cast-on edge and placing
marker after last st of first round (to denote beg
and end of rounds), work in rounds as folls:
Beg and ending rounds as indicated and noting
you are working in **rounds**, not rows, and

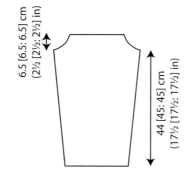

6.5 [6.5: 6.5] cm
(2½ [2½: 2½] in)

44 [45: 45] cm
(17½ [17½: 17½] in)

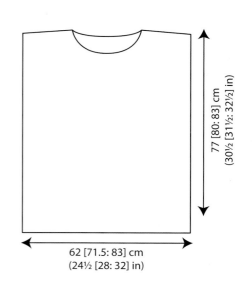

77 [80: 83] cm
(30½ [31½: 32½] in)

62 [71.5: 83] cm
(24½ [28: 32] in)

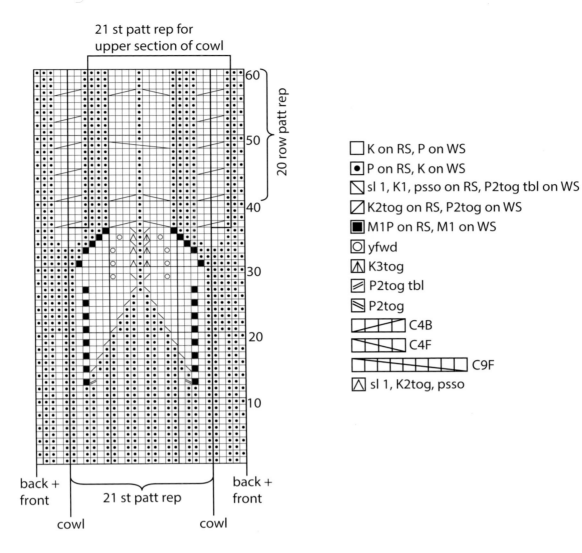

21 st patt rep for
upper section of cowl

20 row patt rep

60
50
40
30
20
10

back +
front

21 st patt rep

back +
front

cowl

cowl

☐ K on RS, P on WS
⦿ P on RS, K on WS
◢ sl 1, K1, psso on RS, P2tog tbl on WS
◢ K2tog on RS, P2tog on WS
◼ M1P on RS, M1 on WS
Ⓞ yfwd
⩕ K3tog
◪ P2tog tbl
◩ P2tog
▭▭ C4B
▭▭ C4F
▭▭▭ C9F
⩓ sl 1, K2tog, psso

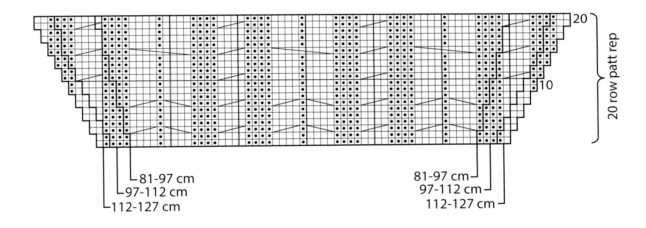

20

10

20 row patt rep

81-97 cm
97-112 cm
112-127 cm

81-97 cm
97-112 cm
112-127 cm

repeating the 21 st patt rep 8 times around each round, cont in patt from chart for body as folls: Work chart rows 1 to 36.
Round 37: Patt to last 3 sts. Re-position marker after last st worked (so that new beg and end point

of rounds moves by 3 sts but position of patt does NOT move).
Now work chart rows 38 to 40.
Now repeating chart rows 41 to 60 as required, cont straight until cowl meas 40 cm.

Change to 4½mm (US 7) circular needle.
Next round (RS): ★K2, P2, rep from ★ to end.
Rep last round 3 times more.
Cast off in rib.

GRANSMOOR

Lisa Richardson

Main image page **10, 11**

● ● ●

SIZE

To fit bust

81–86	91–97	102–107	112–117	122–127	cm
32–34	36–38	40–42	44–46	48–50	in

Actual bust measurement of garment

102	113	121	132	142	cm
40	44½	47½	52	56	in

YARN

Hemp Tweed

A Duck Egg 139

7	8	9	9	10	x 50gm

B Granite 136

4	5	5	6	6	x 50gm

C Almond 141

1	1	1	1	1	x 50gm

NEEDLES

1 pair 4mm (no 8) (US 6) needles
1 pair 4½mm (no 7) (US 7) needles
1 pair 5mm (no 6) (US 8) needles
4mm (no 8) (US 6) circular needle no more than 40 cm long

TENSION

19 sts and 25 rows to 10 cm measured over plain st st using 4½mm (US 7) needles. 19 sts and 20 rows to 10 cm measured over patterned st st using 5mm (US 8) needles.

BACK

Using 4mm (US 6) needles and yarn A cast on 98 [106: 114: 126: 134] sts.
Row 1 (RS): K2, *P2, K2, rep from * to end.
Row 2: P2, *K2, P2, rep from * to end.
These 2 rows form rib.
Work in rib for a further 12 rows, dec [inc: inc: dec: inc] 1 st at end of last row and ending with RS facing for next row. 97 [107: 115: 125: 135] sts.
Change to 4½mm (US 7) needles.
Beg with a K row, work in st st until back meas 18 [20: 21: 23: 24] cm, ending with RS facing for next row.

Change to 5mm (US 8) needles.
Beg and ending rows as indicated and using the **fairisle** technique as described on the information page, cont in patt from chart, which is worked entirely in st st beg with a K row, as folls:
Work 44 [42: 40: 38: 36] rows, ending after chart row 44 [42: 40: 38: 36] and with RS facing for next row. (Back should meas approx 40 [41: 41: 42: 42] cm.)
Shape raglan armholes
Keeping patt correct, cast off 3 sts at beg of next 2 rows. 91 [101: 109: 119: 129] sts.
Dec 1 st at each end of next 22 [24: 26: 28: 30] rows, ending after chart row 68 and with RS facing for next row. 47 [53: 57: 63: 69] sts.
Change to 4½mm (US 7) needles.
Break off contrasts and cont using yarn B **only** as folls:
Beg with a K row, work in st st, dec 1 st at each end of next 1 [5: 7: 11: 13] rows, then on foll 9 [8: 7: 6: 6] alt rows. 27 [27: 29: 29: 31] sts.
Work 1 row, ending with RS facing for next row.
Break yarn and leave sts on a holder.

FRONT

Work as given for back until 35 [35: 39: 39: 43] sts rem in raglan armhole shaping.
Work 1 row, ending with RS facing for next row.
Shape front neck
Next row (RS): K2tog, patt 5 [5: 7: 7: 9] sts and turn, leaving rem sts on a holder. 6 [6: 8: 8: 10] sts.
Work each side of neck separately.
Keeping patt correct, dec 1 st at neck edge of next 3 [3: 4: 4: 4] rows, then on foll 0 [0: 0: 0: 1] alt row
and at same time dec 1 st at raglan armhole edge of 2nd and foll 0 [0: 1: 1: 2] alt rows. 2 sts.
Work 0 [0: 1: 1: 1] row, ending with RS facing for next row.
Next row (RS): K2tog and fasten off.
With RS facing, slip centre 21 sts onto a holder, rejoin yarn and patt to last 2 sts, K2tog.
6 [6: 8: 8: 10] sts.
Complete to match first side, reversing shapings.

SLEEVES

Using 4mm (US 6) needles and yarn A cast on 34 [34: 38: 38: 38] sts.
Work in rib as given for back for 13 rows, ending with **WS** facing for next row.
Row 14 (WS): Rib 2 [1: 4: 4: 3], M1, (rib 5 [4: 5: 5: 4], M1) 6 [8: 6: 6: 8] times, rib 2 [1: 4: 4: 3]. 41 [43: 45: 45: 47] sts.
Change to 4½mm (US 7) needles.

Beg with a K row, work in st st, shaping sides by inc 1 st at each end of 5th [3rd: 3rd: 3rd: 3rd] and 0 [4: 5: 13: 14] foll 4th rows, then on 7 [5: 5: 0: 0] foll 6th rows. 57 [63: 67: 73: 77] sts.
Work 1 [1: 3: 3: 1] rows, ending with RS facing for next row.
Change to 5mm (US 8) needles.
Beg and ending rows as indicated, cont in patt from chart as folls:
Inc 1 st at each end of 5th [5th: 3rd: next: 3rd] and 4 [5: 5: 5: 5] foll 6th [6th: 6th: 6th: 4th] rows, then on 1 [-: -: -: 1] foll 8th [-: -: -: 6th] row, taking inc sts into patt. 69 [75: 79: 85: 91] sts.
Work 7 rows, ending after chart row 44 [42: 40: 38: 36] and with RS facing for next row. (Sleeve should meas approx 46 [46: 47: 47: 47] cm.)
Shape raglan
Keeping patt correct, cast off 3 sts at beg of next 2 rows. 63 [69: 73: 79: 85] sts.
Dec 1 st at each end of next 1 [1: 3: 5: 7] rows, then on 1 [0: 0: 0: 0] foll 4th row, then on foll 8 [11: 11: 11: 11] alt rows. 43 [45: 45: 47: 49] sts.
Work 1 row, ending after chart row 68 and with RS facing for next row.
Change to 4½mm (US 7) needles.
Break off contrasts and cont using yarn B **only** as folls:
Beg with a K row, work in st st, dec 1 st at each end of next and every foll alt row until 27 sts rem.
Work 1 row, ending with RS facing for next row.
Left sleeve only
Dec 1 st at each end of next row, then cast off 8 sts at beg of foll row. 17 sts.
Dec 1 st at beg of next row, then cast off 8 sts at beg of foll row.
Right sleeve only
Cast off 9 sts at beg and dec 1 st at end of next row. 17 sts.
Work 1 row.
Cast off 8 sts at beg and dec 1 st at end of next row.
Work 1 row.
Both sleeves
Cast off rem 8 sts.

MAKING UP

Press as described on the information page.
Join all raglan seams using back stitch, or mattress stitch if preferred.
Neckband
With RS facing, using 4mm (US 6) circular needle and yarn B, pick up and knit 23 sts from top of left sleeve, 3 [3: 4: 4: 7] sts down left side of front neck,

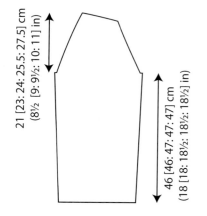

21 [23: 24: 25.5: 27.5] cm
(8½ [9: 9½: 10: 11] in)

46 [46: 47: 47: 47] cm
(18 [18: 18½: 18½: 18½] in)

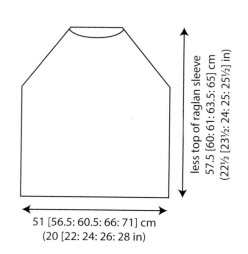

less top of raglan sleeve
57.5 [60: 61: 63.5: 65] cm
(22½ [23½: 24: 25: 25½] in)

51 [56.5: 60.5: 66: 71] cm
(20 [22: 24: 26: 28 in)

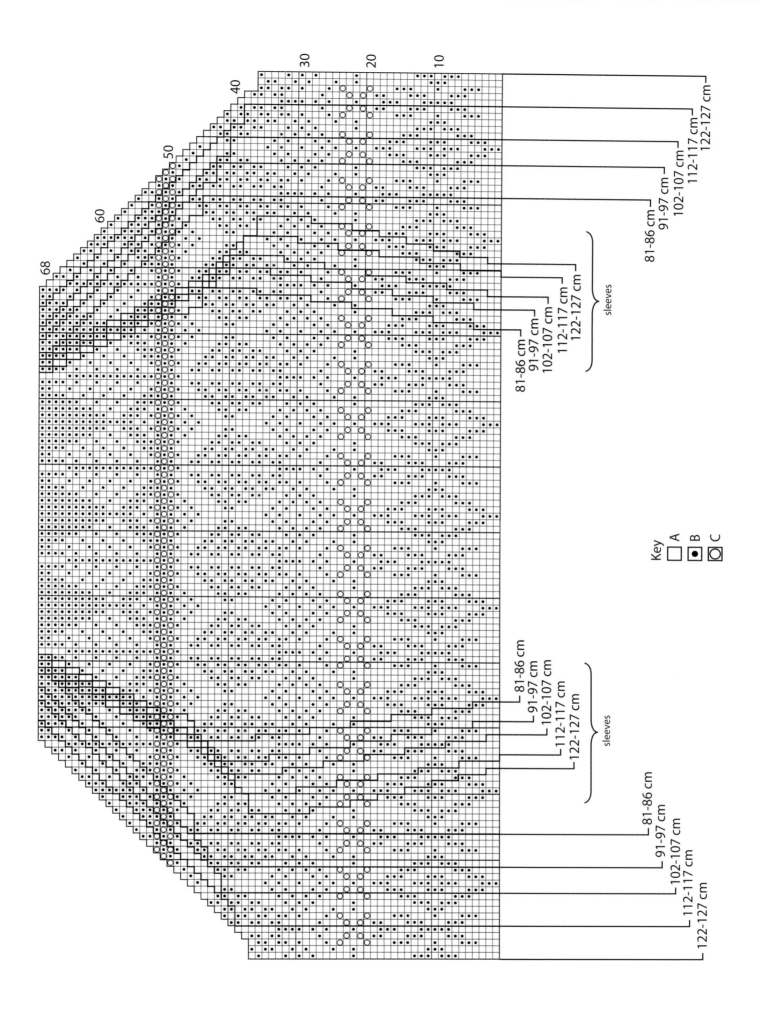

K across 21 sts on front holder, pick up and knit 3 [3: 4: 4: 7] sts up right side of front neck, and 23 sts from top of right sleeve, then K across 27 [27: 29: 29: 31] sts on back holder. 100 [100: 104: 104: 112] sts.

Round 1 (RS): ⋆K2, P2, rep from ⋆ to end.
Rep last round 7 times more.
Round 9: Knit.

Rep last round twice more.
Cast off knitwise.
See information page for finishing instructions.

Key
☐ A
⊡ B
◎ C

30
20
10
40
50
60
68

81-86 cm
91-97 cm
102-107 cm
112-117 cm
122-127 cm

sleeves

81-86 cm
91-97 cm
102-107 cm
112-117 cm
122-127 cm

sleeves

81-86 cm
91-97 cm
102-107 cm
112-117 cm
122-127 cm

MELLOW

Sarah Hatton

Main image page **54, 55, 74**

● ●

SIZE

To fit bust

81-86	91-97	102-107	112-117	122-127	cm
32-34	36-38	40-42	44-46	48-50	in

Actual bust measurement of garment

142	152	163	173	181	cm
56	60	64	68	71½	in

YARN

Kid Classic

13	14	15	16	17	x 50gm

(photographed in Cement 890)

NEEDLES

1 pair 4mm (no 8) (US 6) needles
1 pair 4½mm (no 7) (US 7) needles
Cable needle

TENSION

23½ sts and 28 rows to 10 cm measured over cable patt, 20 sts and 28 rows to 10 cm measured over st st, both using 4½mm (US 7) needles.

SPECIAL ABBREVIATIONS

C6B = slip next 3 sts onto cable needle and leave at back of work, K3, then K3 from cable needle;
C6F = slip next 3 sts onto cable needle and leave at front of work, K3, then K3 from cable needle.

BACK

Using 4mm (US 6) needles cast on 146 [152: 164: 176: 180] sts.
Row 1 (RS): Purl.
Row 2: Knit.
Change to 4½mm (US 7) needles.
Row 3 (RS): K18 [4: 10: 16: 1], ★P1, (K1, M1, K1) 3 times, P1, K9, rep from ★ to last 26 [12: 18: 24: 9] sts, P1, (K1, M1, K1) 3 times, P1, K18 [4: 10: 16: 1]. 167 [179: 191: 203: 213] sts.
Now work in cable patt as folls:
Row 1 and every foll alt row (WS): P18 [4: 10: 16: 1], ★K1, P9, rep from ★ to last 19 [5: 11: 17:

2] sts, K1, P18 [4: 10: 16: 1].
Row 2: K18 [4: 10: 16: 1], ★P1, C6B, K3, P1, K9, rep from ★ to last 29 [15: 21: 27: 12] sts, P1, C6B, K3, P1, K18 [4: 10: 16: 1].
Row 4: K18 [4: 10: 16: 1], ★P1, K9, rep from ★ to last 19 [5: 11: 17: 2] sts, P1, K18 [4: 10: 16: 1].
Row 6: As row 4.
Row 8: K18 [4: 10: 16: 1], ★P1, K3, C6F, P1, K9, rep from ★ to last 29 [15: 21: 27: 12] sts, P1, K3, C6F, P1, K18 [4: 10: 16: 1].
Row 10: As row 4.
Row 12: As row 4.
These 12 rows form cable patt.
Cont in cable patt until back meas 47.5 [48: 48.5: 49: 49.5] cm, ending with RS facing for next row.
Shape armholes
Keeping patt correct, cast off 6 sts at beg of next 2 rows. 155 [167: 179: 191: 201] sts.
Dec 1 st at each end of next and foll 7 alt rows. 139 [151: 163: 175: 185] sts.
Cont straight until armhole meas 20 [21.5: 23: 24.5: 26] cm, ending with RS facing for next row.
Shape shoulders
Cast off 8 [10: 11: 12: 13] sts at beg of next 2 [10: 10: 8: 10] rows, then 9 [-: -: 13: -] sts at beg of foll 8 [-: -: 2: -] rows.
Break yarn and leave rem 51 [51: 53: 53: 55] sts on a holder (for collar).

LEFT FRONT

Using 4mm (US 6) needles cast on 98 [101: 107: 113: 115] sts.
Row 1 (RS): P to last 4 sts, K1, P1, K2.
Row 2: (K1, P1) twice, K to end.
Change to 4½mm (US 7) needles.
Row 3 (RS): K18 [4: 10: 16: 1], ★P1, (K1, M1, K1) 3 times, P1, K9, rep from ★ to last 12 sts, P1, (K1, M1, K1) 3 times, (P1, K1) twice, K1. 113 [119: 125: 131: 136] sts.
Now work in cable patt as folls:
Row 1 and every foll alt row (WS): (K1, P1) twice, ★K1, P9, rep from ★ to last 19 [5: 11: 17: 2] sts, K1, P18 [4: 10: 16: 1].
Row 2: K18 [4: 10: 16: 1], ★P1, C6B, K3, P1, K9, rep from ★ to last 15 sts, P1, C6B, K3, (P1, K1) twice, K1.
Row 4: K18 [4: 10: 16: 1], ★P1, K9, rep from ★ to last 5 sts, (P1, K1) twice, K1.
Row 6: As row 4.
Row 8: K18 [4: 10: 16: 1], ★P1, K3, C6F, P1, K9, rep from ★ to last 15 sts, P1, K3, C6F, (P1, K1) twice, K1.

Row 10: As row 4.
Row 12: As row 4.
These 12 rows set the sts – front opening edge in rib with all other sts in cable patt.
Cont as now set until left front matches back to beg of armhole shaping, ending with RS facing for next row.
Shape armhole
Keeping patt correct, cast off 6 sts at beg of next row. 107 [113: 119: 125: 130] sts.
Work 1 row.
Dec 1 st at armhole edge of next and foll 7 alt rows. 99 [105: 111: 117: 122] sts.
Cont straight until left front matches back to beg of shoulder shaping, ending with RS facing for next row.
Shape shoulder
Cast off 8 [10: 11: 12: 13] sts at beg of next and foll 0 [4: 4: 3: 4] alt rows, then 9 [-: -: 13: -] sts at beg of foll 4 [-: -: 1: -] alt rows.
Work 1 row, ending with RS facing for next row.
Break yarn and leave rem 55 [55: 56: 56: 57] sts on a holder (for collar).

RIGHT FRONT

Using 4mm (US 6) needles cast on 98 [101: 107: 113: 115] sts.
Row 1 (RS): K2, P1, K1, P to end.
Row 2: K to last 4 sts, (P1, K1) twice.
Change to 4½mm (US 7) needles.
Row 3 (RS): K1, (K1, P1) twice, (K1, M1, K1) 3 times, P1, ★K9, P1, (K1, M1, K1) 3 times, P1, rep from ★ to last 18 [4: 10: 16: 1] sts, K18 [4: 10: 16: 1]. 113 [119: 125: 131: 136] sts.
Now work in cable patt as folls:
Row 1 and every foll alt row (WS): P18 [4: 10: 16: 1], K1, ★P9, K1, rep from ★ to last 4 sts, (P1, K1) twice.
Row 2: K1, (K1, P1) twice, C6B, K3, P1, ★K9, P1, C6B, K3, P1, rep from ★ to last 18 [4: 10: 16: 1] sts, K18 [4: 10: 16: 1].
Row 4: K1, (K1, P1) twice, ★K9, P1, rep from ★ to last 18 [4: 10: 16: 1] sts, K18 [4: 10: 16: 1].
Row 6: As row 4.
Row 8: K1, (K1, P1) twice, K3, C6F, P1, ★K9, P1, K3, C6F, P1, rep from ★ to last 18 [4: 10: 16: 1] sts, K18 [4: 10: 16: 1].
Row 10: As row 4.
Row 12: As row 4.
These 12 rows set the sts – front opening edge in rib with all other sts in cable patt.
Complete to match left front, reversing shapings

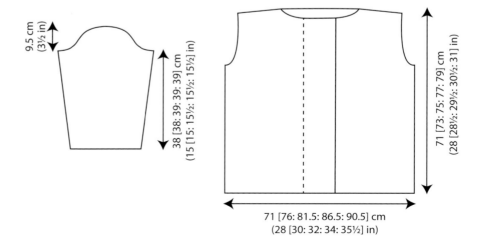

9.5 cm (3½ in)

38 [38: 39: 39: 39] cm (15 [15: 15½: 15½: 15½] in)

71 [73: 75: 77: 79] cm (28 [28½: 29½: 30½: 31] in)

71 [76: 81.5: 86.5: 90.5] cm (28 [30: 32: 34: 35½] in)

and working shoulder shaping as folls:
Shape shoulder
Cast off 8 [10: 11: 12: 13] sts at beg of next and foll 0 [4: 4: 4: 3: 4] alt rows, then 9 [–: –: 13: –] sts at beg of foll 4 [–: –: 1: –] alt rows, ending with RS facing for next row.
Leave rem 55 [55: 56: 56: 57] sts on a holder (for collar). Do NOT break yarn but set aside this ball of yarn to use for collar.

SLEEVES
Using 4mm (US 6) needles cast on 38 [40: 42: 42: 44] sts.
Row 1 (RS): Purl.
Row 2: Knit.
Change to 4½mm (US 7) needles.
Beg with a K row, work in st st throughout as folls:
Inc 1 st at each end of 3rd [3rd: 3rd: 3rd: next] and every foll 4th [4th: 4th: 4th: alt] row to 48 [62: 72: 90: 52] sts, then on every foll 6th [6th: 6th: –: 4th] row until there are 72 [78: 84: –: 96] sts.
Cont straight until sleeve meas 38 [38: 39: 39: 39] cm, ending with RS facing for next row.
Shape top
Cast off 6 sts at beg of next 2 rows. 60 [66: 72: 78: 84] sts.
Dec 1 st at each end of next and foll 6 alt rows, then on foll row, ending with RS facing for next row. 44 [50: 56: 62: 68] sts.
Cast off 3 [3: 3: 4: 4] sts at beg of next 10 [6: 2: 8: 4] rows, then – [4: 4: 5: 5] sts at beg of foll – [4: 8: 2: 6] rows.
Cast off rem 14 [16: 18: 20: 22] sts.

MAKING UP
Press as described on the information page.

Join both shoulder seams using back stitch, or mattress stitch if preferred.
Collar
With RS facing, using 4½mm (US 7) needles and ball of yarn set to one side with right front, patt across 55 [55: 56: 56: 57] sts on right front holder, then patt across 51 [51: 53: 53: 55] sts on back holder, and patt across 55 [55: 56: 56: 57] sts on left front holder. 161 [161: 165: 165: 169] sts.
Cont in patt as set until collar meas 7 cm from pick-up row, ending with **WS** facing for next row.
Work 1 row, working (P2tog, P1) 3 times at top of each cable. 134 [134: 138: 138: 142] sts.
Change to 4mm (US 6) needles.
Next row (RS): Purl.
Cast off knitwise (on **WS**).
See information page for finishing instructions, setting in sleeves using the shallow set-in method.

GREENWOOD
Galina Carroll
Main image page **16, 17**
● ● ● ●

SIZE
To fit bust
81-86 91-97 102-107 112-117 122-127 cm
32-34 36-38 40-42 44-46 48-50 in
Actual bust measurement of garment

| 117 | 126 | 137 | 146 | 157 | cm |
| 46 | 49½ | 54 | 57½ | 62 | in |

YARN
Felted Tweed
A Clay 177

| 6 | 7 | 8 | 8 | 9 | x 50gm |

B Carbon 159

| 4 | 4 | 4 | 5 | 5 | x 50gm |

C Rage 150

| 1 | 1 | 1 | 1 | 1 | x 50gm |

D Peony 183

| 1 | 1 | 1 | 1 | 1 | x 50gm |

E Ginger 154

| 1 | 1 | 1 | 1 | 1 | x 50gm |

F Pine 158

| 1 | 1 | 1 | 1 | 1 | x 50gm |

G Bilberry 151

| 1 | 1 | 1 | 1 | 1 | x 50gm |

NEEDLES
1 pair 3¼mm (no 10) (US 3) needles
1 pair 3¾mm (no 9) (US 5) needles

TENSION
24 sts and 32 rows to 10 cm measured over plain st st, 26 sts and 27 rows to 10 cm measured over patterned st st, both using 3¾mm (US 5) needles.

BACK
Using 3¼mm (US 3) needles and yarn A cast on 151 [163: 177: 189: 203] sts.
Row 1 (RS): K1, ★P1, K1, rep from ★ to end.
Row 2: P1, ★K1, P1, rep from ★ to end.
These 2 rows form rib.
Work in rib for a further 3 rows, inc 1 st at end of last row and ending with **WS** facing for next row. 152 [164: 178: 190: 204] sts.
Change to 3¾mm (US 5) needles.
Noting that chart row 1 is a **WS** row, beg and ending rows as indicated and using the **fairisle** technique as described on the information page, cont in patt from chart for body, which is worked entirely in st st beg with a **purl** row, as folls:
Work chart rows 1 to 28, 3 times.
Now working chart rows 29 to 83 **once only** and then repeating chart rows 84 to 87 as required, cont as folls:
Cont straight until back meas 67 [69: 71: 73: 75] cm, ending with RS facing for next row.
Shape shoulder
Keeping patt correct, cast off 12 [13: 15: 16: 18] sts at beg of next 6 [2: 6: 2: 6] rows, then 13 [14: 16: 17: 19] sts at beg of foll 2 [6: 2: 6: 2] rows.

Break yarns and leave rem 54 [54: 56: 56: 58] sts on a holder.

FRONT
Work as given for back until 12 [12: 14: 14: 16] rows less have been worked than on back to beg of shoulder shaping, ending with RS facing for next row.
Shape front neck
Next row (RS): Patt 59 [65: 72: 78: 85] sts and turn, leaving rem sts on a holder.
Work each side of neck separately.
Keeping patt correct, dec 1 st at neck edge of next 6 rows, then on foll 2 [2: 3: 3: 4] alt rows.
51 [57: 63: 69: 75] sts.
Work 1 row, ending with RS facing for next row.
Shape shoulder
Cast off 12 [13: 15: 16: 18] sts at beg of next and foll 2 [0: 2: 0: 2] alt rows, then – [14: –: 17: –] sts at beg of foll – [2: –: 2: –] alt rows **and at same time** dec 1 st at neck edge of next and foll alt row.
Work 1 row.
Cast off rem 13 [14: 16: 17: 19] sts.
With RS facing, slip centre 34 sts onto a holder, rejoin yarns and patt to end.
Complete to match first side, reversing shapings.

SLEEVE STRIPE SEQUENCE
Rows 1 and 2: Using yarn A.
Rows 3 and 4: Using yarn C.
Rows 5 and 6: Using yarn A.
Rows 7 and 8: Using yarn D.
Rows 9 and 10: Using yarn A.
Rows 11 and 12: Using yarn E.
Rows 13 and 14: Using yarn A.
Rows 15 and 16: Using yarn F.
Rows 17 and 18: Using yarn A.
Rows 19 and 20: Using yarn G.
Rows 21 onwards: Using yarn A.

SLEEVES
Using 3¼mm (US 3) needles and yarn A cast on 49 [51: 53: 53: 55] sts.
Beg with row 1, work in rib as given for back for 3 rows, ending with **WS** facing for next row.

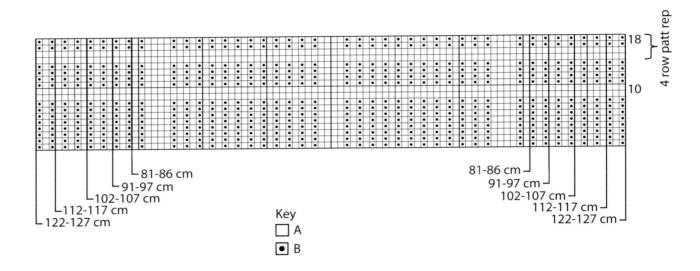

18

10

4 row patt rep

└81-86 cm
└91-97 cm
└102-107 cm
└112-117 cm
└122-127 cm

81-86 cm┘
91-97 cm┘
102-107 cm┘
112-117 cm┘
122-127 cm┘

Key

☐ A
⊡ B

Body chart

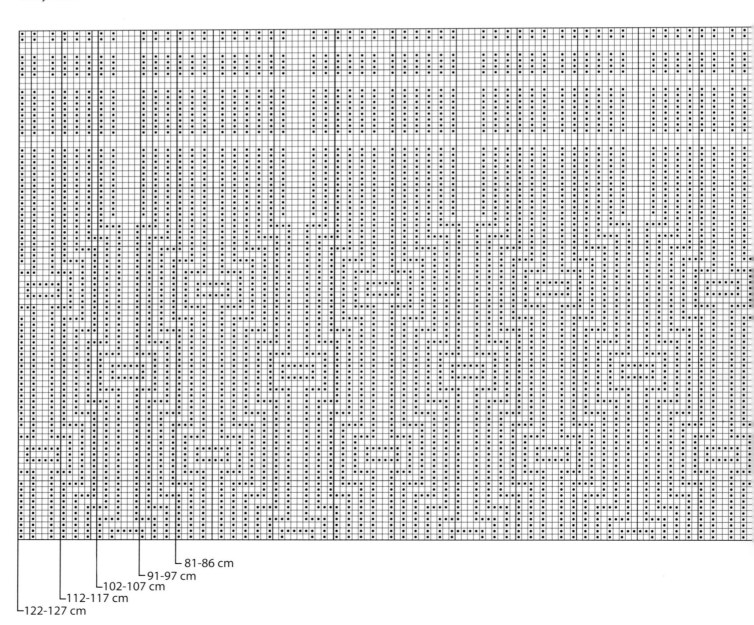

└81-86 cm
└91-97 cm
└102-107 cm
└112-117 cm
└122-127 cm

Change to 3¾mm (US 5) needles.
Beg with a P row, now work in st st throughout
as folls:
Work 1 row, ending with RS facing for next row.
Beg with row 1 and joining in and breaking off
colours as required, cont in sleeve stripe sequence
as folls:
Inc 1 st at each end of 13th [9th: 7th: 3rd: 3rd]
and every foll 16th [10th: 8th: 6th: 4th] row until
there are 57 [57: 69: 79: 69] sts, then on every foll
– [12th: 10th: –: 6th] row until there are – [63: 71:
–: 85] sts.
Cont straight until sleeve meas 36 [36: 37: 37: 37]
cm, ending with **WS** facing for next row.
Next row (WS): Using yarn A, P6 [5: 7: 6: 6],
M1P, (P11 [13: 14: 11: 12], M1P) 4 [4: 4: 6: 6]
times, P7 [6: 8: 7: 7]. 62 [68: 76: 86: 92] sts.
Beg and ending rows as indicated and using the
fairisle technique as described on the information
page, cont in patt from chart for sleeve, which is
worked entirely in st st beg with a K row, as folls:
Work chart rows 1 to 14.
Now repeating chart rows 15 to 18 as required,

cont straight until sleeve meas 44 [44: 45: 45: 45]
cm, ending with RS facing for next row.
Cast off.

UNDERARM GUSSETS (make 2)
Using 3¾mm (US 5) needles and yarn A cast on
43 sts.
Beg with a K row, work in st st in stripes as folls:
Rows 1 and 2: Using yarn A.
Join in yarn B.
Rows 3 and 4: Using yarn B.
These 4 rows form striped st st.
Cont in striped st st for a further 54 rows, ending
after 2 rows using yarn A and with RS facing for
next row.
Cast off.

MAKING UP
Press as described on the information page.
Join right shoulder seam using back stitch, or
mattress stitch if preferred.
Neckband
With RS facing, using 3¼mm (US 3) needles

and yarn A, pick up and knit 18 [18: 20: 20: 22] sts
down left side of front neck, K across 34 sts on
front holder dec 1 st at centre, pick up and knit
18 [18: 20: 20: 22] sts up right side of front neck,
then K across 54 [54: 56: 56: 58] sts on back holder
dec 2 sts evenly. 121 [121: 127: 127: 133] sts.
Beg with row 2, work in rib as given for back for
3 rows, ending with RS facing for next row.
Cast off in rib.
Join left shoulder and neckband seam. Mark
points along side seam edges 12 [13.5: 15: 16.5:
18] cm either side of shoulder seams (to denote
underarm point). Sew cast-off edge of sleeves to
back and front between these points. Join side and
sleeve seams, leaving both seams open for 18 cm
either side of underarm point. Using photograph
as a guide, sew underarm gussets into underarm
openings in side and sleeve seams.
Embroidery
Using photograph as a guide and yarns C, D, E, F
and G at random, swiss darn centres of blocks of
lower section of body chart.
See information page for finishing instructions.

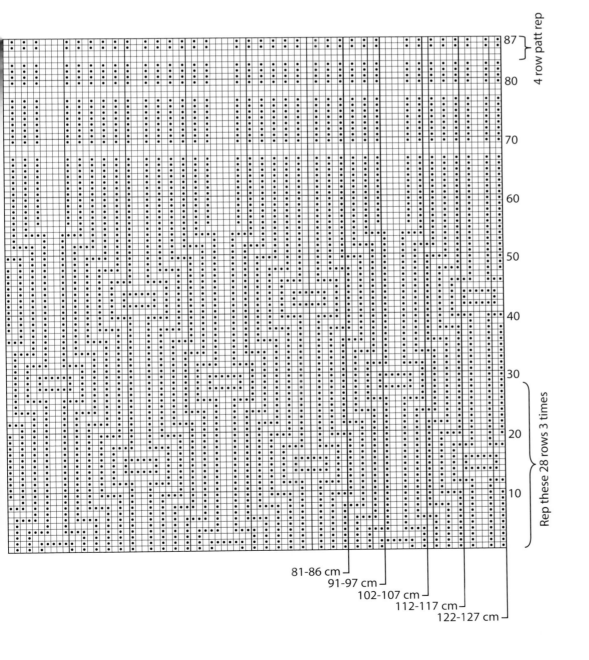

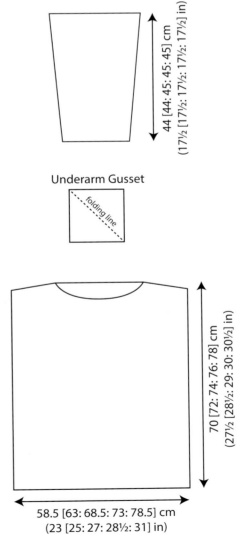

Underarm Gusset

folding line

44 [44: 45: 45: 45] cm
(17½ [17½: 17½: 17½: 17½] in)

70 [72: 74: 76: 78] cm
(27½ [28½: 29: 30: 30½] in)

58.5 [63: 68.5: 73: 78.5] cm
(23 [25: 27: 28½: 31] in)

4 row patt rep

Rep these 28 rows 3 times

81-86 cm
91-97 cm
102-107 cm
112-117 cm
122-127 cm

WHISPERED

Sarah Hatton

Main image page **60, 61**

● ●

YARN

Kid Classic and Kidsilk Haze

A	KCl	Canard 871	3	x 50gm
B	KSH	Peacock 671	2	x 25gm

NEEDLES

1 pair 5mm (no 6) (US 8) needles

TENSION

16 sts and 22 rows to 10 cm measured over patt using 5mm (US 8) needles.

FINISHED SIZE

Completed scarf is approx 35 cm (14 in) wide and 220 cm (86½ in) long.

SPECIAL ABBREVIATION

sl 1 wyaf = slip next st purlwise with yarn at front of work.

SCARF

Using 5mm (US 8) needles and yarn A cast on 65 sts **loosely**. (**Note**: To ensure the cast-on edge is not too tight you may prefer to cast on using larger size needles.)
Row 1 (RS): K1, sl 1 wyaf, *K1, P1, rep from * to last 3 sts, K1, sl 1 wyaf, K1.
Row 2: (Sl 1 wyaf, K1) twice, *P1, K1, rep from * to last 3 sts, sl 1 wyaf, K1, sl 1 wyaf.
These 2 rows set the sts – end 3 sts of rows forming slip st edging and all other sts in rib. Keeping sts correct as set and taking all inc sts into rib, cont as folls:
Row 3: K1, sl 1 wyaf, K1, inc in next st, rib to last 5 sts, work 2 tog, K1, sl 1 wyaf, K1.
Row 4: Sl 1 wyaf, K1, sl 1 wyaf, rib to last 3 sts, sl 1 wyaf, K1, sl 1 wyaf.

Rows 5 to 8: As rows 3 and 4 twice.
Now work in striped st st as folls:
Row 9: Using yarn A K1, sl 1 wyaf, K1, inc in next st, K to last 5 sts, K2tog, K1, sl 1 wyaf, K1.
Row 10: Using yarn A sl 1 wyaf, K1, sl 1 wyaf, P to last 3 sts, sl 1 wyaf, K1, sl 1 wyaf.
Join in yarn B.
Row 11: Using yarn B K1, sl 1 wyaf, K1, inc in next st, K to last 5 sts, K2tog, K1, sl 1 wyaf, K1.
Row 12: Using yarn B sl 1 wyaf, K1, sl 1 wyaf, P to last 3 sts, sl 1 wyaf, K1, sl 1 wyaf.
Last 4 rows form patt.
Cont in patt until scarf meas approx 216 cm, ending after 2 rows using yarn A and with RS facing for next row.
Break off yarn B and cont using yarn A only.
Next row (RS): K1, sl 1 wyaf, K1, inc in next st, *K1, P1, rep from * to last 5 sts, K2tog, K1, sl 1 wyaf, K1.
Next row: Sl 1 wyaf, K1, sl 1 wyaf, P1, *K1, P1, rep from * to last 3 sts, sl 1 wyaf, K1, sl 1 wyaf.
These 2 rows set the sts – end 3 sts of rows still forming slip st edging and all other sts now in rib. Keeping sts correct as set, cont as folls:
Next row: K1, sl 1 wyaf, K1, inc in next st, rib to last 5 sts, work 2 tog, K1, sl 1 wyaf, K1.
Next row: Sl 1 wyaf, K1, sl 1 wyaf, rib to last 3 sts, sl 1 wyaf, K1, sl 1 wyaf.
Rep last 2 rows twice more, ending with RS facing for next row.
Cast off **loosely** in patt. (**Note**: To ensure the cast-off edge is not too tight you may prefer to cast off using a larger size needle.)

MAKING UP

Press as described on the information page.

TWILIGHT

Lisa Richardson

Main image page **67, 68, 80**

● ● ●

SIZE

To fit bust

81-86	91-97	102-107	112-117	122-127	cm
32-34	36-38	40-42	44-46	48-50	in

Actual bust measurement of garment

90	101	110	121	130	cm
35½	40	43½	47½	51	in

YARN

Kidsilk Haze and Fine Lace

A KSH	Trance	582				
6	7	7	8	9	x 25gm
B Lace	Aged	933				
3	4	4	4	4	x 50gm

NEEDLES

1 pair 3¼mm (no 10) (US 3) needles
1 pair 4mm (no 8) (US 6) needles
Cable needle

TENSION

22 sts and 30 rows to 10 cm measured over rev st st using 4mm (US 6) needles and one strand of each of yarns A and B held together. Body patt panel (120 sts) measures 38.5 cm.

SPECIAL ABBREVIATIONS

C6B = slip next 3 sts onto cable needle and leave at back of work, K3, then K3 from cable needle;
C8B = slip next 4 sts onto cable needle and leave

at back of work, K4, then K4 from cable needle;
C8F = slip next 4 sts onto cable needle and leave at front of work, K4, then K4 from cable needle;
Cr3L = slip next 2 sts onto cable needle and leave at front of work, P1, then K2 from cable needle;
Cr3R = slip next st onto cable needle and leave at back of work, K2, then P1 from cable needle;
Cr5L = slip next 3 sts onto cable needle and leave at front of work, P2, then K3 from cable needle;
Cr5R = slip next 2 sts onto cable needle and leave at back of work, K3, then P2 from cable needle;
MB = make bobble as folls: **On RS rows**, (K1, yfwd, K1, yfwd, K1) all into next st, turn, K5, turn, P5, turn, K5, turn, slip next 2 sts, K3tog, then lift the 2 slipped sts over this K3tog and off right needle. **On WS rows**, K into front, back and front again of next st, (turn, K3) 3 times, turn, sl 1, K2tog, psso.

Pattern note: Bobbles are worked on both RS and WS rows. When working the bobbles, take care to ensure that the bobble actually "sits" on the RS of the work, easing it through the knitting if required.

BACK

Using 3¼mm (US 3) needles and one strand each of yarns A and B held together cast on 134 [146: 154: 166: 178] sts.
Row 1 (RS): K2, *P2, K2, rep from * to end.

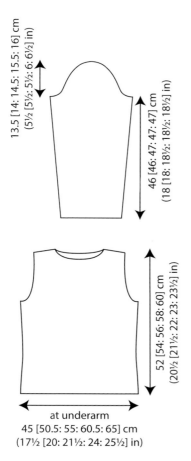

13.5 [14: 14.5: 15.5: 16] cm
(5½ [5½: 5½: 6: 6½] in)

46 [46: 47: 47: 47] cm
(18 [18: 18½: 18½: 18½] in)

52 [54: 56: 58: 60] cm
(20½ [21½: 22: 23: 23½] in)

at underarm
45 [50.5: 55: 60.5: 65] cm
(17½ [20: 21½: 24: 25½] in)

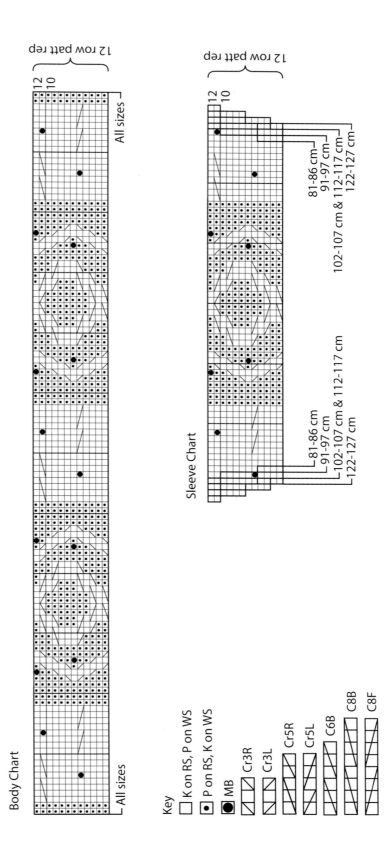

12 row patt rep

12
10

All sizes

Body Chart

All sizes

12 row patt rep

12
10

81-86 cm
91-97 cm
102-107 cm & 112-117 cm
122-127 cm

81-86 cm
91-97 cm
102-107 cm & 112-117 cm
122-127 cm

Sleeve Chart

Key
☐ K on RS, P on WS
• P on RS, K on WS
● MB
Cr3R
Cr3L
Cr5R
Cr5L
C6B
C8B
C8F

Row 2: P2, ★K2, P2, rep from ★ to end.
These 2 rows form rib.
Work in rib for a further 14 rows, inc 0 [0: 1: 1: 0] st at each end of last row and ending with RS facing for next row. 134 [146: 156: 168: 178] sts.
Change to 4mm (US 6) needles.
Now place patt panel as folls:
Row 1 (RS): P7 [13: 18: 24: 29], work next 120 sts as row 1 of patt panel chart for body, P7 [13: 18: 24: 29].
Row 2: K7 [13: 18: 24: 29], work next 120 sts as row 2 of patt panel chart for body, K7 [13: 18: 24: 29].
These 2 rows set the sts – centre 120 sts in patt from chart with rev st st at sides.
Keeping sts correct throughout as now set and repeating the patt panel 12 row rep throughout, cont as folls:
Work 2 [2: 6: 6: 8] rows ending with RS facing for next row.
Keeping patt correct, dec 1 st at each end of next and 3 foll 6th [6th: 6th: 8th: 8th] rows.
126 [138: 148: 160: 170] sts.
Work 11 [13: 13: 13: 13] rows, ending with RS facing for next row.
Inc 1 st at each end of next and 3 foll 10th [10th: 10th: 8th: 8th] rows, taking inc sts into rev st st.
134 [146: 156: 168: 178] sts.
Cont straight until back meas 31 [31.5: 32: 32.5: 33] cm, ending with RS facing for next row.
Shape armholes
Keeping patt correct, cast off 4 [5: 6: 7: 8] sts at beg of next 2 rows. 126 [136: 144: 154: 162] sts.
Dec 1 st at each end of next 3 [5: 5: 7: 7] rows, then on foll 4 [5: 5: 5: 5] alt rows.
112 [116: 124: 130: 138] sts.
Cont straight until armhole meas 19 [20.5: 22: 23.5: 25] cm, ending with RS facing for next row.
Shape back neck and shoulders
Next row (RS): Cast off 7 [7: 8: 9: 10] sts, patt until there are 26 [28: 30: 32: 34] sts on right needle and turn, leaving rem sts on a holder.
Work each side of neck separately.

Dec 1 st at neck edge of next 4 rows **and at same time** cast off 7 [8: 8: 9: 10] sts at beg of 2nd row, then 7 [8: 9: 9: 10] sts at beg of foll alt row.
Work 1 row.
Cast off rem 8 [8: 9: 10: 10] sts.
With RS facing, slip centre 46 [46: 48: 48: 50] sts onto a holder, rejoin yarns and patt to end.
Complete to match first side, reversing shapings.

FRONT
Work as given for back until 12 [12: 14: 14: 16] rows less have been worked than on back to beg of shoulder shaping, ending with RS facing for next row.

Shape front neck
Next row (RS): Patt 38 [40: 44: 47: 51] sts and turn, leaving rem sts on a holder.
Work each side of neck separately.
Keeping patt correct, dec 1 st at neck edge of next 8 rows, then on foll 1 [1: 2: 2: 3] alt rows.
29 [31: 34: 37: 40] sts.
Work 1 row, ending with RS facing for next row.
Shape shoulder
Cast off 7 [7: 8: 9: 10] sts at beg of next and foll 2 [0: 1: 2: 2] alt rows, then – [8: 9: –: –] sts at beg of foll – [2: 1: –: –] alt rows.
Work 1 row.
Cast off rem 8 [8: 9: 10: 10] sts.

With RS facing, slip centre 36 sts onto a holder, rejoin yarns and patt to end.
Complete to match first side, reversing shapings.

SLEEVES

Using 3¼mm (US 3) needles and one strand each of yarns A and B held together cast on 54 [54: 58: 58: 58] sts.
Work in rib as given for back for 16 rows, inc 0 [1: 0: 0: 1] st at each end of last row and ending with RS facing for next row. 54 [56: 58: 58: 60] sts.
Change to 4mm (US 6) needles.
Beg and ending rows as indicated and repeating the 12 row patt repeat throughout, cont in patt from chart for sleeve as folls:
Inc 1 st at each end of 5th [5th: 5th: 3rd: 3rd] and every foll 6th [6th: 6th: 4th: 4th] row to 74 [84: 90: 66: 74] sts, then on every foll 8th [8th: 8th: 6th: 6th] row until there are 86 [90: 94: 98: 102] sts,

taking first few inc sts into cable patt until this 16 st cable column (as worked on back) is complete and rem inc sts into rev st st (so, after all increases are complete, there will be 10 [12: 14: 16: 18] sts in rev st st at each side edge).
Cont straight until sleeve meas 46 [46: 47: 47: 47] cm, ending with RS facing for next row.

Shape top
Keeping patt correct, cast off 4 [5: 6: 7: 8] sts at beg of next 2 rows. 78 [80: 82: 84: 86] sts.
Dec 1 st at each end of next 5 rows, then on every foll alt row until 46 sts rem, then on foll 9 rows, ending with RS facing for next row. 28 sts.
Cast off 4 sts at beg of next 2 rows.
Cast off rem 20 sts.

MAKING UP
Press as described on the information page.
Join right shoulder seam using back stitch, or

mattress stitch if preferred.
Neckband
With RS facing, using 3¼mm (US 3) needles and one strand each of yarns A and B held together, pick up and knit 15 [15: 17: 17: 20] sts down left side of front neck, K across 36 sts on front holder as folls: (K1, K2tog, K1) 9 times, pick up and knit 15 [15: 16: 16: 19] sts up right side of front neck, and 5 sts down right side of back neck, K across 46 [46: 48: 48: 50] sts on back holder as folls: K1 [1: 0: 0: 1], (K1, K2tog, K1) 11 [11: 12: 12: 12] times, K1 [1: 0: 0: 1], then pick up and knit 5 sts up left side of back neck. 102 [102: 106: 106: 114] sts.
Beg with row 2, work in rib as given for back for 15 rows, ending with RS facing for next row.
Cast off **loosely** in rib.
See information page for finishing instructions, setting in sleeves using the set-in method.

LUND
Sarah Hatton
Main image page **39**

SIZE
To fit bust

81-86	91-97	102-107	112-117	122-127	cm
32-34	36-38	40-42	44-46	48-50	in

Actual bust measurement of garment

92	102	111	123	132	cm
36	40	43½	48½	52	in

YARN
Pure Wool Superwash DK

8	9	9	10	12	x 50gm

(photographed in Aegean 112)

NEEDLES
1 pair 3¼mm (no 10) (US 3) needles
1 pair 4mm (no 8) (US 6) needles

TENSION
21 sts and 33 rows to 10 cm measured over patt using 4mm (US 6) needles.

SPECIAL ABBREVIATION
sl 1 wyaf = slip next st purlwise with yarn at front (RS) of work (so a "bar" of yarn is left sitting in front of slipped st on RS of work).

BACK
Using 3¼mm (US 3) needles cast on 97 [107: 117: 129: 139] sts.
Row 1 (RS): K1, *P1, K1, rep from * to end.
Row 2: As row 1.
These 2 rows form moss st.
Work in moss st for a further 10 rows, ending with RS facing for next row.
Change to 4mm (US 6) needles.
Beg and ending rows as indicated and repeating the 18 row patt repeat throughout, cont in patt from chart as folls:
Cont in patt until back meas 13.5 [14.5: 15.5: 17.5: 18.5] cm, ending with RS facing for next row.
Change to 3¼mm (US 3) needles.

Cont straight until back meas 18.5 [19.5: 20.5: 22.5: 23.5] cm, ending with RS facing for next row.
Change to 4mm (US 6) needles.
Cont straight until back meas 35 [35.5: 36: 36.5: 37] cm, ending with RS facing for next row.
Shape armholes
Keeping patt correct, cast off 4 [5: 6: 7: 8] sts at beg of next 2 rows. 89 [97: 105: 115: 123] sts.
Dec 1 st at each end of next 5 [5: 7: 7: 9] rows, then on foll 4 [6: 5: 6: 5] alt rows.
71 [75: 81: 89: 95] sts.
Cont straight until armhole meas 19.5 [21: 22.5: 24: 25.5] cm, ending with RS facing for next row.
Shape back neck and shoulders
Next row (RS): Patt 8 [10: 12: 16: 18] sts and turn, leaving rem sts on a holder.
Work each side of neck separately.
Dec 1 st at neck edge of next 3 rows, ending with RS facing for next row, **and at same time** cast off 2 [3: 4: 6: 7] sts at beg of 2nd row.
Cast off rem 3 [4: 5: 7: 8] sts.
With RS facing, slip centre 55 [55: 57: 57: 59] sts onto a holder, rejoin yarn and patt to end.

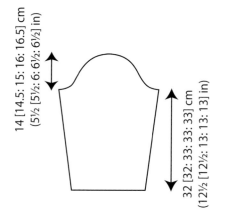

14 [14.5: 15: 16: 16.5] cm
(5½ [5½: 6: 6½: 6½] in)

32 [32: 33: 33: 33] cm
(12½ [12½: 13: 13: 13] in)

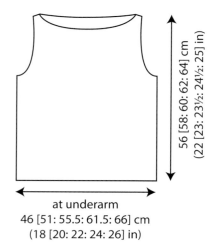

56 [58: 60: 62: 64] cm
(22 [23: 23½: 24½: 25] in)

at underarm
46 [51: 55.5: 61.5: 66] cm
(18 [20: 22: 24: 26] in)

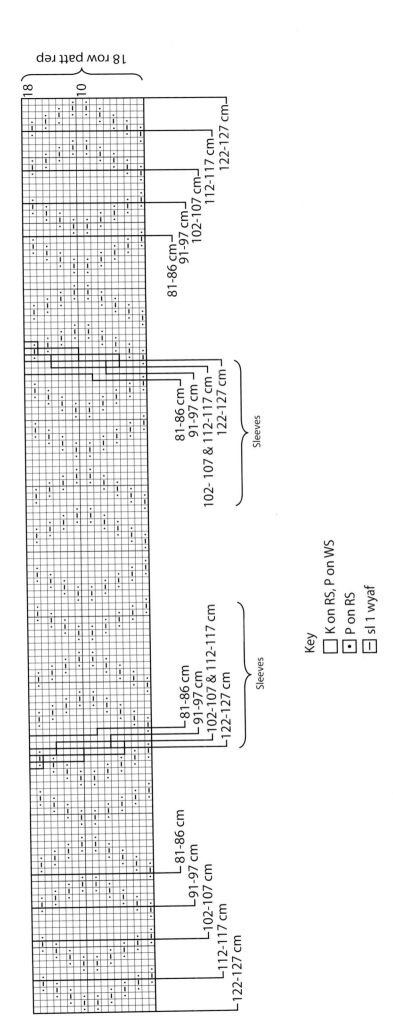

18

10

122-127 cm
112-117 cm
102-107 cm
91-97 cm
81-86 cm

Sleeves

81-86 cm
91-97 cm
102-107 & 112-117 cm
122-127 cm

Sleeves

81-86 cm
91-97 cm
102-107 & 112-117 cm
122-127 cm

81-86 cm
91-97 cm
102-107 cm
112-117 cm
122-127 cm

Key
☐ K on RS, P on WS
• P on RS
— sl 1 wyaf

Complete to match first side, reversing shapings.

FRONT

Work as given for back until 14 [14: 16: 16: 18] rows less have been worked than on back to beg of shoulder shaping, ending with RS facing for next row.

Shape front neck

Next row (RS): Patt 14 [16: 19: 23: 26] sts and turn, leaving rem sts on a holder.

Work each side of neck separately.

Keeping patt correct, dec 1 st at neck edge of next 6 rows, then on foll 3 [3: 4: 4: 5] alt rows.

5 [7: 9: 13: 15] sts.

Work 1 row, ending with RS facing for next row.

Shape shoulder

Cast off 2 [3: 4: 6: 7] sts at beg of next row.

Work 1 row.

Cast off rem 3 [4: 5: 7: 8] sts.

With RS facing, slip centre 43 sts onto a holder, rejoin yarn and patt to end.

Complete to match first side, reversing shapings.

SLEEVES

Using 3¼mm (US 3) needles cast on 53 [55: 57: 57: 59] sts.

Work in moss st as given for back for 12 rows, ending with RS facing for next row.

Change to 4mm (US 6) needles.

Beg and ending rows as indicated and repeating the 18 row patt repeat throughout, cont in patt from chart as folls:

Inc 1 st at each end of 9th [7th: 7th: 5th: 5th] and every foll 10th [8th: 8th: 6th: 6th] row to 69 [65: 75: 71: 81] sts, then on every foll – [10th: 10th: 8th: 8th] row until there are – [73: 77: 81: 85] sts, taking inc sts into patt.

Cont straight until sleeve meas 32 [32: 33: 33: 33] cm, ending with RS facing for next row.

Shape top

Keeping patt correct, cast off 4 [5: 6: 7: 8] sts at beg of next 2 rows. 61 [63: 65: 67: 69] sts.

Dec 1 st at each end of next 3 rows, then on foll 5 alt rows, then on 4 foll 4th rows.

37 [39: 41: 43: 45] sts.

Work 1 row, ending with RS facing for next row.

Dec 1 st at each end of next and every foll alt row until 29 sts rem, then on foll 7 rows, ending with RS facing for next row.

Cast off rem 15 sts.

MAKING UP

Press as described on the information page.

Join right shoulder seam using back stitch, or mattress stitch if preferred.

Neckband

With RS facing and using 3¼mm (US 3) needles, pick up and knit 14 [14: 16: 16: 18] sts down left side of front neck, K across 43 sts on front holder, pick up and knit 14 [14: 16: 16: 18] sts up right side of front neck, and 3 sts down right side of back neck, K across 55 [55: 57: 57: 59] sts on back holder, then pick up and knit 4 sts up left side of back neck. 133 [133: 139: 139: 145] sts.

Work in moss st as given for back for 9 rows, ending with RS facing for next row.

Cast off in moss st.

See information page for finishing instructions, setting in sleeves using the set-in method.

EVE

Jennie Atkinson

Main image page **64, 65**

●●

SIZE

To fit bust

81-86 91-97 102-107 112-117 122-127 cm
32-34 36-38 40-42 44-46 48-50 in

Actual bust measurement of garment

| 90 | 101 | 110 | 121 | 130 | cm |
| 35½ | 40 | 43½ | 47½ | 51 | in |

YARN

Alpaca Merino DK

A Hambleton 110

| 7 | 7 | 8 | 8 | 9 | x 25gm |

B Glenfield 112

| 4 | 4 | 5 | 5 | 5 | x 25gm |

C Ragdale 106

| 6 | 6 | 7 | 8 | 8 | x 25gm |

D Belvoir 107

| 3 | 3 | 3 | 3 | 3 | x 25gm |

NEEDLES

1 pair 4mm (no 8) (US 6) needles
1 pair 4½mm (no 7) (US 7) needles

TENSION

30 sts and 30 rows to 10 cm measured over rib
using 4½mm (US 7) needles.

STRIPE SEQUENCE

Rows 1 to 26: Using yarn A.
Rows 27 to 34: Using yarn B.
Rows 35 to 46: Using yarn C.
Rows 47 and 48: Using yarn D.
Rows 49 to 56: Using yarn A.
Rows 57 to 66: Using yarn B.
Rows 67 to 72: Using yarn C.
Rows 73 to 76: Using yarn D.
Rows 77 and 78: Using yarn A.
Rows 79 to 84: Using yarn B.
Rows 85 to 112: Using yarn C.
Rows 113 to 124: Using yarn D.
Rows 125 to 130: Using yarn A.
Rows 131 to 140: Using yarn B.

Rows 141 to 150: Using yarn C.
Rows 151 to 156: Using yarn D.
These 156 rows form stripe sequence and are
repeated.

BACK

Using 4½mm (US 7) needles and yarn A cast on
135 [151: 165: 181: 195] sts.
Row 1 (RS): K1, *P1, K1, rep from * to end.
Row 2: P1, *K1, P1, rep from * to end.
These 2 rows form rib and rows 1 and 2 of stripe
sequence.
Beg with stripe sequence row 3 (see above), cont
in rib until back meas 34 [34.5: 35: 35.5: 36] cm,
ending with RS facing for next row.
Shape armholes
Keeping rib and stripes correct, cast off 4 [5: 6: 7:
8] sts at beg of next 2 rows.
127 [141: 153: 167: 179] sts.
Dec 1 st at each end of next 3 [5: 5: 7: 7] rows,
then on foll 3 [5: 7: 7: 8] alt rows.
115 [121: 129: 139: 149] sts.
Cont straight until armhole meas 20 [21.5: 23:
24.5: 26] cm, ending with RS facing for next row.
Shape shoulders and back neck
Next row (RS): Cast off 4 [5: 5: 6: 7] sts, rib until
there are 31 [33: 36: 40: 43] sts on right needle and
turn, leaving rem sts on a holder.
Work each side of neck separately.
Dec 1 st at neck edge of next 8 rows **and at
same time** cast off 4 [5: 5: 6: 7] sts at beg of 2nd
and foll 1 [3: 1: 2: 3] alt rows, then 5 [-: 6: 7: -] sts
at beg of foll 2 [-: 2: 1: -] alt rows.
Work 1 row.
Cast off rem 5 [5: 6: 7: 7] sts.
With RS facing, slip centre 45 [45: 47: 47: 49] sts
onto a holder, rejoin appropriate yarn and rib to end.
Complete to match first side, reversing shapings.

LEFT FRONT

Using 4½mm (US 7) needles and yarn A cast on
111 [119: 127: 135: 143] sts.
Beg with rib row 1 and stripe sequence row 1 (see
above), cont in rib as given for back until
22 rows less have been worked than on back to
beg of armhole shaping, ending with RS facing
for next row.
Shape front slope
Keeping rib and stripes correct, dec 1 st at end of
next row and at same edge on foll 21 rows, ending
with RS facing for next row.
89 [97: 105: 113: 121] sts.

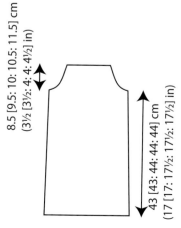

8.5 [9.5: 10: 10.5: 11.5] cm
(3½ [3½: 4: 4: 4½] in)

43 [43: 44: 44: 44] cm
(17 [17: 17½: 17½: 17½] in)

Shape armhole

Keeping rib and stripes correct, cast off 4 [5: 6: 7:
8] sts at beg and dec 1 st at end of next row.
84 [91: 98: 105: 112] sts.
Dec 1 st at front slope edge of next row.
83 [90: 97: 104: 111] sts.
Dec 1 st at armhole edge of next 3 [5: 5: 7: 7]
rows, then on foll 3 [5: 7: 7: 8] alt rows **and at
same time** dec 1 st at front slope edge of next
9 [15: 19: 21: 23] rows. 68 [65: 66: 69: 73] sts.
Dec 1 st at front slope edge **only** on next 38 [28:
22: 16: 14] rows, then on foll 3 [7: 11: 15: 17] alt
rows. 27 [30: 33: 38: 42] sts.
Cont straight until left front matches back to beg
of shoulder shaping, ending with RS facing for
next row.
Shape shoulder
Keeping rib and stripes correct, cast off 4 [5: 5:
6: 7] sts at beg of next and foll 2 [4: 2: 3: 4] alt
rows, then 5 [-: 6: 7: -] sts at beg of foll 2 [-: 2: 1:
-] alt rows.
Work 1 row.
Cast off rem 5 [5: 6: 7: 7] sts.

RIGHT FRONT

Using 4½mm (US 7) needles and yarn A cast on
111 [119: 127: 135: 143] sts.
Beg with rib row 1 and stripe sequence row 1 (see
above), cont in rib as given for back until
22 rows less have been worked than on back to
beg of armhole shaping, ending with RS facing
for next row.
Shape front slope
Keeping rib and stripes correct, dec 1 st at beg of
next row and at same edge on foll 21 rows, ending
with RS facing for next row.
89 [97: 105: 113: 121] sts.
Complete to match left front, reversing shapings.

SLEEVES

Using 4½mm (US 7) needles and yarn A cast on
99 [103: 107: 111: 115] sts.
Beg with rib row 1 and stripe sequence row 1
(see above), cont in rib as given for back until
sleeve meas 43 [43: 44: 44: 44] cm, ending with
RS facing for next row.
Shape top
Keeping rib and stripes correct, cast off 4 [5: 6:
7: 8] sts at beg of next 2 rows.
91 [93: 95: 97: 99] sts.
Dec 1 st at each end of next 24 [26: 28: 30: 32]
rows, ending with RS facing for next row.

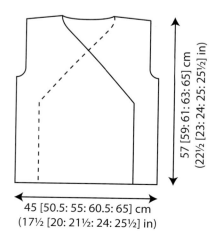

57 [59: 61: 63: 65] cm
(22½ [23: 24: 25: 25½] in)

45 [50.5: 55: 60.5: 65] cm
(17½ [20: 21½: 24: 25½] in)

Cast off rem 43 [41: 39: 37: 35] sts.

MAKING UP
Press as described on the information page.
Join both shoulder seams using back stitch, or mattress stitch if preferred.

Neck trim

With RS facing, using 4mm (US 6) needles and yarn A, beg and ending at beg of front slope shaping, pick up and knit 118 [122: 126: 130: 134]

sts evenly up right front slope, and 9 sts down right side of back neck, K across 45 [45: 47: 47: 49] sts on back holder, pick up and knit 9 sts up left side of back neck, and 118 [122: 126: 130: 134] sts evenly down left front slope. 299 [307: 317: 325: 335] sts.
Beg with row 2, work in rib as given for back for 4 rows, ending with **WS** facing for next row.
Cast off in rib (on **WS**).

Ties (make 2)

Using 4mm (US 6) needles and yarn A cast on 4 sts.
Row 1: (K1, P1) twice.
Rep this row until tie is 105 [115: 125: 135: 145] cm long.
Cast off in rib.
See information page for finishing instructions, setting in sleeves using the set-in method and enclosing one end of each tie in side seams approx 7 cm below armhole.

MARR
Lisa Richardson
Main image page **40, 41**
● ● ●

SIZE
To fit bust

81–86	91–97	102–107	112–117	122–127	cm
32–34	36–38	40–42	44–46	48–50	in

Actual bust measurement of garment

112	122	133	141	152	cm
44	48	52½	55½	60	in

YARN
Alpaca Merino DK
A Medbourne 100

17	18	20	22	23	x 25gm

B Walton 114

11	12	13	15	16	x 25gm

NEEDLES
1 pair 4mm (no 8) (US 6) needles
1 pair 4½mm (no 7) (US 7) needles
4mm (no 8) (US 6) circular needle at least 120 cm long

BUTTONS – 3 x BN1368 B/11 from Bedecked. Please see information page for contact details.

TENSION
27 sts and 52 rows to 10 cm measured over patt using 4½mm (US 7) needles.

Pattern note: When working patt from chart, take care to ensure all slipped sts are worked **keeping yarn at WS of work** – this is back of work on RS rows, and front of work on WS rows.

BACK
Using 4mm (US 6) needles and yarn A cast on 150 [166: 178: 190: 206] sts.
Row 1 (RS): K2, *P2, K2, rep from * to end.
Row 2: P2, *K2, P2, rep from * to end.
These 2 rows form rib.
Work in rib for a further 16 rows, inc [dec: inc: inc: dec] 1 st at end of last row and ending with RS facing for next row.
151 [165: 179: 191: 205] sts.
Change to 4½mm (US 7) needles.
Beg and ending rows as indicated and repeating the 44 row patt repeat throughout, cont in patt from chart (see pattern note) as folls:

Cont straight until back meas 64 [64.5: 65: 65.5: 66] cm, ending with RS facing for next row.
Shape armholes
Keeping patt correct, cast off 7 sts at beg of next 2 rows. 137 [151: 165: 177: 191] sts.
Dec 1 st at each end of next and foll 19 alt rows. 97 [111: 125: 137: 151] sts.
Cont straight until armhole meas 24 [25.5: 27: 28.5: 30] cm, ending with RS facing for next row.
Shape shoulders and back neck
Next row (RS): Cast off 4 [5: 6: 7: 8] sts, patt until there are 29 [35: 40: 45: 50] sts on right needle and turn, leaving rem sts on a holder.
Work each side of neck separately.
Dec 1 st at neck edge of next 8 rows **and at same time** cast off 4 [5: 6: 7: 8] sts at beg of 2nd and foll 3 [2: 2: 2: 2] alt rows, then – [6: 7: 8: 9] sts at beg of foll – [1: 1: 1: 1] alt row.
Work 1 row.
Cast off rem 5 [6: 7: 8: 9] sts.
With RS facing, rejoin yarns and cast off centre 31 [31: 33: 33: 35] sts, then patt to end.
Complete to match first side, reversing shapings.

POCKET LININGS (make 2)
Using 4½mm (US 7) needles and yarn A cast on

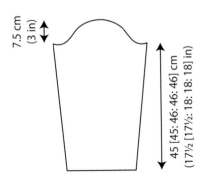

7.5 cm (3 in)

45 [45: 46: 46: 46] cm (17½ [17½: 18: 18: 18] in)

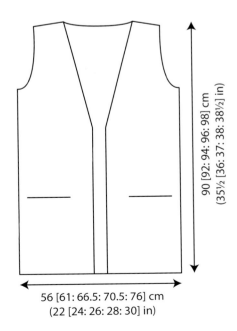

90 [92: 94: 96: 98] cm (35½ [36: 37: 38: 38½] in)

56 [61: 66.5: 70.5: 76] cm (22 [24: 26: 28: 30] in)

34 [34: 36: 36: 38] sts.
Beg with a K row, work in st st for 18 cm, ending with **WS** facing for next row.
Next row (WS): P1 [1: 2: 2: 3], inc purlwise in next st, (P4, inc purlwise in next st) 6 times, P2 [2: 3: 3: 4]. 41 [41: 43: 43: 45] sts.
Break yarn and leave sts on a holder.

LEFT FRONT
Using 4mm (US 6) needles and yarn A cast on 67 [75: 83: 87: 95] sts.
Row 1 (RS): K2, ★P2, K2, rep from ★ to last st, K1.
Row 2: K1, P2, ★K2, P2, rep from ★ to end.
These 2 rows form rib.
Work in rib for a further 16 rows, inc 2 [1: 0: 2: 1] sts evenly across last row and ending with RS facing for next row. 69 [76: 83: 89: 96] sts.
Change to 4½mm (US 7) needles.
Beg and ending rows as indicated, cont in patt from chart (see pattern note) as folls:
Cont straight until left front meas approx 33 [34: 35: 37: 38] cm, ending after a row using yarn A and with RS facing for next row.
Place pocket
Next row (RS): Patt 9 [11: 13: 15: 17] sts, slip next 41 [41: 43: 43: 45] sts onto a holder (for pocket top) and, in their place, patt across 41 [41: 43: 43: 45] sts of first pocket lining, patt 19 [24: 27: 31: 34] sts.
Cont straight until 62 [60: 58: 50: 46] rows less have been worked than on back to beg of armhole shaping, ending with RS facing for next row.
Shape front slope
Place marker at beg of last row (to denote beg of front slope shaping).
Keeping patt correct, dec 1 st at end of next and 6 [5: 5: 4: 4] foll 10th rows. 62 [70: 77: 84: 91] sts.
Work 1 [9: 7: 9: 5] rows, ending with RS facing for next row.
Shape armhole
Keeping patt correct, cast off 7 sts at beg and dec 0 [1: 0: 1: 0] st at end of next row.
55 [62: 70: 76: 84] sts.
Work 1 row.
Dec 1 st at armhole edge of next and foll 19 alt rows **and at same time** dec 1 st at front slope edge of 7th [9th: next: 9th: 3rd] and 3 [1: 3: 3: 3] foll 10th rows, then on 0 [1: 0: 0: 0] foll 12th row. 31 [39: 46: 52: 60] sts.
Dec 1 st at front slope edge **only** on 8th [4th: 2nd: 10th: 4th] and 0 [0: 1: 1: 6] foll 10th rows, then on 5 [6: 6: 6: 3] foll 12th rows. 25 [32: 38: 44: 50] sts.
Cont straight until left front matches back to beg of shoulder shaping, ending with RS facing for next row.
Shape shoulder
Cast off 4 [5: 6: 7: 8] sts at beg of next and foll 4 [3: 3: 3: 3] alt rows, then – [6: 7: 8: 9] sts at beg of foll – [1: 1: 1: 1] alt rows.
Work 1 row.
Cast off rem 5 [6: 7: 8: 9] sts.

RIGHT FRONT
Using 4mm (US 6) needles and yarn A cast on 67 [75: 83: 87: 95] sts.
Row 1 (RS): K3, ★P2, K2, rep from ★ to end.
Row 2: P2, ★K2, P2, rep from ★ to last st, K1.
These 2 rows form rib.

Work in rib for a further 16 rows, inc 2 [1: 0: 2: 1] sts evenly across last row and ending with RS facing for next row. 69 [76: 83: 89: 96] sts.
Change to 4½mm (US 7) needles.
Beg and ending rows as indicated, cont in patt from chart (see pattern note) as folls:
Cont straight until right front meas approx 33 [34: 35: 37: 38] cm, ending after a row using yarn A and with RS facing for next row.
Place pocket
Next row (RS): Patt 19 [24: 27: 31: 34] sts, slip next 41 [41: 43: 43: 45] sts onto a holder (for pocket top) and, in their place, patt across 41 [41: 43: 43: 45] sts of second pocket lining, patt 9 [11: 13: 15: 17] sts.
Cont straight until 62 [60: 58: 50: 46] rows less have been worked than on back to beg of armhole shaping, ending with RS facing for next row.
Shape front slope
Place marker at end of last row (to denote beg of front slope shaping).
Complete to match left front, reversing shapings.

SLEEVES
Using 4mm (US 6) needles and yarn A cast on 58 [62: 66: 66: 66] sts.
Work in rib as given for back for 12 rows, inc [inc: dec: dec: inc] 1 st at end of last row and ending with RS facing for next row. 59 [63: 65: 65: 67] sts.
Change to 4½mm (US 7) needles.
Beg and ending rows as indicated, cont in patt from chart (see pattern note) as folls:
Inc 1 st at each end of 7th [5th: 5th: 5th: 3rd] and every foll 8th [6th: 6th: 6th: 4th] row to 91 [67: 89:

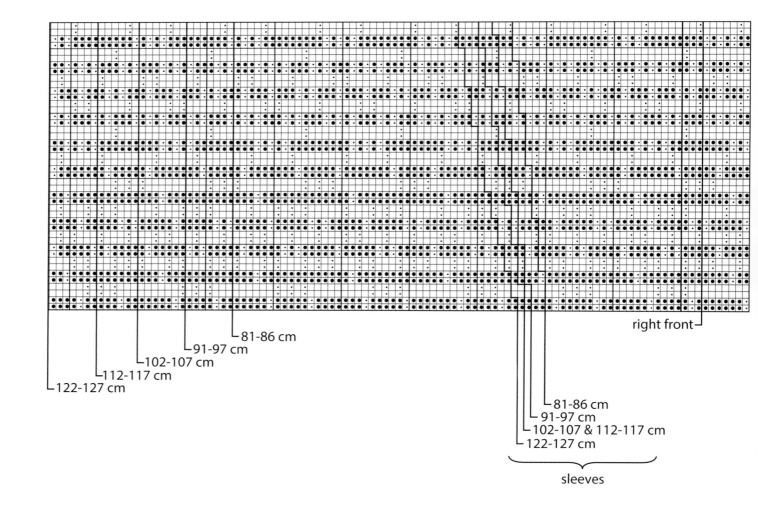

81-86 cm
91-97 cm
102-107 cm
112-117 cm
122-127 cm

right front

81-86 cm
91-97 cm
102-107 & 112-117 cm
122-127 cm

sleeves

121: 79] sts, then on every foll 10th [8th: 8th: 8th: 6th] row until there are 103 [111: 119: 127: 135] sts, taking inc sts into patt.

Cont straight until sleeve meas 45 [45: 46: 46: 46] cm, ending with RS facing for next row.

Shape top

Keeping patt correct, cast off 7 sts at beg of next 2 rows. 89 [97: 105: 113: 121] sts.

Dec 1 st at each end of next and foll 18 alt rows, then on foll row, ending with RS facing for next row.

Cast off rem 49 [57: 65: 73: 81] sts.

MAKING UP

Press as described on the information page.

Join both shoulder seams using back stitch, or mattress stitch if preferred.

Front bands and collar

With RS facing, using 4mm (US 6) circular needle and yarn A, beg and ending at front cast-on edges, pick up and knit 121 [125: 125: 129: 133] sts up right front opening edge to marker at beg of front slope shaping, 84 [87: 90: 93: 96] sts up right front slope, 9 sts down right side of back neck, 31 [31: 34: 34: 34] sts from back neck cast-off edge, 9 sts up left side of back neck, 84 [87: 90: 93: 96] sts down left front slope to marker at beg of front slope shaping, and 121 [125: 125: 129: 133] sts down left front opening edge.

459 [473: 482: 496: 510] sts.

Row 1 (WS of body, RS of collar): K1, (P2, K2) 30 [31: 31: 32: 33] times, (inc purlwise in next st, K2) 72 [74: 77: 79: 81] times, inc purlwise in next st, (K2, P2) 30 [31: 31: 32: 33] times, K1. 532 [548: 560: 576: 592] sts.

Now working all sts in rib as given for back (but with first and last st of every row worked as a K st), cont as folls:

Place markers either side of centre 66 [66: 70: 70: 70] sts – markers should "sit" at shoulder seams and there should be 233 [241: 245: 253: 261] sts either side of markers.

Now shape collar as folls:

Row 2: Rib to **left** shoulder marker, wrap next st (by slipping next st from left needle onto right needle, taking yarn to opposite side of work between needles and then slipping same st back onto left needle - when working back across wrapped sts work the wrapped st and the wrapping loop tog as one st) and turn.

Row 3: Rib to **right** shoulder marker, wrap next st and turn.

Row 4: Rib to 4 sts beyond **left** shoulder marker, wrap next st and turn.

Row 5: Rib to 4 sts beyond **right** shoulder marker, wrap next st and turn.

Row 6: Rib to 8 sts beyond **left** shoulder marker, wrap next st and turn.

Row 7: Rib to 8 sts beyond **right** shoulder marker, wrap next st and turn.

Row 8: Rib to 12 sts beyond **left** shoulder marker, wrap next st and turn.

Row 9: Rib to 12 sts beyond **right** shoulder marker, wrap next st and turn.

Row 10: Rib to 16 sts beyond **left** shoulder marker, wrap next st and turn.

Row 11: Rib to 16 sts beyond **right** shoulder marker, wrap next st and turn.

Cont in this way, working 4 more sts on every row

before wrapping next st and turning, until the foll 2 rows have been worked:

Next row: Rib to 108 [112: 116: 120: 124] sts beyond **left** shoulder marker, wrap next st and turn.

Next row: Rib to 108 [112: 116: 120: 124] sts beyond **right** shoulder marker, wrap next st and turn.

Next row (RS of body): Rib to end.

Collar shaping is now complete – remove markers.

Now working across **all** sts as set, cont as folls:

Work 7 rows, ending with RS of body facing for next row.

Next row (RS): Rib 60 [64: 64: 68: 72], ★cast off 3 sts (to make a buttonhole – cast on 3 sts over these cast-off sts on next row), rib until there are 25 sts on right needle after cast-off, rep from ★ once more, cast off 3 sts (to make 3rd buttonhole – cast on 3 sts over these cast-off sts on next row), rib to end.

Work a further 8 rows, ending with **WS** of body (RS of collar) facing for next row.

Cast off in rib.

Pocket tops (both alike)

Slip 41 [41: 43: 43: 45] sts on pocket holder onto 4mm (US 6) needles and rejoin yarn A with RS facing.

Row 1 (RS): K2 [2: 3: 3: 4], K2tog, (K3, K2tog) 7 times, K2 [2: 3: 3: 4]. 33 [33: 35: 35: 37] sts.

Work in g st for 4 rows, ending with **WS** facing for next row.

Cast off knitwise (on **WS**).

See information page for finishing instructions, setting in sleeves using the shallow set-in method.

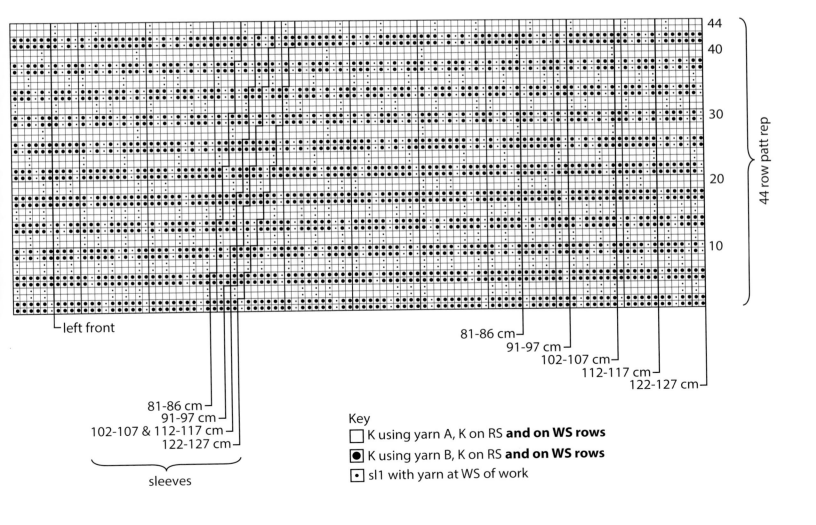

left front

81-86 cm
91-97 cm
102-107 cm
112-117 cm
122-127 cm

81-86 cm
91-97 cm
102-107 & 112-117 cm
122-127 cm

sleeves

Key

☐ K using yarn A, K on RS **and on WS rows**

⦿ K using yarn B, K on RS **and on WS rows**

⊡ sl1 with yarn at WS of work

44
40

30

20

10

44 row patt rep

SIZE

To fit bust

81-86	91-97	102-107	112-117	122-127	cm
32-34	36-38	40-42	44-46	48-50	in

Actual bust measurement of garment

106	117	126	137	146	cm
41½	46	49½	54	57½	in

YARN

Kid Classic

12	13	14	15	16	x 50gm

(photographed in Smoke 831)

NEEDLES

1 pair 4½mm (no 7) (US 7) needles
1 pair 5mm (no 6) (US 8) needles
4½mm (no 7) (US 7) circular needle at least
120 cm long

BUTTONS - 3 x G427230 from Groves & Banks.
Please see information page for contact details.

BEADS – approx 330 [370: 410: 450: 500] beads
(ref Debbie Abrahams size 6, colour 340)

TENSION

20½ sts and 37 rows to 10 cm measured over purl
g st using 4½mm (US 7) needles. 18 sts and 25
rows to 10 cm measured over bodice patt using
5mm (US 8) needles.

SPECIAL ABBREVIATION

bead 1 = place a bead by taking yarn to RS of
work and slipping bead up next to st just worked,
slip next st purlwise from left needle to right
needle and take yarn back to **WS** of work, leaving
bead sitting in front of slipped st on **RS**.

Beading note: Before starting to knit bodice
sections of garment, thread beads onto yarn. To do
this, thread a fine sewing needle (one that will easily
pass through the beads) with sewing thread. Knot

ends of thread and then pass end of yarn through
this loop. Thread a bead onto sewing thread and
then gently slide it along and onto knitting yarn.
Continue in this way until required number of
beads are on yarn. Do not place beads on edge 2 sts
of rows as this will interfere with seaming.

BACK

Using 4½mm (US 7) needles cast on 109 [119:
129: 139: 149] sts.
Work in purl g st (purl every row) until back meas
16 [17: 18: 20: 21] cm, ending with RS facing for
next row.
Dec 1 st at each end of next and foll 18th row,
then on 3 foll 16th rows.
99 [109: 119: 129: 139] sts.
Work 6 rows, ending with **WS** facing for next row.
Next row (WS): P3 [1: 6: 3: 0], P2tog, (P5 [6: 5:
6: 6], P2tog) 13 [13: 15: 15: 17] times, P3 [2: 6: 4:
1]. 85 [95: 103: 113: 121] sts.
Change to 5mm (US 8) needles.
Beg and ending rows as indicated and repeating
the 12 row patt repeat throughout, cont in bodice
patt from chart as folls:
Work 6 [6: 6: 4: 4] rows, ending with RS facing
for next row.
Inc 1 st at each end of next and 0 [1: 2: 3: 3] foll
4th rows, then on 4 [3: 2: 1: 1] foll 6th rows, taking
inc sts into patt. 95 [105: 113: 123: 131] sts.
Work 5 rows, ending with RS facing for next row.
(Back should meas approx 50 [50.5: 51: 51.5: 52]
cm.)
Shape armholes
Place markers at both ends of last row (to denote
base of armhole openings).
Work 50 [54: 58: 62: 66] rows, ending with RS
facing for next row. (Armhole should meas 20
[21.5: 23: 24.5: 26] cm from markers.)
Shape shoulders
Keeping patt correct, cast off 3 [4: 4: 5: 5] sts at beg
of next 6 [10: 8: 10: 10] rows, then 4 [-: 5: -: -] sts
at beg of foll 4 [-: 2: -: -] rows.
61 [65: 71: 73: 81] sts.
Shape back neck
Next row (RS): Cast off 4 [4: 5: 5: 6] sts, patt
until there are 16 [18: 19: 20: 22] sts on right
needle and turn, leaving rem sts on a holder.
Work each side of neck separately.
Dec 1 st at neck edge of next 4 rows **and at
same time** cast off 4 [4: 5: 5: 6] sts at beg of 2nd

row, then 4 [5: 5: 5: 6] sts at beg of foll alt row.
Work 1 row.
Cast off rem 4 [5: 5: 6: 6] sts.
With RS facing, slip centre 21 [21: 23: 23: 25] sts
onto a holder, rejoin yarn and patt to end.
Complete to match first side, reversing shapings.

LEFT FRONT

Using 4½mm (US 7) needles cast on 54 [59: 64:
69: 74] sts.
Work in purl g st (purl every row) until left front
meas 16 [17: 18: 20: 21] cm, ending with RS
facing for next row.
Dec 1 st at beg of next and foll 18th row, then on
3 foll 16th rows. 49 [54: 59: 64: 69] sts.
Work 6 rows, ending with **WS** facing for next row.
Next row (WS): P2 [2: 4: 3: 1], P2tog, (P5 [6: 5:
6: 6], P2tog) 6 [6: 7: 7: 8] times, P3 [2: 4: 3: 2].
42 [47: 51: 56: 60] sts.
Change to 5mm (US 8) needles.
Beg and ending rows as indicated, cont in bodice
patt from chart as folls:
Work 6 [6: 6: 4: 4] rows, ending with RS facing
for next row.
Inc 1 st at beg of next and 0 [1: 2: 3: 3] foll 4th
rows, then on 4 [3: 2: 1: 1] foll 6th rows, taking inc
sts into patt. 47 [52: 56: 61: 65] sts.
Work 1 row, ending with RS facing for next row.
Shape front slope
Keeping patt correct, dec 1 st at end of next row.
46 [51: 55: 60: 64] sts.
Work 3 rows, ending with RS facing for next row.
Shape armhole
Place marker at end of last row (to denote base
of armhole opening).
Keeping patt correct, dec 1 st at front slope edge
of next and 7 [5: 6: 4: 5] foll 4th rows, then on
3 [5: 5: 7: 7] foll 6th rows. 35 [40: 43: 48: 51] sts.
Work 3 rows, ending with RS facing for next row.
Shape shoulder
Cast off 3 [4: 4: 5: 5] sts at beg of next and 2 [6: 3:
7: 4] alt rows, then 4 [5: 5: -: 6] sts at beg of foll
5 [1: 4: -: 3] alt rows **and at same time** dec 1 st
at front slope edge of 3rd and foll 6th row.
Work 1 row.
Cast off rem 4 [5: 5: 6: 6] sts.

RIGHT FRONT

Using 4½mm (US 7) needles cast on 54 [59: 64:
69: 74] sts.

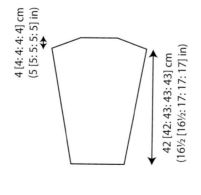

4 [4: 4: 4: 4] cm
(5 [5: 5: 5: 5] in)

42 [42: 43: 43: 43] cm
(16½ [16½: 17: 17: 17] in)

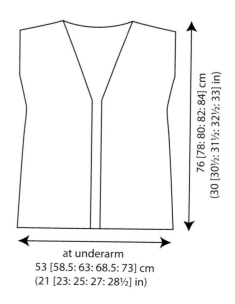

76 [78: 80: 82: 84] cm
(30 [30½: 31½: 32½: 33] in)

at underarm
53 [58.5: 63: 68.5: 73] cm
(21 [23: 25: 27: 28½] in)

Work in purl g st (purl every row) until right front meas 16 [17: 18: 20: 21] cm, ending with RS facing for next row.
Dec 1 st at end of next and foll 18th row, then on 3 foll 16th rows. 49 [54: 59: 64: 69] sts.
Complete to match left front, reversing shapings.

SLEEVES

Using 4½mm (US 7) needles cast on 51 [53: 55: 55: 57] sts.
Work in purl g st (purl every row) throughout as folls:
Inc 1 st at each end of 7th [7th: 5th: 5th: 5th] and every foll 8th [8th: 6th: 6th: 6th] row to 55 [77: 59: 83: 101] sts, then on every foll 10th [10th: 8th: 8th: 8th] row until there are 79 [85: 91: 97: 103] sts.
Cont straight until sleeve meas 42 [42: 43: 43: 43] cm, ending with RS facing for next row.

Shape top
Cast off 3 [4: 4: 4: 4] sts at beg of next 4 [14: 10: 6: 2] rows, then 4 [-: 5: 5: 5] sts at beg of foll 10 [-: 4: 8: 12] rows.
Cast off rem 27 [29: 31: 33: 35] sts.

MAKING UP

Press as described on the information page.
Join both shoulder seams using back stitch, or mattress stitch if preferred.
Front bands and collar
With RS facing and using 4½mm (US 7) circular needle, beg and ending at cast-on edges, pick up and knit 73 [75: 77: 82: 84] sts up right front opening edge to beg of bodice patt, 26 [25: 24: 21: 21] sts up row-end edge of bodice patt to beg of front slope shaping, and 60 [63: 66: 69: 72] sts up right front slope, place (right shoulder) marker on needle, pick up and knit 5 sts down right side of back neck, K across 21 [21: 23: 23: 25] sts on back holder inc 3 sts evenly, pick up and knit 5 sts up left side of back neck, place second (left shoulder) marker on needle, pick up and knit 60 [63: 66: 69: 72] sts down left front slope to beg of front slope shaping, 26 [25: 24: 21: 21] sts down row-end edge of bodice patt to beg of bodice patt, and 73 [75: 77: 82: 84] sts down left front opening edge. 352 [360: 370: 380: 392] sts.
Working in purl g st (P every row) throughout, now shape collar as folls:
Row 1 (WS of body): P to right shoulder marker, wrap next st (by slipping next st from left needle onto right needle, taking yarn to opposite side of work between needles and then slipping same st back onto left needle – when working back across wrapped sts work the wrapped st and the wrapping loop tog as one st) and turn.
Row 2: P to **left** shoulder marker, wrap next st and turn.
Row 3: P to **right** shoulder marker, P3, wrap next st and turn.
Row 4: P to **left** shoulder marker, P3, wrap next st and turn.
Row 5: P to **right** shoulder marker, P6, wrap next st and turn.
Row 6: P to **left** shoulder marker, P6, wrap next st and turn.
Row 7: P to **right** shoulder marker, P9, wrap next st and turn.
Row 8: P to **left** shoulder marker, P9, wrap next st and turn.
Row 9: P to **right** shoulder marker, P12, wrap next st and turn.
Row 10: P to **left** shoulder marker, P12, wrap next st and turn.
Cont in this way, working 3 more sts beyond shoulder marker than on previous row, until the

foll pair of rows have been worked:
Next row: P to right shoulder marker, P60 [63: 66: 69: 72], wrap next st and turn.
Next row: P to left shoulder marker, P60 [63: 66: 69: 72], wrap next st and turn.
This completes short row shaping for collar section.
Next row (WS of body): P to end.
Now working across **all** sts, cont as folls:
Work 4 rows, ending with RS facing for next row.

Next row (RS): P74 [75: 78: 82: 84], yrn, P2tog (to make first buttonhole), (P9 [9: 8: 7: 7], yrn, P2tog) twice (to make 2nd and 3rd buttonholes), P to end.
Work 5 rows, ending with RS facing for next row.
Cast off, taking care to cast-off loosely along collar section.
See information page for finishing instructions, setting in sleeves using the straight cast-off method.

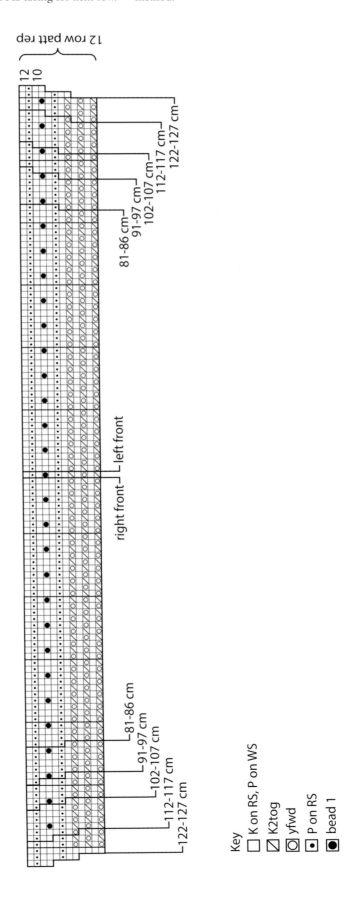

Key
☐ K on RS, P on WS
◩ K2tog
⬭ yfwd
▪ P on RS
● bead 1

BRADSHAW

Martin Storey

Main image page **19, 21**

● ● ● ●

SIZE

To fit bust

81-86 91-97 102-107 112-117 122-127 cm
32-34 36-38 40-42 44-46 48-50 in

Actual bust measurement of garment

107 116 126 136 147 cm
42 45½ 49½ 53½ 58 in

YARN

Kid Classic

11 11 12 13 14 x 50gm

(photographed in Cement 890)

NEEDLES

1 pair 4mm (no 8) (US 6) needles
1 pair 5mm (no 6) (US 8) needles
Cable needle

TENSION

25 sts and 27 rows to 10 cm measured over textured patt using 5mm (US 8) needles. Cable panel (50 sts) measures 15 cm.

SPECIAL ABBREVIATIONS

C6B = slip next 3 sts onto cable needle and leave at back of work, K3, then K3 from cable needle;
C6F = slip next 3 sts onto cable needle and leave at front of work, K3, then K3 from cable needle;
Cr5L = slip next 3 sts onto cable needle and leave at front of work, P2, then K3 from cable needle;
Cr5R = slip next 2 sts onto cable needle and leave at back of work, K3, then P2 from cable needle.

BACK

Using 4mm (US 6) needles cast on 146 [158: 170: 182: 196] sts.
Row 1 (RS): K0 [2: 0: 2: 1], *P2, K2, rep from * to last 2 [0: 2: 0: 3] sts, P2 [0: 2: 0: 2], K0 [0: 0: 0: 1].
Row 2: P0 [2: 0: 2: 1], *K2, P2, rep from * to last 2 [0: 2: 0: 3] sts, K2 [0: 2: 0: 2], P0 [0: 0: 0: 1].
These 2 rows form rib.
Work in rib for a further 20 rows, ending with RS

facing for next row.
Change to 5mm (US 8) needles.
Now work in textured patt, placing cable panel as folls:
Row 1 (RS): K48 [54: 60: 66: 73], work next 50 sts as row 1 of chart, K48 [54: 60: 66: 73].
Row 2: P48 [54: 60: 66: 73], work next 50 sts as row 2 of chart, P48 [54: 60: 66: 73].
Row 3: K3 [1: 3: 1: 4], (sl 1, K3, lift the slipped st over these 3 K sts and off right needle) 11 [13: 14: 16: 17] times, K1, work next 50 sts as row 3 of chart, K1, (sl 1, K3, lift the slipped st over these 3 K sts and off right needle) 11 [13: 14: 16: 17] times, K3 [1: 3: 1: 4].
Row 4: P3 [1: 3: 1: 4], (P3, yrn) 11 [13: 14: 16: 17] times, P1, work next 50 sts as row 4 of chart, P1, (P3, yrn) 11 [13: 14: 16: 17] times, P3 [1: 3: 1: 4].
These 4 rows form textured patt over side edge sts and place cable panel at centre.
(**Note:** As the number of sts varies whilst working textured patt, do **NOT** count sts after patt row 3. All st counts given presume there are 4 sts in each patt rep throughout.)
Keeping sts correct as now set and repeating chart rows 3 to 38 **only** throughout, cont as folls:
Cont straight until back meas 41 [41.5: 42: 42.5: 43] cm, ending with RS facing for next row.
Shape raglan armholes
Keeping patt correct, cast off 3 sts at beg of next 2 rows. 140 [152: 164: 176: 190] sts.
Next row (RS): K2, sl 1, K1, psso, patt to last 4 sts, K2tog, K2.
Next row: P2, P2tog, patt to last 4 sts, P2tog tbl, P2.
Rep last 2 rows 13 [17: 20: 24: 28] times more. 84 [80: 80: 76: 74] sts.
Next row (RS): K2, sl 1, K1, psso, patt to last 4 sts, K2tog, K2.
Next row: P3, patt to last 3 sts, P3.
Rep last 2 rows 12 [10: 9: 7: 5] times more, ending with RS facing for next row. 58 [58: 60: 60: 62] sts.
Break yarn and leave sts on a holder.

FRONT

Work as given for back until 68 [68: 72: 72: 78] sts rem in raglan armhole shaping.
Work 1 [1: 1: 1: 0] row, ending with RS facing for next row.
Shape front neck
Next row (RS): K2, sl 1, K1, psso, patt 5 [5: 7: 7: 10] sts and turn, leaving rem sts on a holder. 8 [8: 10: 10: 13] sts.
Work each side of neck separately.
Keeping patt correct, dec 1 st at neck edge of next 3 [3: 4: 4: 4] rows, then on foll 0 [0: 0: 0: 1] alt row

and at same time dec 1 st at raglan armhole edge of 2nd [2nd: 2nd: 2nd: next] and foll 0 [0: 0: 0: 1] row, then on foll 0 [0: 1: 1: 2] alt rows. 4 sts.
Work 0 [0: 1: 1: 1] row, ending with RS facing for next row.
Next row (RS): K1, sl 1, K2tog, psso.
Next row: P2.
Next row: K2tog and fasten off.
With RS facing, slip centre 50 sts onto a holder, rejoin yarn and patt to last 4 sts, K2tog, K2. 8 [8: 10: 10: 13] sts.
Complete to match first side, reversing shapings.

SLEEVES

Using 4mm (US 6) needles cast on 62 [66: 66: 66: 70] sts.
Row 1 (RS): K2, *P2, K2, rep from * to end.
Row 2: P2, *K2, P2, rep from * to end.
These 2 rows form rib.
Work in rib for a further 20 rows, inc 0 [0: 1: 1: 0] st at each end of last row and ending with RS facing for next row. 62 [66: 68: 68: 70] sts.
Change to 5mm (US 8) needles.
Now work in textured patt as folls:
Row 1 (RS): Knit.
Row 2: Purl.
Row 3: K1 [1: 2: 2: 1], (sl 1, K3, lift the slipped st over these 3 K sts and off right needle) 15 [16: 16: 16: 17] times, K1 [1: 2: 2: 1].
Row 4: P1 [1: 2: 2: 1], (P3, yrn) 15 [16: 16: 16: 17] times, P1 [1: 2: 2: 1].
These 4 rows form textured patt.
(**Note:** As the number of sts varies whilst working textured patt, do NOT count sts after patt row 3. All st counts given presume there are 4 sts in each patt rep throughout.)
Cont in patt, shaping sides by inc 1 st at each end of 3rd [3rd: next: next: next] and 8 [12: 2: 11: 17] foll 6th [6th: 4th: 4th: 4th] rows, then on 4 [1: 13: 7: 3] foll 8th [8th: 6th: 6th: 6th] rows, taking inc sts into st st until there are sufficient to work in patt. 88 [94: 100: 106: 112] sts.
Cont straight until sleeve meas 45 [45: 46: 46: 46] cm, ending with RS facing for next row.
Shape raglan
Keeping patt correct, cast off 3 sts at beg of next 2 rows. 82 [88: 94: 100: 106] sts.
Working all raglan decreases in same way as back and front raglan armhole decreases, dec 1 st at each end of next 11 [13: 15: 17: 19] rows, then on every foll alt row until 22 sts rem.
Work 1 row, ending with RS facing for next row.
Left sleeve only
Dec 1 st at each end of next row, then cast off 5 sts

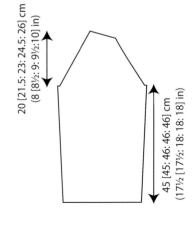

20 [21.5: 23: 24.5: 26] cm
(8 [8½: 9: 9½:10] in)

45 [45: 46: 46: 46] cm
(17½ [17½: 18: 18: 18] in)

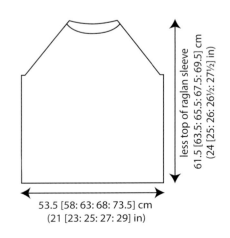

less top of raglan sleeve
61.5 [63.5: 65.5: 67.5: 69.5] cm
(24 [25: 26: 26½: 27½] in)

53.5 [58: 63: 68: 73.5] cm
(21 [23: 25: 27: 29] in)

Key

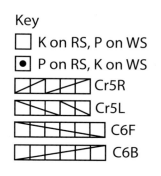

☐ K on RS, P on WS

◉ P on RS, K on WS

[chart symbol] Cr5R

[chart symbol] Cr5L

[chart symbol] C6F

[chart symbol] C6B

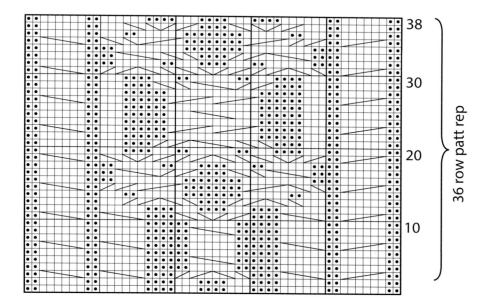

38

30

20

10

36 row patt rep

at beg of foll row. 15 sts.

Dec 1 st at beg of next row, then cast off 7 sts at beg of foll row.

Right sleeve only

Cast off 6 sts at beg and dec 1 st at end of next row. 15 sts.

Work 1 row.

Cast off 7 sts at beg and dec 1 st at end of next row.

Work 1 row.

Both sleeves

Cast off rem 7 sts.

MAKING UP

Press as described on the information page.

Join both front and right back raglan seams using back stitch, or mattress stitch if preferred.

Collar

With RS facing and using 4mm (US 6) needles, pick up and knit 18 sts from top of left sleeve, and 5 [5: 8: 8: 9] sts down left side of front neck, K across 50 sts on front holder as folls: K1, (K1, K2tog, K1) 12 times, K1, pick up and knit 5 [5: 8:

8: 9] sts up right side of front neck, and 18 sts from top of right sleeve, then K across 58 [58: 60: 60: 62] sts on back holder as folls: K5 [5: 6: 6: 7], (K1, K2tog, K1) 12 times, K5 [5: 6: 6: 7].

130 [130: 138: 138: 142] sts.

Beg with row 1, work in rib as given for sleeves for 20 cm, ending with **WS** facing for next row.

Cast off in rib.

See information page for finishing instructions, reversing collar seam for last 11 cm (for turn back).

FARNLEY

Emma Wright

Main image page **12, 13**

● ●

YARN

Big Wool

6   x 100gm

(photographed in Biscotti 082)

NEEDLES

1 pair 10mm (no 000) (US 15) needles

Cable needle

TENSION

Based on a st st tension of 9 sts and 12½ rows to 10 cm using 10mm (US 15) needles.

FINISHED SIZE

Completed scarf is approx 19 cm (7½ in) wide and 193 cm (76 in) long, excluding pompons.

SPECIAL ABBREVIATIONS

C4B = slip next 2 sts onto cable needle and leave at back of work, K2, then K2 from cable needle;

C4F = slip next 2 sts onto cable needle and leave at front of work, K2, then K2 from cable needle.

SCARF

First section

Using 10mm (US 15) needles and waste yarn cast on 28 sts.

Work in st st for 2 rows, ending with RS facing for next row.

Break waste yarn and join in main yarn, leaving a fairly long end (this will be used to gather end of section).

Now work in patt as folls:

Row 1 (RS): K10, C4B, C4F, K10.

Row 2 and every foll alt row: K6, P16, K6.

Row 3: K8, C4B, K4, C4F, K8.

Row 5: K6, C4B, K8, C4F, K6.

Row 6: As row 2.

These 6 rows form patt.

Cont in patt until work meas 96.5 cm **from waste yarn**, ending with RS facing for next row.★★

Break yarn and leave sts on a holder.

Second section

Work as given for first section to ★★.

Break yarn, leaving a long end.

Join sections

Carefully graft together last rows of both sections to form completed scarf.

MAKING UP

Press as described on the information page.

Carefully unravel waste yarn and, using strand of main yarn left at beg of section in main yarn, thread this end through all 28 sts. Pull up tight and fasten off securely. Make two 10 cm diameter pompons and attach one to each end of scarf as in photograph.

SUNDOWN

Martin Storey

Main image page **88, 89**

● ●

SIZE

To fit bust

81-86	91-97	102-107	112-117	122-127	cm
32-34	36-38	40-42	44-46	48-50	in

Actual bust measurement of garment

85	96	106	117	125	cm
33½	38	41½	46	49	in

YARN

Kid Classic

6	6	7	7	8	x 50gm

(photographed in Tattoo 856)

NEEDLES

1 pair 4mm (no 8) (US 6) needles
1 pair 5mm (no 6) (US 8) needles

BUTTONS - 6 x Metal Filigree Buttons from Groves & Banks. Please see information page for contact details.

BEADS – approx 270 [320: 360: 400: 450] beads (ref Debbie Abrahams size 6, colour 562)

TENSION

19 sts and 32 rows to 10 cm measured over patt using 5mm (US 8) needles.

SPECIAL ABBREVIATION

bead 1 = place a bead by taking yarn to RS of work and slipping bead up next to st just worked, slip next st purlwise from left needle to right needle and take yarn back to WS of work, leaving bead sitting in front of slipped st on RS.

Beading note: Before starting to knit, thread beads onto yarn. To do this, thread a fine sewing needle (one that will easily pass through the beads) with sewing thread. Knot ends of thread and then pass end of yarn through this loop. Thread a bead onto sewing thread and then gently slide it along and onto knitting yarn. Continue in this way until required number of beads are on yarn. Do not place beads on edge 2 sts of rows as this will interfere with seaming.

BACK

Using 4mm (US 6) needles cast on 77 [87: 97: 107: 115] sts.

Work in g st for 10 rows, ending with RS facing for next row.

Change to 5mm (US 8) needles.

Beg and ending rows as indicated and repeating the 12 row patt repeat throughout, cont in patt from chart as folls:

Work 20 [20: 18: 16: 16] rows, ending with RS facing for next row.

Inc 1 st at each end of next and foll 20th [20th: 20th: 18th: 18th] row, taking inc sts into patt.
81 [91: 101: 111: 119] sts.

Cont straight until back meas 22 [21.5: 21: 19.5: 19] cm, ending with RS facing for next row.

Shape armholes

Keeping patt correct, cast off 3 [4: 5: 6: 7] sts at beg of next 2 rows. 75 [83: 91: 99: 105] sts.

Dec 1 st at each end of next 3 [3: 5: 5: 5] rows, then on foll 3 [5: 4: 6: 5] alt rows.
63 [67: 73: 77: 85] sts.

Cont straight until armhole meas 18 [19.5: 21: 22.5: 24] cm, ending with RS facing for next row.

Shape shoulders and back neck

Next row (RS): Cast off 3 [3: 4: 4: 5] sts, patt until there are 14 [16: 17: 19: 21] sts on right needle and turn, leaving rem sts on a holder.

Work each side of neck separately.

Dec 1 st at neck edge of next 4 rows **and at same time** cast off 3 [4: 4: 5: 5] sts at beg of 2nd row, then 3 [4: 4: 5: 6] sts at beg of foll alt row.

Work 1 row.

Cast off rem 4 [4: 5: 5: 6] sts.

With RS facing, slip centre 29 [29: 31: 31: 33] sts onto a holder, rejoin yarn and patt to end.

Complete to match first side, reversing shapings.

LEFT FRONT

Using 4mm (US 6) needles cast on 38 [43: 48: 53: 57] sts.

Work in g st for 10 rows, ending with RS facing for next row.

Change to 5mm (US 8) needles.

Beg and ending rows as indicated, cont in patt from chart as folls:

Work 20 [20: 18: 16: 16] rows, ending with RS facing for next row.

Inc 1 st at beg of next and foll 20th [20th: 20th: 18th: 18th] row, taking inc sts into patt.
40 [45: 50: 55: 59] sts.

Cont straight until left front matches back to beg of armhole shaping, ending with RS facing for next row.

Shape armhole

Keeping patt correct, cast off 3 [4: 5: 6: 7] sts at beg of next row. 37 [41: 45: 49: 52] sts.

Work 1 row.

Dec 1 st at armhole edge of next 3 [3: 5: 5: 5] rows, then on foll 3 [5: 4: 6: 5] alt rows.
31 [33: 36: 38: 42] sts.

Cont straight until 20 [20: 22: 22: 24] rows less have been worked than on back to beg of shoulder shaping, ending with RS facing for next row.

Shape front neck

Next row (RS): Patt 23 [25: 28: 30: 34] sts and turn, leaving rem 8 sts on a holder (for neckband).

Keeping patt correct, dec 1 st at neck edge of next 6 rows, then on foll 2 [2: 3: 3: 4] alt rows, then on 2 foll 4th rows. 13 [15: 17: 19: 22] sts.

Work 1 row, ending with RS facing for next row.

Shape shoulder

Cast off 3 [3: 4: 4: 5] sts at beg of next and foll 2 [0: 2: 0: 1] alt rows, then – [4: -: 5: 6] sts at beg of foll – [2: -: 2: 1] alt rows.

Work 1 row.

Cast off rem 4 [4: 5: 5: 6] sts.

RIGHT FRONT

Using 4mm (US 6) needles cast on 38 [43: 48: 53: 57] sts.

Work in g st for 10 rows, ending with RS facing for next row.

Change to 5mm (US 8) needles.

Beg and ending rows as indicated, cont in patt from chart as folls:

Work 20 [20: 18: 16: 16] rows, ending with RS facing for next row.

Inc 1 st at end of next and foll 20th [20th: 20th: 18th: 18th] row, taking inc sts into patt.
40 [45: 50: 55: 59] sts.

Complete to match left front, reversing shapings and working first row of neck shaping as folls:

Shape front neck

Next row (RS): Patt 8 sts and slip these sts onto a holder (for neckband), patt to end.
23 [25: 28: 30: 34] sts.

SLEEVES

Using 4mm (US 6) needles cast on 43 [45: 47: 47: 49] sts.

Work in g st for 10 rows, ending with RS facing for next row.

Change to 5mm (US 8) needles.

Beg and ending rows as indicated, cont in patt from chart as folls:

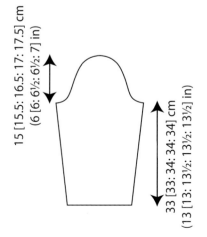

15 [15.5: 16.5: 17: 17.5] cm
(6 [6: 6½: 6½: 7] in)

33 [33: 34: 34: 34] cm
(13 [13: 13½: 13½: 13½] in)

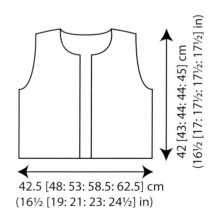

42 [43: 44: 44: 45] cm
(16½ [17: 17½: 17½: 17½] in)

42.5 [48: 53: 58.5: 62.5] cm
(16½ [19: 21: 23: 24½] in)

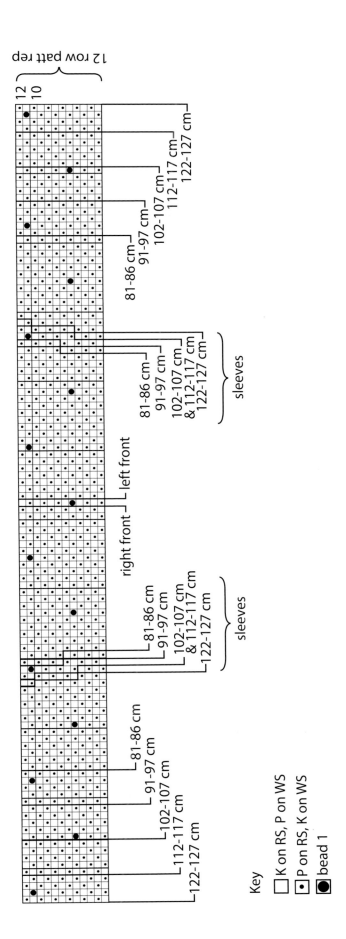

Key

☐ K on RS, P on WS

• P on RS, K on WS

● bead 1

Inc 1 st at each end of 7th [7th: 5th: 5th: 5th] and every foll 8th [8th: 6th: 6th: 6th] row to 53 [65: 51: 67: 77] sts, then on every foll 10th [-: 8th: 8th: -] row until there are 61 [-: 69: 73: -] sts, taking inc sts into patt.

Cont straight until sleeve meas 33 [33: 34: 34: 34] cm, ending with RS facing for next row.

Shape top

Keeping patt correct, cast off 3 [4: 5: 6: 7] sts at beg of next 2 rows. 55 [57: 59: 61: 63] sts.

Dec 1 st at each end of next 3 rows, then on foll alt row, then on 6 foll 4th rows.

35 [37: 39: 41: 43] sts.

Work 1 row.

Dec 1 st at each end of next and every foll alt row until 23 sts rem, then on foll 5 rows, ending with RS facing for next row.

Cast off rem 13 sts.

MAKING UP

Press as described on the information page.

Join both shoulder seams using back stitch, or mattress stitch if preferred.

Neckband

With RS facing and using 4mm (US 6) needles, slip 8 sts from right front holder onto right needle, rejoin yarn and pick up and knit 18 [18: 20: 20: 22] sts up right side of front neck, and 5 sts down right side of back neck, K across 29 [29: 31: 31: 33] sts on back holder, pick up and knit 5 sts up left side of back neck, and 18 [18: 20: 20: 22] sts down left side of front neck, then patt across 8 sts on left front holder. 91 [91: 97: 97: 103] sts.

Work in g st for 8 rows, ending with **WS** facing for next row.

Cast off knitwise (on **WS**).

Button band

With RS facing and using 4mm (US 6) needles, pick up and knit 69 [71: 71: 71: 73] sts evenly down entire left front opening edge, from top of neckband to cast-on edge.

Work in g st for 10 rows, ending with **WS** facing for next row.

Cast off knitwise (on **WS**).

Buttonhole band

Work to match button band, picking up sts along right front opening edge and making buttonholes in row 6 as folls:

Row 6 (buttonhole row) (RS): K5 [7: 7: 7: 8], ★yfwd, K2tog (to make a buttonhole), K10, rep from ★ 4 times more, yfwd, K2tog (to make 6th buttonhole), K2 [2: 2: 2: 3].

See information page for finishing instructions, setting in sleeves using the set-in method.

SWEETING

Lisa Richardson

Main image page **20, 21**

● ● ● ●

SIZE

To fit bust

81-86	91-97	102-107	112-117	122-127 cm
32-34	36-38	40-42	44-46	48-50 in

Actual bust measurement of garment

115	123	134	144	155 cm
45½	48½	53	56½	61 in

YARN

Kid Classic

19	20	22	23	24	x 50gm

(photographed in Cement 890)

NEEDLES

1 pair 4½mm (no 7) (US 7) needles
1 pair 5mm (no 6) (US 8) needles

BUTTONS – 5 x A0480 from Groves & Banks.
Please see information page for contact details.

TENSION

19 sts and 26 rows to 10 cm measured over patt
using 5mm (US 8) needles.

Pattern note: The number of sts varies whilst
working patt. All st counts given relate to the
original number of sts and do NOT include
any sts made whilst working patt. When shaping
through patt, treat each group of 3 "bubble" sts
as one st, working these 3 sts together. Do NOT
work a "bubble" on end sts of rows – instead, work
these sts in rev st st.

BACK

Using 4½mm (US 7) needles cast on 103 [111:
121: 131: 141] sts.
Beg with a P row, work in rev st st for 12 rows,
ending with RS facing for next row.
Change to 5mm (US 8) needles.
Place markers at both ends of last row (to denote
hem fold line).
Beg and ending rows as indicated and repeating

the 12 row patt repeat throughout, cont in patt
from chart (see pattern note) as folls:
Work 36 rows, ending with RS facing for next row.
Inc 1 st at each end of next and 2 foll 32nd rows,
taking inc sts into patt. 109 [117: 127: 137: 147] sts.
Cont straight until back meas 51 [51.5: 52: 52.5:
53] cm **from markers**, ending with RS facing for
next row.

Shape raglan armholes
Keeping patt correct, cast off 3 sts at beg of next
2 rows. 103 [111: 121: 131: 141] sts.
Dec 1 st at each end of next 3 [7: 11: 17: 21] rows,
then on foll 27 [27: 27: 26: 26] alt rows.
43 [43: 45: 45: 47] sts.
Work 1 row, ending with RS facing for next row.
Break yarn and leave sts on a holder.

LEFT POCKET BAG
Using 5mm (US 8) needles cast on 1 st.
Beg with a P row, work in rev st st throughout
as folls:
Work 1 row, ending with **WS** facing for next row.
Row 2 (WS): Inc in st. 2 sts.
Work 1 row.
Inc 1 st at end of next row, then at beg of foll row.
4 sts.
Work 1 row.
Inc 1 st at beg of next row, then at end of foll row.
6 sts.
Rep last 6 rows 3 times more, then first 5 of these
rows again, ending with **WS** facing for next row.
21 sts.
Work 59 rows, ending with RS facing for next
row.
Break yarn and leave sts on a holder.

LEFT FRONT
Using 4½mm (US 7) needles cast on 45 [49: 54:
59: 64] sts.
Beg with a P row, work in rev st st as folls:
Work 1 row, ending with **WS** facing for next row.
Inc 1 st at beg of next row and at same edge on
foll 10 rows, ending with RS facing for next row.
56 [60: 65: 70: 75] sts.
Change to 5mm (US 8) needles.
Place markers at both ends of last row (to
denote hem fold line).
Now cont to shape for facings and, beg and
ending rows as indicated, cont in patt from chart
(see pattern note) as folls:

Next row (RS): Work chart row 1, inc in last st.
Next row: Inc knitwise in first st, place marker
on needle, work rem 56 [60: 65: 70: 75] sts as chart
row 2.
Next row: Work first 56 [60: 65: 70: 75] sts as
chart row 3, slip marker onto right needle, P to last
st, inc in last st.
Next row: Inc knitwise in first st, K to marker,
slip marker onto right needle, work rem 56 [60:
65: 70: 75] sts as chart row 4.
Working appropriate rows of chart, rep last 2 rows
3 times more, ending with RS facing for next row.
66 [70: 75: 80: 85] sts.
Remove marker.
Next row (RS): Patt to last 10 sts, P10.
Next row: K10, patt to end.
Last 2 rows set the sts – front opening edge 10 sts
in rev st st (for front facing) and all rem sts in patt
from chart.
Keeping sts correct as now set throughout, cont
as folls:
Work 24 rows, ending with RS facing for next row.
Inc 1 st at beg of next row. 67 [71: 76: 81: 86] sts.
Work 15 rows, ending with RS facing for next row.

Place pocket
Next row (RS): Patt 10 [14: 15: 20: 21] sts, slip
rem 57 [57: 61: 61: 65] sts onto a holder (for
pocket front) and, in their place, patt across 21 sts
of left pocket bag. 31 [35: 36: 41: 42] sts.
Working all sts in patt, work 30 rows on these sts,
inc 1 st at beg of 16th of these rows and ending
with **WS** facing for next row.
32 [36: 37: 42: 43] sts.
Break yarn and leave sts on another holder.
Rejoin yarn to 57 [57: 61: 61: 65] sts on first
holder with RS facing and, keeping sts correct as
set, shape pocket front as folls:
Dec 1 st at beg of next row.
Work 1 row.
Dec 1 st at beg of next row, then at end of foll row.
Work 1 row.
Dec 1 st at end of next row, then at beg of foll row.
Rep last 6 rows 4 times more, ending with **WS**
facing for next row. 36 [36: 40: 40: 44] sts.
Join sections
Next row (WS): Patt across 36 [36: 40: 40: 44] sts
of pocket front, then patt across 32 [36: 37: 42: 43]
sts on holder. 68 [72: 77: 82: 87] sts.
Work 16 rows, ending with RS facing for next row.
Inc 1 st at beg of next row. 69 [73: 78: 83: 88] sts.

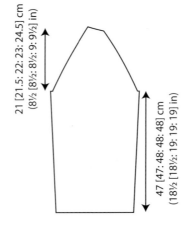

21 [21.5: 22: 23: 24.5] cm
(8½ [8½: 8½: 9: 9½] in)

47 [47: 48: 48: 48] cm
(18½ [18½: 19: 19: 19] in)

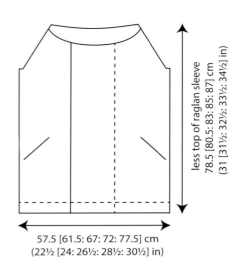

less top of raglan sleeve
78.5 [80.5: 83: 85: 87] cm
(31 [31½: 32½: 33½: 34½] in)

57.5 [61.5: 67: 72: 77.5] cm
(22½ [24: 26½: 28½: 30½] in)

Cont straight until left front matches back to beg of raglan armhole shaping, ending with RS facing for next row.

Shape raglan armhole
Keeping patt correct, cast off 3 sts at beg of next row. 66 [70: 75: 80: 85] sts.
Work 1 row.
Dec 1 st at raglan armhole edge of next 3 [7: 11: 17: 21] rows, then on foll 23 [23: 22: 21: 20] alt rows. 40 [40: 42: 42: 44] sts.
Work 1 row, ending with RS facing for next row.

Shape front neck
Next row (RS): P2tog, patt 10 [10: 12: 12: 14] sts and turn, leaving rem 28 sts on a holder (for hood). 11 [11: 13: 13: 15] sts.
Keeping patt correct, dec 1 st at neck edge of next 6 rows, then on foll 0 [0: 1: 1: 2] alt rows **and at same time** dec 1 st at raglan armhole edge of 2nd and foll 2 [2: 3: 3: 4] alt rows. 2 sts.
Work 1 row, ending with RS facing for next row.
Next row (RS): P2tog and fasten off.
Mark positions for 5 buttons along left front opening edge – first button to come level with top of pocket opening, top button to come 3 cm above sts left on holder at neck, and rem 3 buttons evenly spaced between.

RIGHT POCKET BAG
Using 5mm (US 8) needles cast on 1 st.
Beg with a P row, work in rev st st throughout as folls:
Work 1 row, ending with **WS** facing for next row.
Row 2 (WS): Inc in st. 2 sts.
Work 1 row.
Inc 1 st at beg of next row, then at end of foll row. 4 sts.
Work 1 row.
Inc 1 st at end of next row, then at beg of foll row. 6 sts.
Rep last 6 rows 3 times more, then first 5 of these rows again, ending with **WS** facing for next row. 21 sts.
Work 59 rows, ending with RS facing for next row.
Break yarn and leave sts on a holder.

RIGHT FRONT
Using 4½mm (US 7) needles cast on 45 [49: 54: 59: 64] sts.
Beg with a P row, work in rev st st as folls:
Work 1 row, ending with **WS** facing for next row.
Inc 1 st at end of next row and at same edge on foll 10 rows, ending with RS facing for next row. 56 [60: 65: 70: 75] sts.
Change to 5mm (US 8) needles.
Place markers at both ends of last row (to denote hem fold line).
Now cont to shape for facings and, beg and ending rows as indicated, cont in patt from chart (see pattern note) as folls:
Next row (RS): Inc in first st, work chart row 1.
Next row: Work first 56 [60: 65: 70: 75] sts as chart row 2, place marker on needle, inc knitwise in last st.
Next row: Inc in first st, P to marker, slip marker onto right needle, work rem 56 [60: 65: 70: 75] sts as chart row 3.
Next row: Work first 56 [60: 65: 70: 75] sts as chart row 4, slip marker onto right needle, K to last st, inc knitwise in last st.
Working appropriate rows of chart, rep last 2 rows 3 times more, ending with RS facing for next row. 66 [70: 75: 80: 85] sts.
Remove marker.

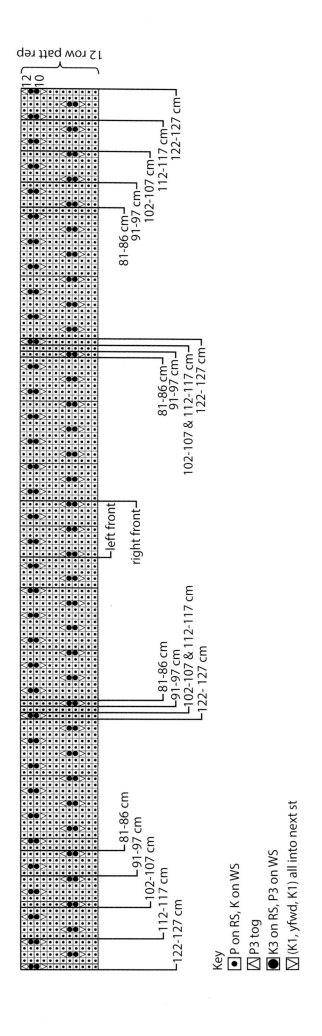

Key
⊡ P on RS, K on WS
◩ P3 tog
⬤ K3 on RS, P3 on WS
▽ (K1, yfwd, K1) all into next st

Next row (RS): P10, patt to end.

Next row: Patt to last 10 sts, K10.

Last 2 rows set the sts – front opening edge 10 sts in rev st st (for front facing) and all rem sts in patt from chart.

Keeping sts correct as now set throughout, cont as folls:

Work 24 rows, ending with RS facing for next row.

Inc 1 st at end of next row. 67 [71: 76: 81: 86] sts.

Work 15 rows, ending with RS facing for next row.

Place pocket

Next row (RS): Patt 55 [55: 59: 59: 63] sts, P2tog and turn, leaving rem 10 [14: 15: 20: 21] sts on a holder (for side front).

Keeping patt correct, work on this set of 56 [56: 60: 60: 64] sts for pocket front as folls:

Work 1 row.

Dec 1 st at end of next row, then at beg of foll row.

Work 1 row.

Dec 1 st at beg of next row, then at end of foll row.

Rep last 6 rows 3 times more, then first 5 of these rows again, ending with RS facing for next row. 37 [37: 41: 41: 45] sts.

Next row (buttonhole row) (RS): P4, cast off 2 sts purlwise (to make first buttonhole of first pair of buttonholes – cast on 2 sts over these cast-off sts on next row), patt until there are 8 sts on right needle after cast-off, cast off 2 sts purlwise (to make second buttonhole of first pair of buttonholes – cast on 2 sts over these cast-off sts on next row), patt to last 2 sts, P2tog. 36 [36: 40: 40: 44] sts.

Making a further 3 pairs of buttonholes in this way to correspond with positions marked for buttons on left front and noting that no further reference will be made to buttonholes, cont as folls:

Break yarn and leave sts on another holder.

With RS facing, now work pocket lining and side front as folls:

Rejoin yarn to right pocket bag sts and P these 21 sts, then patt across 10 [14: 15: 20: 21] sts on side front holder. 31 [35: 36: 41: 42] sts.

Working all sts in patt, work 30 rows on these sts, inc 1 st at end of 16th of these rows and ending with **WS** facing for next row. 32 [36: 37: 42: 43] sts.

Join sections

Next row (WS): Patt across 32 [36: 37: 42: 43] sts of side front, then patt across 36 [36: 40: 40: 44] sts on holder. 68 [72: 77: 82: 87] sts.

Complete to match left front, reversing shapings and working first row of neck shaping as folls:

Shape front neck

Next row (RS): Break yarn and slip first 28 sts onto a holder (for hood), rejoin yarn and patt to last 2 sts, P2tog. 11 [11: 13: 13: 15] sts.

SLEEVES

Using 4½mm (US 7) needles cast on 55 [57: 59: 59: 61] sts.

Beg with a P row, work in rev st st for 12 rows, ending with RS facing for next row.

Change to 5mm (US 8) needles.

Place markers at both ends of last row (to denote hem fold line).

Beg and ending rows as indicated, cont in patt from chart (see pattern note) as folls:

Work 12 rows, ending with RS facing for next row.

Inc 1 st at each end of next and every foll 8th [6th: 6th: 4th: 4th] row to 71 [67: 83: 65: 79] sts, then on every foll 10th [8th: 8th: 6th: 6th] row until there are 79 [85: 91: 95: 101] sts, taking inc sts into patt.

Cont straight until sleeve meas approx 47 [47: 48: 48: 48] cm **from markers**, ending after same point in patt as on back to beg of raglan armhole shaping and with RS facing for next row.

Shape raglan

Keeping patt correct, cast off 3 sts at beg of next 2 rows. 73 [79: 85: 89: 95] sts.

Dec 1 st at each end of next and 5 [4: 3: 3: 2] foll 4th rows, then on foll 18 [22: 26: 28: 32] alt rows. 25 sts.

Work 1 row, ending with RS facing for next row.

Break yarn and leave sts on a holder (for hood).

MAKING UP

Press as described on the information page.

Join all raglan seams using back stitch, or mattress stitch if preferred.

Left side hood and hood lining

With RS facing and using 5mm (US 8) needles, beg at left back raglan seam, P across 25 sts on left sleeve holder (decreasing if required, depending on point reached in patt – see pattern note), pick up and knit 7 [7: 9: 9: 11] sts down left side of front neck, patt across first 18 sts on left front holder, place marker on needle, then **patt** across rem 10 sts from holder, turn and cast on 40 [40: 42: 42: 44] sts. 100 [100: 104: 104: 108] sts – marker is at centre of these sts and denotes fold line for hood lining.

Now working **all** sts in patt as set by 18 sts from front holder, cont as folls:

Work 3 rows, ending with RS facing for next row.

Inc 1 st at each end of next and foll 4th row, then on foll 6th row, taking inc sts into patt. 106 [106: 110: 110: 114] sts.

Cont straight until work meas 28 cm from pick-up row, ending with RS facing for next row.

Keeping patt correct, dec 1 st at each end of next and foll 4th row, then on foll 3 alt rows, then on foll 9 rows, ending with RS facing for next row. 78 [78: 82: 82: 86] sts.

Cast off 4 sts at beg of next 2 rows, 5 sts at beg of foll 2 rows, and 6 sts at beg of next 2 rows.

Cast off rem 48 [48: 52: 52: 56] sts, placing marker between centre 2 cast-off sts (to denote fold line for hood lining).

Right side hood and hood lining

Using 5mm (US 8) needles, cast on 40 [40: 42: 42: 44] sts, then, with RS facing, **patt** first 10 sts on right front holder, place marker on needle, patt across rem 18 sts on holder, pick up and knit 7 [7: 9: 9: 11] sts up right side of front neck, then P across 25 sts on right sleeve holder (decreasing if required, depending on point reached in patt – see pattern note) to right back raglan seam. 100 [100: 104: 104: 108] sts – marker is at centre of these sts and denotes fold line for hood lining.

Now working **all** sts in patt as set by 18 sts from front holder, complete as given for left side hood and hood lining making 5th buttonhole when work meas 3 cm from pick-up row as folls:

Buttonhole row (RS): Patt to within 6 sts of fold line marker, cast off 2 sts purlwise (to make first buttonhole of 5th pair of buttonholes – cast on 2 sts over these cast-off sts on next row), patt until there are 8 sts on right needle after cast-off, cast off 2 sts purlwise (to make second buttonhole of 5th pair of buttonholes – cast on 2 sts over these cast-off sts on next row), patt to end.

Hood and hood lining back panel

Slip 43 [43: 45: 45: 47] sts from back neck holder onto 5mm (US 8) needles and rejoin yarn with RS facing.

Cont in patt as set until this centre back panel fits up row-end edges of side hood sections, across cast-off edges and then down other row-end edge to cast-on edge of side hood lining sections, ending with RS facing for next row.

Cast off.

Sew row-end edges of back panel to side panels. Fold hood lining sections to inside along fold lines and then neatly sew cast-on and cast-off edges of lining sections to neck edge.

Pocket tops (both alike)

With RS facing and using 5mm (US 8) needles, pick up and knit 29 sts evenly along sloped pocket opening edge.

Row 1 (WS): Knit.

Row 2: P2, (K1, yfwd, K1) all into next st, *P3, (K1, yfwd, K1) all into next st, rep from * to last 2 sts, P2.

Row 3: K2, P3, (P3, K3) 6 times, K2.

Row 4: P2, K3, (P3, K3) 6 times, P2.

Row 5: K2, P3tog, (K3, P3tog) 6 times, K2.

Row 6: Purl.

Row 7: Knit.

Row 8: P4, (K1, yfwd, K1) all into next st, *P3, (K1, yfwd, K1) all into next st, rep from * to last 4 sts, P4.

Row 9: K4, P3, (K3, P3) 5 times, K4.

Row 10: P4, K3, (P3, K3) 5 times, P4.

Row 11: K4, P3tog, (K3, P3tog) 5 times, K4.

Row 12: Purl.

Row 13: Knit.

Place markers at both ends of last row (to denote fold line).

Change to 4½mm (US 7) needles.

Beg with a P row, work in rev st st for 13 rows, ending with **WS** facing for next row.

Cast off knitwise (on **WS**).

Fold pocket bag in half so that shaped row-end edge of first part of pocket bag matches shaped pocket opening edge and neatly sew pocket bag to pocket top pick-up row. Join row-end edges of pocket bag. Fold pocket top in half to inside along fold line row and neatly sew cast-off edge in place on inside, then neatly sew ends of pocket top in place on front.

See information page for finishing instructions. Around lower edges of sleeves, fold first 12 rows to inside along fold line row and neatly sew in place. Across lower hem edge of back and fronts, fold first 12 rows to inside along fold line row and neatly sew in place. Along front opening edges, fold 10 sts to inside along fold line and neatly sew in place, joining shaped row-end edges of front opening and hem edges at base of front opening edges.

THACKREY

Martin Storey

Main image page **28, 29**

● ● ●

YARN

Felted Tweed	Scarf	Hat	Scarf and Hat	
A Stone 190	3	1	4	x 50gm
B Seafarer 170	3	1	4	x 50gm
C Tawny 186	1	1	1	x 50gm

NEEDLES

Set of 4 double-pointed 3¼mm (no 10) (US 3) needles
Set of 4 double-pointed 3¾mm (no 9) (US 5) needles

TENSION

24 sts and 27 rounds to 10 cm measured over patterned st st using 3¾mm (US 5) needles.

FINISHED SIZE

Completed scarf is 20 cm (7¾ in) wide and 210 cm (82½ in) long. Hat to fit average size adult head.

SCARF

Using double-pointed 3¼mm (US 3) needles and yarn C cast on 96 sts.
Distribute sts evenly over 3 of the 4 needles and, using 4th needle and taking care not to twist cast-on edge, work in rounds as folls:
Round 1 (RS): ★K2, P2, rep from ★ to end.
This round forms rib.
Cont in rib until scarf meas 8 cm.
Change to double-pointed 3¾mm (US 5) needles.
Joining in and breaking off colours as required, using the **fairisle** technique as described on the information page and repeating the 4 st patt repeat 24 times around each round, cont in patt from chart, which is worked entirely in st st (K every round), as folls:
Work chart rounds 1 to 10, 4 times.
Now work chart rounds 11 to 20 once.
Now rep chart rounds 1 to 10 **only** until scarf meas approx 183.5 cm, ending after chart round 10.
Now work chart rounds 11 to 20 once.
Work chart rounds 1 to 10, 4 times.
Break off contrast and cont using yarn C **only**.
Change to double-pointed 3¼mm (US 3) needles.
Work in rib as given for cast-on edge for 8 cm.
Cast off in rib.

HAT

Using double-pointed 3¼mm (US 3) needles and yarn C cast on 124 sts.
Distribute sts evenly over 3 of the 4 needles and, using 4th needle and taking care not to twist cast-on edge, work in rounds as folls:
Round 1 (RS): ★K2, P2, rep from ★ to end.
This round forms rib.
Cont in rib until hat meas 2 cm.
Change to double-pointed 3¾mm (US 5) needles.
Joining in and breaking off colours as required, using the **fairisle** technique as described on the information page and repeating the 4 st patt repeat 31 times around each round, cont in patt from chart, which is worked entirely in st st (K every round), as folls:

Work chart rounds 1 to 20 once.
Now rep chart rounds 1 to 10 **only** twice more, ending after chart round 10.
Break off contrasts and complete hat in st st (K every round) using yarn C **only** as folls:
Next round (RS): (K14, K2tog, K15) 4 times. 120 sts.
Shape top
Round 1: (K10, K2tog) 10 times. 110 sts.
Work 3 rounds.
Round 5: (K9, K2tog) 10 times. 100 sts.
Work 1 round.
Round 7: (K8, K2tog) 10 times. 90 sts.
Work 1 round.
Round 9: (K7, K2tog) 10 times. 80 sts.
Work 1 round.
Round 11: (K6, K2tog) 10 times. 70 sts.
Work 1 round.
Round 13: (K5, K2tog) 10 times. 60 sts.
Work 1 round.
Round 15: (K4, K2tog) 10 times. 50 sts.
Work 1 round.
Round 17: (K3, K2tog) 10 times. 40 sts.
Round 18: (K2, K2tog) 10 times. 30 sts.
Round 19: (K1, K2tog) 10 times. 20 sts.
Round 20: (K2tog) 10 times.
Break yarn and thread through rem 10 sts. Pull up tight and fasten off securely.

MAKING UP

Press as described on the information page.

Key

A □
B ■
C ☒

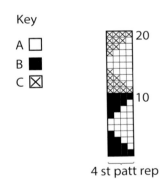

4 st patt rep

SYKES

Martin Storey

Main image page **14, 15**

● ● ●

SIZE

To fit bust

81-86	91-97	102-107	112-117	122-127	cm
32-34	36-38	40-42	44-46	48-50	in

Actual bust measurement of garment

106	116	126	136	146	cm
41½	45½	49½	53½	57½	in

YARN

Kid Classic

12	13	14	16	17	x 50gm

(photographed in Pumice 888)

NEEDLES

1 pair 4mm (no 8) (US 6) needles
1 pair 5mm (no 6) (US 8) needles
Cable needle

TENSION

28 sts and 25 rows to 10 cm measured over patt using 5mm (US 8) needles.

SPECIAL ABBREVIATIONS

C2B = slip next st onto cable needle and leave at back of work, K1, then K1 from cable needle; **C2F** = slip next st onto cable needle and leave at front of work, K1, then K1 from cable needle; **C4B** = slip next 2 sts onto cable needle and leave at back of work, K2, then K2 from cable needle; **C4F** = slip next 2 sts onto cable needle and leave at front of work, K2, then K2 from cable needle; **Cr3L** = slip next 2 sts onto cable needle and leave at front of work, P1, then K2 from cable needle; **Cr3R** = slip next st onto cable needle and leave at back of work, K2, then P1 from cable needle.

BACK

Using 4mm (US 6) needles cast on 148 [162: 176: 190: 204] sts.

Beg and ending rows as indicated, cont in patt from chart as folls:

Row 1 (RS): K1, work next 146 [160: 174: 188: 202] sts as row 1 of chart, K1.

Row 2: K1, work next 146 [160: 174: 188: 202]

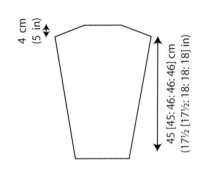

4 cm (5 in)

45 [45: 46: 46: 46] cm (17½ [17½: 18: 18: 18] in)

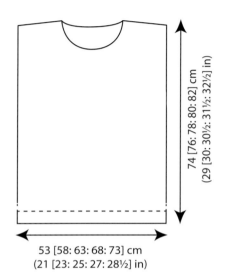

74 [76: 78: 80: 82] cm (29 [30: 30½: 31½: 32½] in)

53 [58: 63: 68: 73] cm (21 [23: 25: 27: 28½] in)

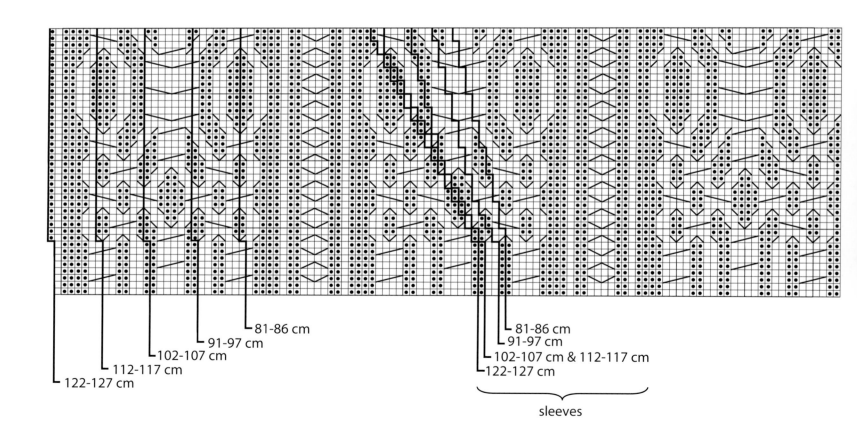

81-86 cm
91-97 cm
102-107 cm
112-117 cm
122-127 cm

81-86 cm
91-97 cm
102-107 cm & 112-117 cm
122-127 cm

sleeves

sts as row 2 of chart, K1.

These 2 rows set the sts – first and last st of every row worked as a K st with all other sts in patt from chart.**

Now work chart rows 3 and 4 **once only**, then chart rows 5 to 8, 7 times, ending with RS facing for next row.

Place markers at both ends of last row (to denote top of side seam openings).

Change to 5mm (US 8) needles.

Now repeating chart rows 9 to 40 **throughout** (and noting that first and last sts of rows are now worked in patt from chart), cont in patt from chart as folls:

Cont straight until back meas 60 [62: 64: 66: 68] cm **from markers**, ending with RS facing for next row.

Shape shoulders and back neck

Keeping patt correct, cast off 7 [8: 9: 11: 12] sts at beg of next 2 rows, then 7 [9: 10: 11: 12] sts at beg of foll 2 rows. 120 [128: 138: 146: 156] sts.

Next row (RS): Cast off 8 [9: 10: 11: 12] sts, patt until there are 28 [31: 34: 37: 40] sts on right needle and turn, leaving rem sts on a holder.

Work each side of neck separately.

Dec 1 st at neck edge of next 4 rows **and at same time** cast off 8 [9: 10: 11: 12] sts at beg of 2nd and foll alt row.

Work 1 row.

Cast off rem 8 [9: 10: 11: 12] sts.

With RS facing, slip centre 48 [48: 50: 50: 52] sts onto a holder, rejoin yarn and patt to end.

Complete to match first side, reversing shapings.

FRONT

Work as given for back to **.

Now work chart rows 3 and 4 **once only**, then chart rows 5 to 8, 3 times, ending with RS facing

for next row.

Place markers at both ends of last row (to denote top of side seam openings). (**Note:** Front rib is 16 rows shorter than back rib.)

Change to 5mm (US 8) needles.

Now repeating chart rows 9 to 40 **throughout** (and noting that first and last sts of rows are now worked in patt from chart), cont in patt from chart as folls:

Measuring from markers and remembering that front is 16 rows shorter than back below markers, cont straight until 20 [20: 22: 22: 24] rows less have been worked than on back to beg of shoulder shaping, ending with RS facing for next row.

Shape front neck

Next row (RS): Patt 61 [68: 75: 82: 89] sts and turn, leaving rem sts on a holder.

Work each side of neck separately.

Keeping patt correct, dec 1 st at neck edge of next 10 rows, then on foll 4 [4: 5: 5: 6] alt rows. 47 [54: 60: 67: 73] sts.

Work 1 row, ending with RS facing for next row.

Shape shoulder

Cast off 7 [8: 9: 11: 12] sts at beg of next and foll 1 [0: 0: 4: 4] alt rows, then 8 [9: 10: –: –] sts at beg of foll 3 [4: 4: –: –] alt rows **and at same time** dec 1 st at neck edge of 3rd row.

Work 1 row.

Cast off rem 8 [9: 10: 11: 12] sts.

With RS facing, slip centre 26 sts onto a holder, rejoin yarn and patt to end.

Complete to match first side, reversing shapings.

SLEEVES

Using 4mm (US 6) needles cast on 70 [72: 76: 76: 78] sts.

Beg and ending rows as indicated, cont in patt

from chart as folls:

Work chart rows 1 to 4 **once only**, then chart rows 5 to 8, 3 times, ending with RS facing for next row.

Change to 5mm (US 8) needles.

Now repeating chart rows 9 to 40 **throughout**, cont in patt from chart as folls:

Inc 1 st at each end of 3rd [next: next: next: next] and every foll 4th [alt: alt: alt: alt] row to 106 [80: 90: 106: 120] sts, then on every foll 6th [4th: 4th: 4th: 4th] row until there are 110 [118: 126: 134: 142] sts, taking inc sts into patt.

Cont straight until sleeve meas 45 [45: 46: 46: 46] cm, ending with RS facing for next row.

Shape top

Keeping patt correct, cast off 7 [7: 8: 9: 9] sts at beg of next 6 [2: 6: 10: 6] rows, then 8 [8: 9: –: 10] sts at beg of foll 4 [8: 4: –: 4] rows.

Cast off rem 36 [40: 42: 44: 48] sts.

Key

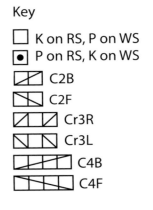

☐ K on RS, P on WS
⊡ P on RS, K on WS
▱ C2B
▱ C2F
▱ Cr3R
▱ Cr3L
▱ C4B
▱ C4F

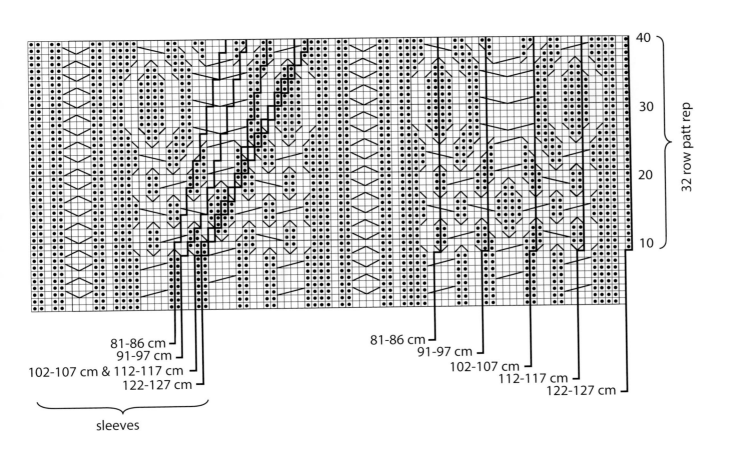

81-86 cm
91-97 cm
102-107 cm & 112-117 cm
122-127 cm

81-86 cm
91-97 cm
102-107 cm
112-117 cm
122-127 cm

sleeves

40
30
20
10

32 row patt rep

MAKING UP

Press as described on the information page. Join left shoulder seam using back stitch, or mattress stitch if preferred.

Neckband

With RS facing and using 4mm (US 6) needles, pick up and knit 26 [26: 29: 29: 30] sts down left side of front neck, K across 26 sts on front holder as folls: K1, (K1, K2tog, K1) 6 times, K1, pick up and knit 26 [26: 29: 29: 30] sts up right side of front neck, and 5 sts down right side of back neck, K across 48 [48: 50: 50: 52] sts on back holder as folls: K0 [0: 1: 1: 2], (K1, K2tog, K1) 12 times, K0 [0: 1: 1: 2], then pick up and knit 5 sts up left side of back neck. 118 [118: 126: 126: 130] sts.

Row 1 (WS): P2, *K2, P2, rep from * to end.
Row 2: K2, *P2, K2, rep from * to end.
These 2 rows form rib.
Work in rib for a further 5 rows, ending with RS facing for next row.

Cast off in rib.

Join left shoulder and neckband seam. Mark points along side seam edges 20 [21.5: 23: 24.5: 26] cm either side of shoulder seams (to denote base of armhole openings). See information page for finishing instructions, setting in sleeves using the straight cast-off method and leaving side seams open below markers.

EASTBURY

Emma Wright

Main image page **43**

●●●●

SIZE

To fit bust

81-86	91-97	102-107	112-117	122-127	cm
32-34	36-38	40-42	44-46	48-50	in

Actual bust measurement of garment

87	98	107	118	127	cm
34½	38½	42	46½	50	in

YARN

Alpaca Merino DK

A Saxon 101

11	12	13	15	16	x 25gm

B Stamford 111

1	1	1	1	1	x 25gm

NEEDLES

4½mm (no 7) (US 7) circular needle no more than 80 cm long
Set of 4 double-pointed 4½mm (no 7) (US 7) needles
Cable needle

TENSION

22 sts and 30 rounds to 10 cm measured over st st using 4½mm (US 7) needles. Cable panel (13 sts) meas 4 cm.

SPECIAL ABBREVIATIONS

C5B = slip next 3 sts onto cable needle and leave at back of work, K2, then (P1, K2) from cable needle; **Cr3L** = slip next 2 sts onto cable needle and leave at front of work, P1, then K2 from cable needle; **Cr3R** = slip next st onto cable needle and leave at back of work, K2, then P1 from cable needle; **MB** = make bobble as folls: K into front, back and front again of next st, turn, P3, turn, K3, turn, P3, turn, K3tog.

BODY (worked in one piece to armholes)
Using 4½mm (US 7) circular needle and yarn B cast on 188 [212: 232: 256: 276] sts.
Break off yarn B and join in yarn A.
Taking care not to twist cast-on edge, work in rounds as folls:
Round 1 (RS): K1, *P2, K2, rep from * to last 3 sts, P2, K1, rep from * to end.
This round forms rib.
Place markers to denote side seams as folls: place marker after last st of last round (this is left side "seam"), then place second marker after 94 [106: 116: 128: 138] sts (this is right side "seam").
Cont in rib for a further 8 rounds.

Now working in st st (K every round) throughout, cont as folls:
Cont straight until body meas 9 [10: 11: 13: 14] cm.
Next round: (K1, sl 1, K1, psso, K to within 3 sts of marker, K2tog, K1) twice.
Working all side seam decreases as set by last round, dec 1 st at each side of both side seam markers on 8th and 2 foll 8th rounds.
172 [196: 216: 240: 260] sts.
Work 15 rounds.
Next round: (K2, M1, K to within 2 sts of marker, M1, K2) twice.
Working all side seam increases as set by last round, inc 1 st at each side of both side seam markers on 8th and 3 foll 8th rounds.
192 [216: 236: 260: 280] sts.
Cont straight until body meas 38 [38.5: 39: 39.5: 40] cm.
Break yarn and leave sts on holders as folls: Slip first 3 sts onto a holder for left underarm, next 90 [102: 112: 124: 134] sts onto another holder for front, next 6 sts onto another holder for right underarm, next 45 [51: 56: 62: 67] sts onto another holder for right back, next 45 [51: 56: 62: 67] sts onto another holder for left back, and rem 3 sts onto same holder as first 3 sts (for rest of left underarm sts).

SLEEVE STRIPE SEQUENCE

Rounds 1 and 2: Using yarn A.

45 [45: 46: 46: 46] cm
(17½ [17½: 18: 18: 18] in)

at underarm
43.5 [49: 53.5: 59: 63.5] cm
(17 [19½: 21: 23: 25] in)

59 [61: 63: 65: 67] cm
(23 [24: 25: 25½: 26½] in)

Rounds 3 and 4: Using yarn B.
Rounds 5 to 12: Using yarn A.
Rounds 13 to 32: As rounds 3 to 12, twice.
Rounds 33 and 34: Using yarn B.
Round 35 onwards: Using yarn A.

SLEEVES

Using 4½mm (US 7) double-pointed needles and yarn A cast on 40 [42: 44: 44: 46] sts.
Taking care not to twist cast-on edge, distribute sts over 3 of the 4 needles and, using 4th needle, work in rounds as folls:
Round 1 (RS): K1 [2: 1: 1: 2], *P2, K2, rep from * to last 3 [4: 3: 3: 4] sts, P2, K1 [2: 1: 1: 2].
This round forms rib.
Place marker after last st of last round – this denotes sleeve "seam".
Cont in rib for a further 8 rounds.
Beg with sleeve stripe sequence round 1, now work in st st (K every round) in stripe sequence (see above) as folls:
Work 5 [5: 3: 3: 3] rounds.
Next round: K1, M1, K to last st, M1, K1.
Working all sleeve increases as set by last round, inc 1 st at each end of 6th [6th: 4th: 4th: 4th] and every foll 6th [6th: 4th: 4th: 4th] round to 48 [74: 56: 74: 94] sts, then on every foll 8th [8th: 6th: 6th: 6th] round until there are 70 [78: 86: 92: 100] sts.
Cont straight until sleeve meas 45 [45: 46: 46: 46] cm.
Break yarn and leave sts on holders as folls: Slip first 3 sts onto a holder for underarm, next 64 [72: 80: 86: 94] sts onto another holder for sleeve, and rem 3 sts onto same holder as first 3 sts (for rest of underarm sts).

YOKE

Using 4½mm (US 7) circular needle and yarn A, join body and sleeves as folls:
Round 1 (RS): K across 45 [51: 56: 62: 67] sts on left back holder as folls: K to last 5 sts, place first green marker on needle, (K1, inc in next st) twice, K1, K across 64 [72: 80: 86: 94] sts on left sleeve holder as folls: (inc in next st, K1) twice, place first red marker on needle, K to last 4 sts, place second red marker on needle, (K1, inc in next st) twice, K across 90 [102: 112: 124: 134] sts on front holder as folls: (K1, inc in next st) twice, K1, place first blue marker on needle, K to last 5 sts, place second blue marker on needle, (K1, inc in next st) twice, K1, K across 64 [72: 80: 86: 94] sts on right sleeve holder as folls: (inc in next st, K1) twice, place third red marker on needle, K to last 4 sts, place fourth red marker on needle, (K1, inc in next st) twice, then K across 45 [51: 56: 62: 67] sts on right back holder as folls: (K1, inc in next st) twice, K1, place second green marker on needle, K to end.
324 [364: 400: 436: 472] sts.
There should be 8 markers in total – sts between blue markers are front sts, sts between green markers are back sts, and sts between each pair of red markers are sleeve sts. Between each pair of NON-matching markers there should be 13 sts – these are for cable panel. Each cable panel "sits" along raglan "seam".
Round 2: K to first marker, *slip marker onto right needle, work next 13 sts as row 1 of cable panel, slip next marker onto right needle, K to next marker, rep from * twice more, slip marker onto right needle, work next 13 sts as row 1 of cable panel, slip next marker onto right needle, K to end.
This round sets position of 4 cable panels.
Keeping cable panels correct as now set, cont as folls:
Round 3: K to within 3 sts of first green marker, K2tog (for left back raglan armhole dec), K1, slip green marker onto right needle, patt 13 sts, slip next red marker onto right needle, K1, sl 1, K1, psso (for left back raglan sleeve dec), K to within 3 sts of next red marker, K2tog (for left front raglan sleeve dec), K1, slip red marker onto right needle, patt 13 sts, slip next blue marker onto right needle, K1, sl 1, K1, psso (for left front raglan armhole dec), K to within 3 sts of next blue marker, K2tog (for right front raglan armhole dec), K1, slip blue marker onto right needle, patt 13 sts, slip next red marker onto right needle, K1, sl 1, K1, psso (for right front raglan sleeve dec), K to within 3 sts of next red marker, K2tog (for right back raglan sleeve dec), K1, slip red marker onto right needle, patt 13 sts, slip next green marker onto right needle, K1, sl 1, K1, psso (for right back raglan armhole dec), K to end.
316 [356: 392: 428: 464] sts.
(**Note:** As the number of sts decreases whilst working yoke, change to double-pointed needles.)
Working all raglan decreases as set by last round, cont as folls:
Dec 1 st next to each blue and green marker (on front and back) on next 16 [24: 26: 34: 38] rounds, then on foll 6 [4: 6: 4: 4] alt rounds **and at same time** dec 1 st next to each red marker (sleeves) on 4th [4th: 2nd: next: next] and foll 0 [0: 0: 1: 5] rounds, then on 2 [0: 0: 0: 0] foll 4th rounds, then on foll 8 [14: 18: 20: 20] alt rounds. 184 [184: 188: 188: 192] sts in total, with 34 [34: 36: 36: 38] sts between blue markers and green markers, and 32 sts between each pair of red markers.
Keeping cable panel and decreases correct as set, now shape neck as folls:
Row 1 (RS): Patt to first blue marker, slip blue marker onto right needle, K8, wrap next st (by slipping next st from left needle onto right needle, taking yarn to opposite side of work between needles and then slipping same st back onto left needle - when working back across wrapped sts work the wrapped st and the wrapping loop tog as one st) and turn.
Row 2 (WS): P5, P2tog tbl, P1, patt 13 sts, P1, P2tog, P26, P2tog tbl, P1, patt 13 sts, P1, P2tog, P5, wrap next st and turn.
Row 3: K7, patt 13 sts, K30, patt 13 sts, K3, wrap next st and turn.
Row 4: P2tog tbl, P1, patt 13 sts, P1, P2tog, P24, P2tog tbl, P1, patt 13 sts, P1, P2tog, wrap next st and turn.
Row 5: K2, patt 13 sts, K28, patt 11 sts, wrap next st and turn.
Row 6: Patt 11 sts, P1, P2tog, P22, P2tog tbl, P1, patt 11 sts and turn.
Row 7: Patt 11 sts, K26, patt 7 sts, wrap next st and turn.
Row 8: Patt 7 sts, P1, P2tog, P20, P2tog tbl, P1, patt 7 sts, wrap next st and turn.

Row 9: Patt 7 sts, K24, patt 3 sts, wrap next st and turn.
Row 10: Patt 3 sts, P1, P2tog, P18, P2tog tbl, P1, patt 3 sts, wrap next st and turn.
These 10 rows complete shaping for left side of neck and shoulder.
Row 11: Patt to green right back raglan marker, slip green marker onto right needle, K8, wrap next st and turn.
Now rep rows 2 to 10 once more – this completes shaping for right side of neck and shoulder.
Next row: Patt to end of round, ending at centre back. 156 [156: 160: 160: 164] sts.
Now working in rounds again, cont as folls:
Next round: K to end, inc 0 [0: 1: 1: 1] st at centre front, working across each set of 13 cable sts as folls: P2tog, patt 1 st, work 2 tog, patt 3 sts, work 2 tog, patt 1 st, P2tog, and inc 0 [0: 0: 0: 1] st at end of round. 140 [140: 145: 145: 150] sts.
Next round: K1, *P3, K2, rep from * to last 4 sts, P3, K1.
Rep last round 7 times more.
Next round: K1, *P2tog, P1, K2, rep from * to last 4 sts, P2tog, P1, K1.
112 [112: 116: 116: 120] sts.
Next round: K1, *P2, K2, rep from * to last 3 sts, P2, K1.
Rep last round 8 times more.
Cast off in rib.

MAKING UP
Press as described on the information page.
Join sets of 6 underarm sts by grafting sets of sts together.
See information page for finishing instructions.

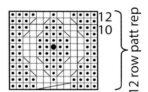

Key

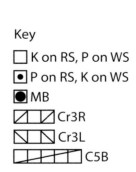

K on RS, P on WS

P on RS, K on WS

MB

Cr3R

Cr3L

C5B

MIDNIGHT

Lisa Richardson

Main image page **78, 84**

Cowl **85, 87**

● ● ●

SIZE

To fit bust

81-86	91-97	102-107	112-117	122-127	cm
32-34	36-38	40-42	44-46	48-50	in

Actual bust measurement of garment

90	102	114	120	132	cm
35½	40	45	47	52	in

YARN

Kidsilk Haze and Fine Lace

Sweater and cowl

A KSH

9	10	11	11	12	x 25gm

B Lace

4	4	4	4	5	x 50gm

Sweater

A KSH

7	8	8	8	9	x 25gm

B Lace

4	4	4	4	5	x 50gm

Cowl

A KSH

2	2	2	2	2	x 25gm

B Lace

1	1	1	1	1	x 50gm

(both photographed in Kidsilk Haze in Mulberry 679 with Fine lace in Dark Burgundy 951)

CROCHET HOOK

3.50mm (no 9) (US E4) crochet hook

TENSION

3 patt repeats (18 sts) to **9** cm and 16 rows to 10 cm measured over patt using 3.50mm (US E4) crochet hook and one strand of each of yarns A and B held together.

COWL FINISHED SIZE

Completed cowl is 25 cm (10 in) deep and meas 75 cm (29½ in) all round.

CROCHET ABBREVIATIONS

ch = chain; **dc** = double crochet; **puff st** = (yoh and insert hook as indicated, yoh and draw loop through) 5 times, yoh and draw through all 11 loops on hook, then work 1 ch tightly to close puff st (note: once completed, there will be 2 sts at top of each puff st – when working back across a puff st treat these 2 sts as one st, working into the top of the actual puff section);
ss = slip stitch; **tr** = treble; **yoh** = yarn over hook.

BACK and FRONT (both alike)

Using 3.50mm (US E4) crochet hook and one strand of each of yarns A and B held together make 92 [104: 116: 122: 134] ch.

Foundation row (RS): 1 dc into 2nd ch from hook, ★3 ch, miss 2 ch, 1 puff st into next ch, 3 ch, miss 2 ch, 1 dc into next ch, rep from ★ to end, turn. 15 [17: 19: 20: 22] patt reps.

Now work in patt as folls:

Row 1 (WS): 1 ch (does NOT count as st), 1 dc into first dc, ★3 ch, miss 3 ch, 1 dc into next st, rep from ★ to end, turn.

Row 2: 6 ch (counts as 1 tr and 3 ch), miss dc at base of 6 ch and next 3 ch, ★1 dc into next dc, 3 ch, miss 3 ch★★, 1 puff st into next dc, 3 ch, miss 3 ch, rep from ★ to end, ending last rep at ★★, 1 tr into last dc, turn.

Row 3: 1 ch (does NOT count as st), 1 dc into tr at base of 1 ch, ★3 ch, miss 3 ch, 1 dc into next st, rep from ★ to end, working dc at end of last rep into 3rd of 6 ch at beg of previous row, turn.

Row 4: 1 ch (does NOT count as st), 1 dc into first dc, ★3 ch, miss 3 ch, 1 puff st into next dc, 3 ch, miss 3 ch, 1 dc into next dc, rep from ★ to end, turn. These 4 rows form patt.

Cont in patt for a further 60 rows, ending after patt row 4 and with **WS** facing for next row. (Work should meas approx 40.5 cm.)

Shape armholes

Next row (WS): Ss across and into top of first puff st, 1 ch (does NOT count as st), 1 dc into top of puff st at base of 1 ch, patt until dc has been worked into last puff st and turn, leaving rem (3 ch and 1 dc) unworked. 14 [16: 18: 19: 21] patt reps.

Next row: As patt row 4.

Rep last 2 rows 2 [3: 4: 4: 5] times more. 12 [13: 14: 15: 16] patt reps.

Beg with patt row 1, cont in patt for a further 24 [24: 26: 28: 28] rows, ending with **WS** facing for next row. (Armhole should meas approx 19 [20: 22.5: 24: 25] cm.)

Fasten off.

SLEEVES

Using 3.50mm (US E4) crochet hook and one strand of each of yarns A and B held together make 44 [44: 50: 50: 50] ch.

Work foundation row as given for back and front. 7 [7: 8: 8: 8] patt reps.

Beg with patt row 1, now work in patt as given for back and front as folls:

Work 7 rows, ending after patt row 3 and with RS facing for next row.

★★★**Row 9 (RS):** 7 ch (counts as 3 ch, 1 dc and 3 ch), 1 dc into first dc, ★3 ch, miss 3 ch, 1 puff st into next dc, 3 ch, miss 3 ch★★, 1 dc into next dc, rep from ★ to end, ending last rep at ★★, (1 dc, 3 ch and 1 tr) into last dc, turn.

Row 10: 1 ch (does NOT count as st), 1 dc into tr at base of 1 ch, ★3 ch, miss 3 ch, 1 dc into next st, rep from ★ to end, working dc at end of last rep into 4th of 7 ch at beg of previous row, turn. 8 [8: 9: 9: 9] patt reps.

Beg with patt row 4, work 12 [8: 8: 8: 4] rows, ending after patt row 3.

Rep from ★★★ 0 [0: 0: 3: 1] times more. 8 [8: 9: 12: 10] patt reps.

★★★★Rep rows 9 and 10 once more.

Beg with patt row 4, work 16 [12: 12: 8: 8] rows, ending after patt row 3.

Rep from ★★★★ 1 [2: 2: 0: 3] times more. 10 [11: 12: 13: 14] patt reps.

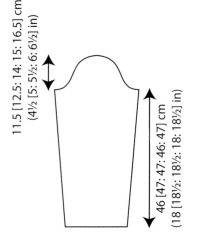

11.5 [12.5: 14: 15: 16.5] cm
(4½ [5: 5½: 6: 6½] in)

46 [47: 47: 46: 47] cm
(18 [18½: 18½: 18: 18½] in)

45 [51: 57: 60: 66] cm
(17½ [20: 22½: 23½: 26] in)

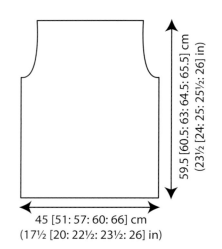

59.5 [60.5: 63: 64.5: 65.5] cm
(23½ [24: 25: 25½: 26] in)

Rep rows 9 and 10 once more.
11 [12: 13: 14: 15] patt reps.
Beg with patt row 4, work 13 rows, ending after patt row 4. (Sleeve should meas approx 46 [47: 47: 46: 47] cm.)

Shape top

Next row (WS): Ss across and into top of first puff st, 1 ch (does NOT count as st), 1 dc into top of puff st at base of 1 ch, patt until dc has been worked into last puff st and turn, leaving rem (3 ch and 1 dc) unworked. 10 [11: 12: 13: 14] patt reps.
Next row: As patt row 4.
Rep last 2 rows 8 [9: 10: 11: 12] times more. 2 patt reps.
Fasten off.

COWL

Using 3.50mm (US E4) crochet hook and one strand of each of yarns A and B held together make 150 ch and join with a ss to form a ring, taking care not to twist ch.
Foundation round (RS): 1 ch (does NOT count as st), 1 dc into same place as ss closing ring, *3 ch, miss 2 ch, 1 puff st into next ch, 3 ch, miss 2 ch**, 1 dc into next ch, rep from * to end, ending last rep at **, ss to first dc, turn. 25 patt reps.
Now work in patt as folls:
Round 1 (WS): 1 ch (does NOT count as st), 1 dc into st at base of 1 ch, *3 ch, miss 3 ch, 1 dc into next st, rep from * to end, replacing dc at end of last rep with ss to first dc, turn.
Round 2: 3 ch (does NOT count as st), 1 puff st into st at base of 3 ch, 3 ch, miss 3 ch, *1 dc into next dc, 3 ch, miss 3 ch**, 1 puff st into next dc, 3 ch, miss 3 ch, rep from * to end, ending last rep at **, ss to top of puff st at beg of round, turn.

Round 3: As round 1.
Round 4: 1 ch (does NOT count as st), 1 dc into st at base of 1 ch, *3 ch, miss 3 ch, 1 puff st into next dc, 3 ch, miss 3 ch, 1 dc into next dc, rep from * to end, replacing dc at end of last rep with ss to first dc, turn.
These 4 rounds form patt.
Cont in patt for a further 35 rounds, ending after patt round 3 and with RS facing for next round.
Fasten off.

MAKING UP

Press as described on the information page.
Join both shoulder seams using back stitch and leaving centre 27 [27: 28: 28: 29] cm open (for neck opening).
See information page for finishing instructions, setting in sleeves using the set-in method.

WEETON

Lisa Richardson

Main image page **11**

●

YARN
Alpaca Merino DK
    7   x 25gm
(photographed in Saxon 101)

CROCHET HOOK
15mm (US P/Q19) crochet hook

TENSION
Due to construction, the tension is irrelevant – but make sure you do not work too tightly.

FINISHED SIZE
Completed scarf is approx 12 cm (4½ in) wide and 155 cm (61 in) long, excluding fringe.

CROCHET ABBREVIATIONS
ch = chain.

SCARF
Using 15mm (US P/Q) crochet hook and 6 strands of yarn held together, starting at least 12 cm from yarn ends, make a length of ch approx 210 cm long.
Fasten off and cut yarn, leaving ends of at least 12 cm.
Make a further 9 lengths in this way.
Knot together 5 pairs of 2 lengths so that there is 12 cm of yarn left free beyond knots.
Now weave all 10 strands together as shown in diagram – you may find it easiest to do if you pin

the knots onto a firm surface and then place pins along side edges as well, to stop the woven section pulling in too much.
Cont to weave all 10 lengths together in this way until all lengths of ch are used up – you may find it necessary to unpick a little of some lengths so that all lengths finish at the same point.
Once all weaving is complete, knot together 5 pairs of lengths at this end of scarf in same way as at opposite end.
If necessary, unravel ch back to knots and then trim ends to 12 cm.

MAKING UP
Press as described on the information page.

SIZE

To fit bust

81-86 91-97 102-107 112-117 122-127 cm
32-34 36-38 40-42   44-46   48-50   in
Actual bust measurement of garment
 92   102   112   122   132   cm
 36   40   44   48   52   in

YARN

Kidsilk Haze

7   8   8   9   9   x 25gm

(photographed in Liqueur 595)

NEEDLES

1 pair 3mm (no 11) (US 2/3) needles
Cable needle

TENSION

28 sts and 38 rows to 10 cm measured over st st using 3mm (US 2/3) needles. Cable panel (20 sts) measures 4 cm.

SPECIAL ABBREVIATIONS

C8B = slip next 4 sts onto cable needle and leave at back of work, K4, then K4 from cable needle; **C8F** = slip next 4 sts onto cable needle and leave at front of work, K4, then K4 from cable needle.

BACK

Using 3mm (US 2/3) needles cast on 186 [200: 214: 228: 242] sts **loosely**.
Work in g st for 5 rows, ending with **WS** facing for next row.
Next row (WS): K89 [96: 103: 110: 117], inc once in each of next 8 sts, K89 [96: 103: 110: 117]. 194 [208: 222: 236: 250] sts.
Now work in patt as folls:
Row 1 (RS): K87 [94: 101: 108: 115], P2, K4, P3, K2, P3, K4, P2, K87 [94: 101: 108: 115].
Row 2: P87 [94: 101: 108: 115], K2, P4, K3, P2, K3, P4, K2, P87 [94: 101: 108: 115].
Rows 3 and 4: As rows 1 and 2.

Row 5: K2, sl 1, K1, psso, K83 [90: 97: 104: 111], P2, C8F, C8B, P2, K83 [90: 97: 104: 111], K2tog, K2. 192 [206: 220: 234: 248] sts.
Row 6: P86 [93: 100: 107: 114], K2, P4, K3, P2, K3, P4, K2, P86 [93: 100: 107: 114].
Row 7: K86 [93: 100: 107: 114], P2, K4, P3, K2, P3, K4, P2, K86 [93: 100: 107: 114].
Rows 8 and 9: As rows 6 and 7.
Row 10: As row 6.
These 10 rows form patt and beg side seam shaping.
Keeping patt correct and working all side seam shaping as set (by patt row 5), cont as folls:
Dec 1 st at each end of next and 13 foll 6th rows, then on 13 foll 4th rows.
138 [152: 166: 180: 194] sts.
Cont straight until back meas 42 [42.5: 43: 43.5: 44] cm, ending with RS facing for next row.

Shape armholes

Keeping patt correct, cast off 5 [6: 7: 8: 9] sts at beg of next 2 rows. 128 [140: 152: 164: 176] sts.
Dec 1 st at each end of next 5 [7: 7: 9: 9] rows, then on foll 4 [5: 7: 7: 8] alt rows.
110 [116: 124: 132: 142] sts.
Cont straight until armhole meas 18 [19.5: 21: 22.5: 24] cm, ending with RS facing for next row.

Shape back neck and shoulders

Next row (RS): Cast off 4 [5: 5: 6: 7] sts, patt until there are 25 [27: 30: 33: 36] sts on right needle and turn, leaving rem sts on a holder.
Work each side of neck separately.
Dec 1 st at neck edge of next 6 rows **and at same time** cast off 4 [5: 6: 6: 7] sts at beg of 2nd and foll 0 [2: 2: 0: 1] alt rows, then 5 [-: -: 7: 8] sts at beg of foll 2 [-: -: 2: 1] alt rows.
Work 1 row.
Cast off rem 5 [6: 6: 7: 8] sts.
With RS facing, slip centre 52 [52: 54: 54: 56] sts onto a holder, rejoin yarn and K to end.
Complete to match first side, reversing shapings.

FRONT

Work as given for back until 14 [14: 18: 18: 22] rows less have been worked than on back to beg of shoulder shaping, ending with RS facing for next row.

Shape front neck

Next row (RS): Patt 34 [37: 41: 45: 50] sts and turn, leaving rem sts on a holder.
Work each side of neck separately.
Dec 1 st at neck edge of next 6 rows, then on foll

3 [3: 4: 4: 4] alt rows, then on 0 [0: 0: 0: 1] foll 4th row. 25 [28: 31: 35: 39] sts.
Work 1 [1: 3: 3: 3] rows, ending with RS facing for next row.

Shape shoulder

Cast off 4 [5: 5: 6: 7] sts at beg of next and foll 1 [3: 0: 1: 2] alt rows, then 5 [-: 6: 7: 8] sts at beg of foll 2 [-: 3: 2: 1] alt rows **and at same time** dec 1 st at neck edge of next and foll 4th row.
Work 1 row.
Cast off rem 5 [6: 6: 7: 8] sts.
With RS facing, slip centre 42 sts onto a holder, rejoin yarn and K to end.
Complete to match first side, reversing shapings.

SLEEVES

Using 3mm (US 2/3) needles cast on 52 [54: 56: 56: 60] sts **loosely**.
Work in g st for 5 rows, ending with **WS** facing for next row.
Next row (WS): K22 [23: 24: 24: 26], inc once in each of next 8 sts, K22 [23: 24: 24: 26].
60 [62: 64: 64: 68] sts.
Now work in patt as folls:
Row 1 (RS): K20 [21: 22: 22: 24], P2, K4, P3, K2, P3, K4, P2, K20 [21: 22: 22: 24].
Row 2: P20 [21: 22: 22: 24], K2, P4, K3, P2, K3, P4, K2, P20 [21: 22: 22: 24].
Row 3: (Inc in first st) 0 [0: 0: 1: 1] times, K20 [21: 22: 21: 23], P2, K4, P3, K2, P3, K4, P2, K20 [21: 22: 21: 23], (inc in last st) 0 [0: 0: 1: 1] times. 60 [62: 64: 66: 70] sts.
Row 4: P20 [21: 22: 23: 25], K2, P4, K3, P2, K3, P4, K2, P20 [21: 22: 23: 25].
Row 5: (Inc in first st) 1 [1: 1: 0: 0] times, K19 [20: 21: 23: 25], P2, C8F, C8B, P2, K19 [20: 21: 23: 25], (inc in last st) 1 [1: 1: 0: 0] times. 62 [64: 66: 66: 70] sts.
Row 6: P21 [22: 23: 23: 25], K2, P4, K3, P2, K3, P4, K2, P21 [22: 23: 23: 25].
Row 7: (Inc in first st) 0 [0: 0: 1: 1] times, K21 [22: 23: 22: 24], P2, K4, P3, K2, P3, K4, P2, K21 [22: 23: 22: 24], (inc in last st) 0 [0: 0: 1: 1] times. 62 [64: 66: 68: 72] sts.
Row 8: P21 [22: 23: 24: 26], K2, P4, K3, P2, K3, P4, K2, P21 [22: 23: 24: 26].
Row 9: K21 [22: 23: 24: 26], P2, K4, P3, K2, P3, K4, P2, K21 [22: 23: 24: 26].
Row 10: As row 8.
These 10 rows form patt and beg sleeve shaping.

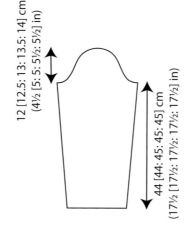

12 [12.5: 13: 13.5: 14] cm
(4½ [5: 5: 5½: 5½] in)

44 [44: 45: 45: 45] cm
(17½ [17½: 17½: 17½: 17½] in)

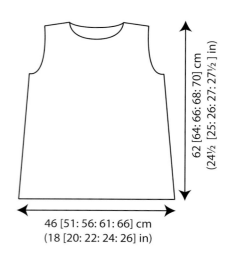

62 [64: 66: 68: 70] cm
(24½ [25: 26: 27: 27½] in)

46 [51: 56: 61: 66] cm
(18 [20: 22: 24: 26] in)

Keeping patt correct, cont as folls:
Inc 1 st at each end of next and every foll 6th [6th: 6th: 4th: 4th] row to 92 [102: 108: 72: 76] sts, then on every foll 8th [8th: 8th: 6th: 6th] row until there are 104 [108: 112: 116: 120] sts, taking inc sts into st st.
Cont straight until sleeve meas 44 [44: 45: 45: 45] cm, ending with RS facing for next row.
Shape top
Keeping patt correct, cast off 5 [6: 7: 8: 9] sts at beg of next 2 rows. 94 [96: 98: 100: 102] sts.
Dec 1 st at each end of next 5 rows, then on every foll alt row until 62 sts rem, then on foll 17 rows, ending with RS facing for next row.
Cast off rem 28 sts.

MAKING UP
Press as described on the information page.
Join right shoulder seam using back stitch, or mattress stitch if preferred.
Neckband
With RS facing and using 3mm (US 2/3) needles, pick up and knit 19 [19: 22: 22: 25] sts down left side of front neck, K across 42 sts on front holder as folls: K13, (K2tog) 8 times, K13, pick up and knit 19 [19: 22: 22: 25] sts up right side of front neck, and 7 sts down right side of back neck, K across 52 [52: 54: 54: 56] sts on back holder as folls: K18 [18: 19: 19: 20], (K2tog) 8 times, K18 [18: 19: 19: 20], then pick up and knit 7 sts up left side of back neck. 130 [130: 138: 138: 146] sts.
Work in g st for 4 rows, ending with **WS** facing for next row.
Cast off **loosely** knitwise (on **WS**).
See information page for finishing instructions, setting in sleeves using the set-in method.

HUTTON
Lisa Richardson
Main image page **15, 67**
● ●

YARN
Kidsilk Haze and Felted Tweed
1st colourway

A	KSH Candy Girl 606	1	x	25gm
B	KSH Blackcurrant 641	1	x	25gm
C	KSH Turkish Plum 660	2	x	25gm
D	KSH Peacock 671	2	x	25gm
E	FTwd Tawny 186	2	x	50gm
F	FTwd Bilberry 151	3	x	50gm
G	FTwd Seafarer 170	2	x	50gm
H	FTwd Watery 152	1	x	50gm

2nd colourway

A	KSH Jelly 597	1	x	25gm
B	KSH Trance 582	1	x	25gm
C	KSH Anthracite 639	2	x	25gm
D	KSH Steel 664	2	x	25gm
E	FTwd Avocado 161	2	x	50gm
F	FTwd Delft 194	3	x	50gm
G	FTwd Boulder 195	2	x	50gm
H	FTwd Alabaster 197	1	x	50gm

CROCHET HOOK
4.00mm (no 8) (US G6) crochet hook

FASTENINGS – decorative shawl pin

TENSION
16 sts and 20 rows to 10 cm measured over dc fabric using 4.00mm (US G6) crochet hook and one strand each of Kidsilk Haze and felted Tweed held together.

FINISHED SIZE
Completed shawl is 26.5 cm (10½ in) wide at narrow end, approx 75 cm (29½ in) wide at wider end, and 125 cm (49 in) long.

CROCHET ABBREVIATIONS
ch = chain; **dc** = double crochet; **htr** = half treble; **tr** = yarn treble; **dtr** = double treble; **ttr** = triple treble.

SHAWL
Using 4.00mm (US G6) crochet hook and one strand each of yarns A and E held together, make 201 ch.
Row 1 (RS): 1 dc into 2nd ch from hook, 1 dc into each ch to end, turn. 200 sts.
Row 2: 5 ch (counts as first st), miss dc at base of 5 ch, 1 ttr into each of next 39 dc, 1 dtr into each of next 40 dc, 1 tr into each of next 40 dc, 1 htr into each of next 40 dc, 1 dc into each of last 40 dc, turn.
Joining in and breaking off colours as required, now work in patt as folls:
Row 3: Using one strand each of yarns B and F held together, 1 ch (does NOT count as st), 1 dc into each st to end, working last dc into top of 5 ch at beg of previous row, turn.
Row 4: Using one strand each of yarns B and F held together, 5 ch (counts as first st), miss dc at base of 5 ch, 1 ttr into each of next 39 dc, 1 dtr into each of next 40 dc, 1 tr into each of next 40 dc, 1 htr into each of next 40 dc, 1 dc into each of last 40 dc, turn.
Rows 3 and 4 form patt.
Keeping patt correct, now work in stripes as folls:
Rows 5 and 6: Using one strand each of yarns C and F held together.
Rows 7 and 8: Using one strand each of yarns C and G held together.
Rows 9 and 10: Using one strand each of yarns D and G held together.
Rows 11 and 12: Using one strand each of yarns D and H held together.
Rows 13 and 14: Using one strand each of yarns A and E held together.
Rows 3 to 14 form stripe sequence.
Now rep rows 3 to 14, 3 times more, then rows 3 and 4 again.
Row 53: As row 3.
Fasten off.

MAKING UP
Press as described on the information page.
Fasten shawl using shawl pin as in photograph.

VEILED

Martin Storey

Main image page **71, 81**

● ●

YARN
Kid Classic
    3   x 50gm
(photographed in Cherry Red 847)

NEEDLES
1 pair 4mm (no 8) (US 6) needles
1 pair 5mm (no 6) (US 8) needles

BEADS - 162 beads (ref Debbie Abrahams size 6, col Night Sky 754)

BUTTONS - 3 x BN1729 from Bedecked. Please see information page for contact details.

TENSION
19 sts and 32 rows to 10 cm measured over beaded moss st using 5mm (US 8) needles.

FINISHED SIZE
Completed cowl scarf is 24 cm (9½ in) wide and 130 cm (51 in) long.

SPECIAL ABBREVIATION

bead 1 = place a bead by taking yarn to RS of work and slipping bead up next to st just worked, slip next st purlwise from left needle to right needle and take yarn back to WS of work, leaving bead sitting in front of slipped st on RS.

Beading note: Before starting to knit, thread beads onto yarn. To do this, thread a fine sewing needle (one that will easily pass through the beads) with sewing thread. Knot ends of thread and then pass end of yarn through this loop. Thread a bead onto sewing thread and then gently slide it along and onto knitting yarn. Continue in this way until required number of beads are on yarn.

SCARF
Using 4mm (US 6) needles cast on 45 sts.
Row 1 (RS): K2, *P1, K1, rep from * to last st, K1.
Row 2: K1, *P1, K1, rep from * to end.
These 2 rows form rib.
Work in rib for a further 4 rows, ending with RS facing for next row.
Row 7 (RS): Rib 5, *yrn, work 2 tog (to make a buttonhole), rib 15, rep from * once more, yrn, work 2 tog (to make 3rd buttonhole), rib 4.
Work in rib for a further 5 rows, ending with RS facing for next row.
Change to 5mm (US 8) needles.
Now work in beaded moss st as folls:
Row 1 (RS): P1, *K1, P1, rep from * to end.
Rows 2 to 4: As row 1, 3 times.
Row 5: (P1, K1) 7 times, bead 1, K1, (P1, K1) 7 times, bead 1, (K1, P1) 7 times.
Rows 6 to 10: As row 1, 5 times.
Row 11: (P1, K1) 3 times, *bead 1, K1, (P1, K1) 7 times, rep from * once more, bead 1, (K1, P1) 3 times.
Row 12: As row 1.
These 12 rows form beaded moss st.
Rep last 12 rows 31 times more, and then rows 1 to 8 again, ending with RS facing for next row.
Change to 4mm (US 6) needles.
Beg with row 1, work in rib as given for cast-on edge for 12 rows, ending with RS facing for next row.
Cast off in rib.

MAKING UP
Press as described on the information page.
Sew on buttons to correspond with buttonholes.

ECLIPSE

Martin Storey

Main image page **66**

● ● ●

YARN
Kidsilk Haze and Fine Lace
A KSH Purplicious 678
      2   x 25gm
B Lace Twilight Magenta 952
      1   x 50gm

NEEDLES
1 pair 2¾mm (no 12) (US 2) needles
3¼mm (no 10) (US 3) circular needle no more than 40 cm long

BEADS - 91 beads (ref Debbie Abrahams size 6, col 562)

TENSION
24 sts and 33 rounds to 10 cm measured over st st using 3¼mm (US 3) circular needle and one strand of each of yarns A and B held together.

FINISHED SIZE
Completed cowl meas 76 cm (30 in) all round at lower edge, 54 cm (21½ in) all round at upper edge and is 35 cm (14 in) deep.

SPECIAL ABBREVIATION

bead 1 = place a bead by taking yarn to RS of work and slipping bead up next to st just worked, slip next st purlwise from left needle to right needle and take yarn back to WS of work, leaving bead sitting in front of slipped st on RS.

Beading note: Before starting to knit, thread beads onto yarn – as yarns A and B are held together, beads need to be threaded onto BOTH yarns together. To do this, thread a fine sewing needle (one that will easily pass through the beads) with sewing thread. Knot ends of thread and then pass ends of BOTH yarns through this loop. Thread a bead onto sewing thread and then gently slide it along and onto BOTH knitting yarns. Continue in this way until required number of beads are on yarns.

COWL
Edging
Using 2¾mm (US 2) needles and one strand each of yarns A and B held together cast on 13 sts.
Row 1 (RS): K1, K1 tbl, yfwd, K1, yfwd, sl 1, K1, psso, yfwd, K2tog, K6. 14 sts.
Row 2: K1, P to last st, K1.
Now work in patt as folls:
Row 1 (RS): K1, K1 tbl, yfwd, K3, yfwd, sl 1, K1, psso, yfwd, K2tog, K5. 15 sts.
Row 2: K1, P to last st, K1.
Row 3: K1, K1 tbl, yfwd, K5, yfwd, sl 1, K1, psso, yfwd, K2tog, K4. 16 sts.
Row 4: As row 2.
Row 5: K1, K1 tbl, yfwd, K7, yfwd, sl 1, K1, psso, yfwd, K2tog, K3. 17 sts.

Row 6: As row 2.
Row 7: K1, K1 tbl, yfwd, K9, yfwd, sl 1, K1, psso, yfwd, K2tog, K2. 18 sts.
Row 8: As row 2.
Row 9: K1, K1 tbl, yfwd, K11, yfwd, sl 1, K1, psso, yfwd, K2tog, K1. 19 sts.
Row 10: K1, P8, bead 1, P1, bead 1, P6, K1.
Row 11: K1, K1 tbl, yfwd, K13, yfwd, sl 1, K1, psso, yfwd, K2tog. 20 sts.
Row 12: K1, P7, (bead 1, P1) twice, bead 1, P6, K1.
Row 13: Sl 1, K1, psso, K1, yfwd, K2tog, K9, sl 1, K1, psso, yfwd, K2tog, yfwd, K2. 19 sts.
Row 14: As row 10.
Row 15: Sl 1, K1, psso, K1, yfwd, K2tog, K7, sl 1, K1, psso, yfwd, K2tog, yfwd, K3. 18 sts.
Row 16: As row 2.
Row 17: Sl 1, K1, psso, K1, yfwd, K2tog, K5, sl 1, K1, psso, yfwd, K2tog, yfwd, K4. 17 sts.
Row 18: As row 2.
Row 19: Sl 1, K1, psso, K1, yfwd, K2tog, K3, sl 1, K1, psso, yfwd, K2tog, yfwd, K5. 16 sts.

Row 20: As row 2.
Row 21: Sl 1, K1, psso, K1, yfwd, K2tog, K1, sl 1, K1, psso, yfwd, K2tog, yfwd, K6. 15 sts.
Row 22: As row 2.
Row 23: Sl 1, K1, psso, K1, yfwd, slip next 2 sts as though to K2tog, K1, pass 2 slipped sts over, yfwd, K2tog, yfwd, K7. 14 sts.
Row 24: As row 2.
These 24 rows form patt.
Rep last 24 rows 12 times more, ending with RS facing for next row. 14 sts.
Cast off but do **NOT** break yarn.

Main section
With RS facing, using 3¼mm (US 3) circular needle and one strand each of yarns A and B held together, pick up and knit 182 sts evenly along straight row-end edge of edging (this is 14 sts for each rep of edging).
Taking care not to twist cast-on edge, work in rounds as folls:
Round 1 (RS): Knit.

This round forms st st.
Working in rounds of st st throughout, cont as folls:
Work 3 rounds.
Round 5: (K12, K2tog) 13 times. 169 sts.
Work 4 rounds.
Round 10: (K11, K2tog) 13 times. 156 sts.
Work 4 rounds.
Round 15: (K10, K2tog) 13 times. 143 sts.
Work 4 rounds.
Round 20: (K9, K2tog) 13 times. 130 sts.
Cont straight until cowl meas 32 cm from lower edge of edging, inc 2 sts evenly around last round. 132 sts.
Next round (RS): ⋆K2, P2, rep from ⋆ to end.
Rep last round 9 times more.
Cast off in rib.

MAKING UP
Press as described on the information page.
Join cast-on and cast-off ends of edging. See information page for finishing instructions.

WILSHAW
Georgia Farrell
Main image page **36, 37**
● ● ●

SIZE
To fit bust

81-86	91-97	102-107	112-117	122-127	cm
32-34	36-38	40-42	44-46	48-50	in

Actual bust measurement of garment

104	116	124	136	144	cm
41	45½	49	53½	56½	in

YARN
Big Wool

12	13	14	16	17	x 100gm

(photographed in Concrete 061)

NEEDLES
1 pair 9mm (no 00) (US 13) needles
Cable needle

TENSION
11 sts and 16 rows to 10 cm measured over patt, 10 sts and 14 rows to 10 cm measured over st st, 10 sts and 22 rows to 10 cm measured over g st, all using 9mm (US 13) needles.

SPECIAL ABBREVIATIONS
C2B = slip next st onto cable needle and leave at back of work, K1, then K1 from cable needle; **C2F** = slip next st onto cable needle and leave at front of work, K1, then K1 from cable needle.

Pattern note: All slipped sts should be worked purlwise, keeping yarn at **front** of work – this is

RS of work on RS rows, and WS of work on WS rows.

LEFT FRONT AND BACK
Using 9mm (US 13) needles cast on 54 [60: 64: 70: 74] sts.
Beg and ending rows as indicated, place patt from chart (see pattern note) as folls:
Row 1 (RS): K3, work next 48 [54: 58: 64: 68] sts as row 1 of chart, K1, sl 1, K1.
Row 2: Sl 1, P1, sl 1, work next 48 [54: 58: 64: 68] sts as row 2 of chart, K3.
These 2 rows set the sts – front opening edge 3 sts in slip st patt, centre back seam 3 sts in g st with all other sts in patt from chart.
⋆⋆Cont as set until all 76 rows of chart have been completed, ending with RS facing for next row. (Work should meas approx 47.5 cm.)

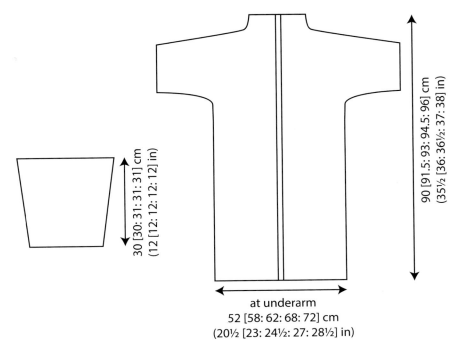

30 [30: 31: 31: 31] cm
(12 [12: 12: 12: 12] in)

90 [91.5: 93: 94.5: 96] cm
(35½ [36: 36½: 37: 38] in)

at underarm
52 [58: 62: 68: 72] cm
(20½ [23: 24½: 27: 28½] in)

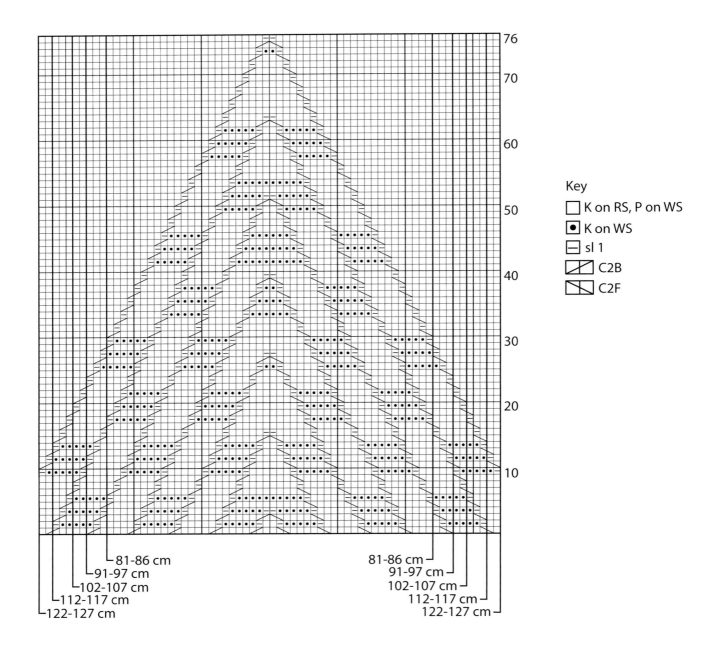

76

70

60

50

40

30

20

10

Key
☐ K on RS, P on WS
⊡ K on WS
⊟ sl 1
▨ C2B
▧ C2F

81-86 cm
91-97 cm
102-107 cm
112-117 cm
122-127 cm

81-86 cm
91-97 cm
102-107 cm
112-117 cm
122-127 cm

Row 77 (RS): Patt 3 sts, K48 [54: 58: 64: 68], patt 3 sts.

Row 78: Patt 3 sts, P48 [54: 58: 64: 68], patt 3 sts. These 2 rows set the sts for rest of work – front opening and centre back sts still worked as before but with all other sts now worked in st st.

Keeping all sts correct as now set throughout, cont as folls:

Divide for back and front

Next row (RS): Patt 26 [29: 31: 34: 36] sts, inc in next st and slip these 28 [31: 33: 36: 38] sts onto a holder (for left back), inc in next st, patt to end. Work on this set of 28 [31: 33: 36: 38] sts only for left front section as folls:

Work 1 row, ending with RS facing for next row. Inc 1 st at beg of next and foll alt row, then at same edge on foll 5 rows, taking inc sts into st st and ending with RS facing for next row. 35 [38: 40: 43: 45] sts.

Cast on 7 sts at beg of next and foll alt row, then 8 sts at beg of foll alt row. 57 [60: 62: 65: 67] sts. Place marker at beg of last row (to denote base of armhole opening).

Cont straight until work meas 16 [17.5: 19: 20.5: 22] cm from marker, ending with RS facing for next row.

Shape shoulder

Cast off 4 sts at beg of next and foll 8 [5: 4: 1: 0] alt rows, then 5 sts at beg of foll 1 [4: 5: 8: 9] alt rows, then 4 sts at beg of foll alt row, ending with WS facing for next row. 12 [12: 13: 13: 14] sts.

Dec 1 st at end of next row, then at beg of foll row. 10 [10: 11: 11: 12] sts.

Work a further 11 rows on these sts (for funnel neck extension), ending with RS facing for next row.

Cast off.

Rejoin yarn to 28 [31: 33: 36: 38] sts on left back holder with **WS** facing and patt to end.

Complete to match left front section, reversing shapings.

RIGHT FRONT AND BACK

Using 9mm (US 13) needles cast on 54 [60: 64: 70: 74] sts.

Beg and ending rows as indicated, place patt from chart (see pattern note) as folls:

Row 1 (RS): K1, sl 1, K1, work next 48 [54: 58: 64: 68] sts as row 1 of chart, K3.

Row 2: K3, work next 48 [54: 58: 64: 68] sts as row 2 of chart, sl 1, P1, sl 1.

These 2 rows set the sts – front opening edge 3 sts

in slip st patt, centre back seam 3 sts in g st with all other sts in patt from chart.

Complete as given for left front and back from ******, noting that right back section will be worked before right front section.

SLEEVES

Join funnel neck and shoulder seams using back stitch, or mattress stitch if preferred.

With RS facing and using 9mm (US 13) needles, pick up and knit 31 [34: 37: 40: 43] sts evenly along straight row-end edge of sleeve extensions between markers.

Cont in g st, shaping sides by dec 1 st at each end of 10th and 2 foll 20th rows. 25 [28: 31: 34: 37] sts.

Cont straight until sleeve meas 30 [30: 31: 31: 31] cm from pick-up row, ending with **WS** facing for next row.

Cast off knitwise (on **WS**).

MAKING UP

Press as described on the information page.

Join centre back seam using back stitch, or mattress stitch if preferred. Join sleeve and underarm seams from cuff edge to dividing row at underarm.

See information page for finishing instructions.

SIZING GUIDE

ROWAN

When you knit and wear a Rowan design we want you to look and feel fabulous. This all starts with the size and fit of the design you choose. To help you to achieve a great knitting experience we have looked at the sizing of our womens and menswear patterns.

The menswear designs are now available to knit in a wider range of sizes from 81 cm (32") chest to a 137 cm (54") chest.

Dimensions in the charts below are body measurements, not garment dimensions, therefore please refer to the measuring guide to help you to determine which is the best size for you to knit. We also now give full garment measurements around chest/bust at the beginning of each pattern so that you can see how much ease there will be for your size.

STANDARD WOMENS SIZING GUIDE

The sizing within this chart is also based on the larger size within the range.

To fit bust	32 – 34	36 – 38	40 – 42	44 – 46	48 – 50	inches
	81 – 86	91 – 97	102 – 107	112 – 117	122 – 127	cm
To fit waist	24 – 26	28 – 30	32 – 34	36 – 38	40 – 42	inches
	61 – 66	71 – 76	81 – 86	91 – 97	102 – 107	cm
To fit hips	34 – 36	38 – 40	42 – 44	46 – 48	50 – 52	inches
	86 – 91	97 – 102	107 – 112	117 – 122	127 – 132	cm

STANDARD MENS AND UNISEX SIZING GUIDE

The sizing within this chart is also based on the larger size within the range.

To fit Chest	32-34	36-38	40-42	44-46	48-50	52-54	inches
	81-86	91-97	102-107	112-117	122-127	132-137	cm
To fit waist	24-26	28-30	32-34	36-38	40-42	44-46	inches
	61-66	71-76	81-86	91-97	102-107	112-117	cm

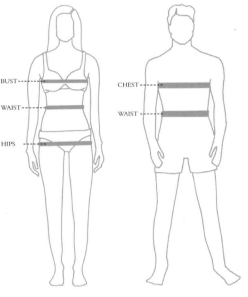

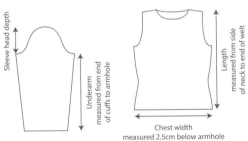

SIZING & SIZE DIAGRAM NOTE

The instructions are given for the smallest size. Where they vary, work the figures in brackets for the larger sizes. **One set of figures refers to all sizes.** Included with most patterns in this magazine is a '**size diagram**' - see image on the right, of the finished garment and its dimensions. The measurement shown at the bottom of each '**size diagram**' shows the garment width 2.5cm below the armhole shaping. To help you choose the size of garment to knit please refer to the sizing guide. Generally in the majority of designs the welt width (at the cast on edge of the garment) is the same width as the chest. However, some designs are 'A-Line' in shape or have a flared edge and in these cases the welt width will be wider than the chest width.

MEASURING GUIDE

For maximum comfort and to ensure the correct fit when choosing a size to knit, please follow the tips below when checking your size.

Measure yourself close to your body, over your underwear and don't pull the tape measure too tight!

Bust/chest – measure around the fullest part of the bust/chest and across the shoulder blades.

Waist – measure around the natural waistline.

Hips – measure around the fullest part of the bottom.

To be extra sure, measure your favourite jumper and then compare these measurements with the Rowan size diagram given at the end of the individual instructions.

Finally, once you have decided which size is best for you, please ensure that you achieve the tension required for the design you wish to knit.

Remember if your tension is too loose, your garment will be bigger than the pattern size. If your tension is too tight, your garment could be smaller than the pattern size both of which will alter the amount of yarn used to that stated in the pattern.

Furthermore if your tension is incorrect, the handle of your fabric will be too stiff or floppy and will not fit properly. It really does make sense to check your tension before starting every project.

TENSION

Obtaining the correct tension is perhaps the single factor which can make the difference between a successful garment and a disastrous one. It controls both the shape and size of an article, so any variation, however slight, can distort the finished garment. Different designers feature in our books and it is **their** tension, given at the **start** of each pattern, which you must match. We recommend that you knit a square in pattern and/or stocking stitch (depending on the pattern instructions) of perhaps 5 - 10 more stitches and 5 - 10 more rows than those given in the tension note. Mark out the central 10cm square with pins. If you have too many stitches to 10cm try again using thicker needles, if you have too few stitches to 10cm try again using finer needles. Once you have achieved the correct tension your garment will be knitted to the measurements indicated in the size diagram shown at the end of the pattern.

CHART NOTE

Many of the patterns in the book are worked from charts. Each square on a chart represents a stitch and each line of squares a row of knitting. Each colour used is given a different letter and these are shown in the **materials** section, or in the **key** alongside the chart of each pattern. When working from the charts, read odd rows (K) from right to left and even rows (P) from left to right, unless otherwise stated. When working lace from a chart it is important to note that all but the largest size may have to alter the first and last few stitches in order not to lose or gain stitches over the row.

WORKING A LACE PATTERN

When working a lace pattern it is important to remember that if you are unable to work both the increase and corresponding decrease and vica versa, the stitches should be worked in stocking stitch.

KNITTING WITH COLOUR

There are two main methods of working colour into a knitted fabric: **Intarsia** and **Fairisle** techniques. The first method produces a single thickness of fabric and is usually used where a colour is only required in a particular area of a row and does not form a repeating pattern across the row, as in the fairisle technique.

Fairisle type knitting: When two or three colours are worked repeatedly across a row, strand the yarn **not** in use loosely behind the stitches being worked. If you are working with more than two colours, treat the "floating" yarns as if they were one yarn and always spread the stitches to their correct width to keep them elastic. It is advisable not to carry the stranded or "floating" yarns over more than three stitches at a time, but to weave them under and over the colour you are working. The "floating" yarns are therefore caught at the back of the work.

Intarsia: The simplest way to do this is to cut short lengths of yarn for each motif or block of colour used in a row. Then joining in the various colours at the appropriate point on the row, link one colour to the next by twisting them around each other where they meet on the wrong side to avoid gaps. All ends can then either be darned along the colour join lines, as each motif is completed or then can be "knitted-in" to the fabric of the knitting as each colour is worked into the pattern. This is done in much the same way as "weaving- in" yarns when working the Fairisle technique and does save time darning-in ends. It is essential that the tension is noted for intarsia as this may vary from the stocking stitch if both are used in the same pattern.

FINISHING INSTRUCTIONS

After working for hours knitting a garment, it seems a great pity that many garments are spoiled because such little care is taken in the pressing and finishing process. Follow the text below for a truly professional-looking garment.

PRESSING

Block out each piece of knitting and following the instructions on the ball band press the garment pieces, omitting the ribs. Tip: Take special care to press the edges, as this will make sewing up both easier and neater. If the ball band indicates that the fabric is not to be pressed, then covering the blocked out fabric with a damp white cotton cloth and leaving it to stand will have the desired effect. Darn in all ends neatly along the selvage edge or a colour join, as appropriate.

STITCHING

When stitching the pieces together, remember to match areas of colour and texture very carefully where they meet. Use a seam stitch such as back stitch or mattress stitch for all main knitting seams and join all ribs and neckband with mattress stitch, unless otherwise stated.

CONSTRUCTION

Having completed the pattern instructions, join left shoulder and neckband seams as detailed above. Sew the top of the sleeve to the body of the garment using the method detailed in the pattern, referring to the appropriate guide:

Straight cast-off sleeves: Place centre of cast-off edge of sleeve to shoulder seam. Sew top of sleeve to body, using markers as guidelines where applicable.

Square set-in sleeves: Place centre of cast-off edge of sleeve to shoulder seam. Set sleeve head into armhole, the straight sides at top of sleeve to form a neat right-angle to cast-off sts at armhole on back and front.

Shallow set-in sleeves: Place centre of cast off edge of sleeve to shoulder seam. Match decreases at beg of armhole shaping to decreases at top of sleeve. Sew sleeve head into armhole, easing in shapings.

Set-in sleeves: Place centre of cast-off edge of sleeve to shoulder seam. Set in sleeve, easing sleeve head into armhole.

Join side and sleeve seams.

Slip stitch pocket edgings and linings into place. Sew on buttons to correspond with buttonholes. Ribbed welts and neckbands and any areas of garter stitch should not be pressed.

ABBREVIATIONS

K	knit
P	purl
st(s)	stitch(es)
inc	increas(e)(ing)
dec	decreas(e)(ing)
st st	stocking stitch (1 row K , 1 row P)
g st	garter stitch (K every row)
beg	begin(ning)
foll	following
rem	remain(ing)
rev st st	reverse stocking stitch (1 row K , 1 row P)
rep	repeat
alt	alternate
cont	continue
patt	pattern
tog	together
mm	millimetres
cm	centimetres
in(s)	inch(es)
RS	right side
WS	wrong side
sl 1	slip one stitch
psso	pass slipped stitch over
p2sso	pass 2 slipped stitches over
tbl	through back of loop
M1	make one stitch by picking up horizontal loop before next stitch and knitting into back of it
M1P	make one stitch by picking up horizontal loop before next stitch and purling into back of it
yfwd	yarn forward
yrn	yarn round needle
meas	measures
0	no stitches, times or rows
-	no stitches, times or rows for that size
yon	yarn over needle
yfrn	yarn forward round needle
wyib	with yarn at back

CROCHET TERMS

UK crochet terms and abbreviations have been used throughout. The list below gives the US equivalent where they vary.

ABBREV.	UK	US
dc (sc)	double crochet	(single crochet)
htr (hdc)	half treble	(half double crochet)
tr (dc)	treble	(double crochet)
dtr (tr)	double treble	(treble)

EXPERIENCE RATING - for guidance only

● Beginner Techniques
For the beginner knitter, basic garment shaping and straight forward stitch technique.

● ● Simple Techniques
Simple straight forward knitting, introducing various, shaping techniques and garments.

● ● ● Experienced Techniques
For the more experienced knitter, using more advanced shaping techniques at the same time as colourwork or more advanced stitch techniques.

● ● ● ● Advanced Techniques
Advanced techniques used, using advanced stitches and garment shaping along with more challenging techniques

BUTTONS, BEADS AND RIBBONS USED IN THIS MAGAZINE ARE SOURCED FROM:

Bedecked Haberdashery
Barningham Park Coach House
Barningham, Nr Richmond
North Yorkshire
DL11 7DW
United Kingdom
Tel: +44 (0)1833 621 451
Email: thegirls@bedecked.co.uk

Groves
Eastern Bypass
Thame, Oxfordshire
OX9 3FU
Web: www.grovesltd.co.uk
Email: groves@stockistenquiries.co.uk

Debbie Abrahams Beads
26 Church Drive
Nottingham
NG5 2BA
Tel: 0115 960 7991
Email: beads@debbieabrahams.com
Web: www.debbieabrahamsbeads.co.uk

WASH CARE INFORMATION

To help you to care for your knitting and crochet more easily below are the symbols you are likely to on our ball bands and shade cards and a brief explanation of each.

MACHINE WASH SYMBOLS

Machine Wash, Cold   Machine Wash, Cold, Gentle   Machine Wash, Warn   Machine Wash, Warm, Gentle

HAND WASH SYMBOLS

Do Not Wash   Hand Wash, Normal   Hand Wash, Cold   Hand Wash, Warm

DRY CLEAN SYMBOLS

Do Not Dry Clean   Dry Clean   Dry Clean, in Certain Solvents, Consult Cleaner   Dry Clean, Any Solvent

IRONING SYMBOLS

Do Not Iron   Iron Low Heat   Iron Medium Heat

DO NOT BLEACH SYMBOL

Do Not Bleach

DRYING SYMBOLS

Do Not Tumble Dry   Tumble Dry, Gentle, Low Heat   Dry Flat in Shade   Do Not Wring

STOCKISTS

For more information on overseas stockists and mail order details, please contact the Rowan distributor listed under each country.
'ROWAN AT ....' stockists, carry a large range of Rowan Yarns.

ROWAN

County	Town / City	Stockist	Address	Postcode	Email	Website	Telephone	Rowan At	Yarn	Fabric	Online	Instore
AUSTRALIA												
VIC	**Melbourne**	**Australian Country Spinners Pty Ltd (Distributor)**	**Level 7, 409 St. Kilda Road**	**3004**	**customerservices@auspinners.com.au**		**(03) 9380 3888**		•			•
ACT	Mawson	Stitch N Time	P O BOX 145	2607	dalenalan@bigpond.com		(02) 6282 8383		•			•
NSW	Avalon Beach	Avalon Fabrics & Crafts	Shop 4, 24 Avalon Parade	2107	info@avalonfabrics.com		(02) 99182978		•			•
NSW	Orange	Caboodle of Orange Gifts	186a Anson Street	2800	greenbrook@bigpond.com		(02) 6362 6310		•			•
NSW	Tweed Heads	Fantazia Fabricland	P O BOX 6113	2486	raso@netspace.net.au		(07) 5523 2220		•			•
NSW	Holbrook	Grandma's Closet	128 Albury Street	2644	grandmascloset@southernphone.com.au		(02) 6036 2322		•			•
NSW	Hornsby	Hornsby Wool & Craft Nook	Shop 3-3A, 25-31 Florence St	2077	hornsbywoolcraft@optusnet.com		(02) 9482 4924		•			•
NSW	Mosman	Mosman Needlecraft	Shop 3, 529 Military Road	2088	mosmanneedlecraft@bigpond.com		(02) 9969 5105		•			•
NSW	MERIMBULA	Pins & Needles	P O BOX 758	2548	tara.birdinatree@gmail.com		(02) 6495 3646		•			•
NSW	Pennant Hills	Sue's Cherryhills	Shop 7, 354 Pennant Hills Road	2120	cherryhills@live.com.au		(02) 9484 0212		•			•
NSW	Smeaton Grange	Tijuana	Unit 1/8 Blackmore Road	2567	sharon@tijuana-alpacas.com.au		(02) 4647 1155		•			•
NSW	Wollombi	Wollombi Wool Store	2883 Wollombi Road	2325	enquiries@wollombiwoolstore.com		(02) 4998 3154		•			•
NSW	Bowral	Wool Addiction	Shop 4, 31 Station Street	2576	jill@wooladdiction.com.au		(02) 4862 4799		•			•
NSW	Penrith	The Wool Inn	Shop 14 N & K Centre, 450 High Street	2750	penrith@the-wool-inn.com.au		(02) 4732 2201		•			•
NSW	Beecroft	Yarns & Gifts	Shop 8a 16-24 Hannah St	2119	yarns_and_gifts@optusnet.com.au		(02) 8407 9512		•			•
NSW	Sydney	Morris and Sons	50 York Street	2000		morrisandsons.com.au	(02) 92998588		•			•
QLD	Booval	John Watts Sewing Machines	168 Brisbane Street	4304	info@johnwattssewing.com.au		(07) 3282 4711		•			•
SA	Gelenelg	Barb's Sew & Knits	2 Byron Street	5045	barb@barbssewandknits.com.au		(08)8294 7441		•			•
TAS	Moonah	The Wool Shop	P O Box 394	7009	woolsuppliers@bigpond.com		(03) 6278 1800		•			•
VIC	Melbourne	Morris and Sons	Level 1, 234 Collins Street	3000		morrisandsons.com.au	(03) 9654 0888		•			•
VIC	Brunswick	Clegs	P O BOX 185	3057	clegsbrunswick@clegs.com.au		(03) 9654 7677		•			•
VIC	LWR Templestowe	Wollybutt PTY Ltd	P O BOX 2493	3107	lorraine@woolybutt.com.au		(03) 9458 3101		•			•
VIC	Mansfield	Country Folk	P O BOX 233	3724	lafolk@bigpond.com		(03) 5775 2044		•			•
VIC	Oakleigh	Craftee Cottage	Shop 5 52-54 Atherton Road	3166	info@crafteecottage.com.au		(03) 9568 3606		•			•
VIC	Healesville	Crumbz Craft	P O BOX 1714	3777	shop@crumbz.com.au		0412 389192		•			•
VIC	Sassafras	Dalcheri Sassafras	Shop 2, 372 Mt. Dandenong Tourist Road	3787	dalcheri2@bigpond.com		(03) 9755 2510		•			•
VIC	Warrandyte	Needles And Pins	102 Melbourne Hill Road	3113	kayjay15@bigpond.com		(03) 9844 1720		•			•
VIC	Kyneton	Pick Up Stitches Pty Ltd	30 Piper Street	3444	sharon@pickupstitches.com.au		(03) 5422 6614		•			•
VIC	Blackburn	Sunspun	15 Myrtle Grove	3130	amy.doran@sunspun.com.au		(03) 9830 1609		•			•
VIC	Croydon	Threads of Nature	Shop 8, 30-32 Mcadam Square	3136	office@threadsofnature.com.au		(03) 9723 9242		•			•
VIC	Geelong	Twisted Threads	106 Ryrie Street	3220	mandy@twistedthreads.com.au		(03) 5221 0099		•			•
VIC	Mount Eliza	Windmills & Roses	36-38 Ranelagh Drive	3930	windmillsandroses@bigpond.com		(03) 9787 4949		•			•
VIC	Albert Park	Albert Park Wool Baa	124 Bridport Street	3206	sales@woolbaa.com		(03) 9690 6633		•			•
VIC	Northcote	Woolarium	211 A High Street	3070	sharron@woolarium.com		(03) 9486 5275		•			•
VIC	Surrey Hills	Wool Shop	486 Whitehorse Road	3127	woolshop@thewoolshop.com		(03) 9836 9614		•			•
WA	Mosman Park	Calico and Ivy	10 Glyde Street	6012	info@calicoandivy.com		(08) 9383 3794		•			•
WA	Subiaco	Crossways Wool & Fabrics	Shop 15, Crossways S/CTR	6008	sales@crosswayswoolandfabrics.com.aucom.au		(08) 9381 4286		•			•
AUSTRIA												
	Wien	**MEZ Harlander GmbH (Distributor)**	**Schulhof 6, 1. Stock, 1010**		**verkauf.harlander@mezcrafts.com**	**www.mezcrafts.at**	**0800 262 72 8 00**					
	Kitzbuehel	Kitzbuehel Handarbeiten	Im Gries Nr. 23	6370	kbhandarbeiten@networld.at		0043/535672646		•			•
	Kolsass	Wolle + Staune (Sabine Schatz)	Auweg 2a	6114	kahn@wolleundstaune.at	www.wolleundstaune.at	0043/522467198		•			•
	Wien	Laniato - das Wiener Wollcafe	Beatrixgasse 4	1030	wolle@laniato.com	www.laniato.com	0043/69915249911		•			•
	Wien	Sonja Hager-Vedadinejad	Mariahilfer-Straße 45/48	1060	sonja@strickwerk.at		0043/06503190575		•			•
	Wien	Stick + Strick	Simmeringer Hauptstrasse 86	1110	susanne.hasieber@stickundstrick.at	www.stickundstrick.at	0043/1/7494268		•			•
	Wien	Strickwerk	Mariahilfer Straße 45/48	1060	sonja@strickwerk.at		01 89 09 071		•			•
	Wien	Wollboutique Pinguin	Alserstrasse 21	1080	pinguin.wolle@yahoo.de		0043/1/4080010		•			•
	Wien	Wolle fuer Mode Fleischmann	Neubaugasse 59/3	1070	evafleischmann@aon.at		0043/1/5233394		•			•
	Wien	Zwei Glatt Zwei Verkehrt	Josefstädter Str. 14	1080	wolle@zweiglattzweiverkehrt.at	www.zweiglattzweiverkehrt.at	0043/1/4035736	•	•			•
		Wollerei			shop@wollerei.at	www.wollerei.at	43 0 2689 42528		•		•	•
	Mödling	Krawany GmbH	Hauptstrasse 83	2340	handarbeit@krawany.com		0043/2236 41500 15		•	•		•
	Wien	Wollsalon	Schliessmanngasse 11	1130	wolle@wollsalon.com		43 01 2900 300		•			•
BELGIUM												
	Kenzingen	**MEZ crafts Belgium NV (Distributor)**	**c/o MEZ GmbH, Kaiserstr.1, 79341**		**sales.be-nl@mezcrafts.com**	**www.mezcrafts.com**						
Oost-Vlaanderen	Lede	Petit Bear	Kasteeldreef 34	9340	kathba@hotmail.com		0486 31.37.94		•			•
	Antwerpen	Lana	Anselmostraat 92	2018	info@lana-antwerpen.be	www.lana-antwerpen.be	03/ 238 70 17	•	•			•
	Arlon	Brin De Soi	Rue des Faubourg 19	6700	brindesoi@skynet.be		063/ 445 680		•			•
	Assenede	Kashmire	Kloosterstraat 46	9960	info@kashmire.be		09 343 05 93		•			•
	BRASSCHAAT	GENIOUS	Augustijnslei 99	2930	greet@wollebolleke.be		0468 11 81 51		•			•
	Brugge	Cathie's breiboetiek	Karel De Stoutelaan 22	8000	info@cathiesbreiboetiek.be	www.cathiesbreiboetiek.be	050/31.87.87		•			•
	Brugge	Veritas	Steenstraat 20	8000	aankoopcreatief@veritas.be	www.veritas.eu	050.33.77.90		•			•
	Brussel	Be creative by schleiper	63 Rue de l'Etang	1040	becreative@schleiper.be	www.becreativebyschleiper.com	02.541.05.12	•	•	•		•
	Chenée	Rêve de quilts	Rue d'Embourg 29	4032	quiltsdream@skynet.be	www.revedequilts.be	0475 66 76 61		•	•		•
	Deinze	Perfecta	Markt 123	9800	info@perfectadeinze.be		09 386 71 74		•	•		•
	Eeklo	Hobbyfarm	Pastoor Bontestraat, 37	9900	hobbyfarm@pandora.be	www.hobbyfarm.be	09/3786664		•			•
	GEMBLOUX	LA BOITE AU BOUTONS	Rue Léopold 2	5030	info@buromatix.net		081 61 18 10	•				•
	Gent	Stoffenidee	Burgstraat 38A	9000	stoffenidee@skynet.be	www.stoffenidee.net	09/233.37.48	•	•			•
	Geraardsbergen	Maxime's Hobby	Guilleminlaan 237	9500	info@maximeshobby.com	www.maximeshobby.com	054/411145		•			•
	Hamme	Guy's Naaicentrum	Roodkruisstraat 98	9220	info@guysnaaicentrum.be	www.guysnaaicentrum.be	052/ 47 18 05		•	•	•	•
	Hasselt	Veritas	Koning albertstraat 5	3500	aankoopcreatief@veritas.be	www.veritas.eu	011.23.62.93		•	•		•
	Huy	Au Fil Des Laines	Rue du Pont 8	4500	roche.nathalie.34@gmail.com		085 84 64 32		•			•
	Kalken	Calcken	Brugstraat 12	9270	info@calcken.be	www.calcken.be	0494.37.56.35		•	•		•
	Keerbergen	Linnenmandje	Mechelsebaan 3	3140	linnenmand@hotmail.com		015 515 753		•			•
	Kraainem	Atelier de la passion	Avenue des Tarins 24	1950			02 731 85 83		•			•
	Landen	Nodo	Stationstraat 93	3400	info@nodo-mercerie.be		011.83.18.00		•	•		•
	Leper	Origami	Jules Capronstraat 10	8900	nicolie.origami@scarlet.be	www.hobbyshop-origami@skynet.be	057/216022		•	•	•	•
	Leuven	t Wolwinkeltje	Parijsstraat 25	3000	deforcerosemie@hotmail.com	www.twolwinkeltje.be	016 22 75 48	•	•	•		•
	Leuven	Veritas	Brusselsestraat 26-30	3000	aankoopcreatief@veritas.be	www.veritas.eu	016.23.90.65		•	•		•
	LIEGE	TRICOTEA	Rue du Laveu 30	4000	info@valeureux.be		0477.91.25.02		•			•
	Lokeren	De Wolkamer	Gentsesteenweg 477	9160	therese.coens@telenet.be		09/355 20 55		•			•
	Mechelen	Huis Inge Goderis	O.L.V. straat 131-133	2800	info@dehandwerkwinkel.be	www.dehandwerkwinkel.be	015.41.40.54		•			•
	Ronse	Creasis VOF	Jan van Nassaustraat 10	9600	creasis@telenet.be	www.creasis.be	0495 70 81 90		•	•	•	•
	ROESELARE	CLARA'S WOL	Lepersestraat 199	8800	info@claraswol.be			•				•
	Sint Truiden	mercerie GOVAERTS bvba	Markt 61	3800		www.merceriegovaerts.be	011/682288		•	•	•	•
	Sint-Genesius-Rode	The Cosy Cottage	Lindestraat 16	1640	thecosycottage@skynet.be		02 361 70 72			•		•
	Sint-Niklaas	Baele Naaicentrum	Ankerstraat 53	9100	info@baelenaaicentrum.be	www.baelenaaicentrum.be	03.776.16.26					
	Stabroek	Dolce Lana	Laageind 3B	2940	info@dolcelana.be	www.dolcelana.be	03/689.24.88					
	Torhout	Lana Exclusief	Oostendestraat 88A	8820	retrans@skynet.be	www.lana-exclusief.be	050/213632		•		•	•
	Tournai	Paprika Cotton	Rue Saint-Martin 62	7500		www.paprikacotton.be	069/235383		•			•
	Waanrode	t Vlijtig Bijtje	Dorp 12	3473	het.vlijtig.bijtje@skynet.be		016.49.00.16		•	•		•
	Werchter	t Vlijtig Bijtje	Hoge Weg 1	3118	het.vlijtig.bijtje@skynet.be		016.53.16.16		•	•		•
	Westerlo	Atelier Salgarollo	Koning Leopoldlaan 16	2260	kristel.salgarollo@telenet.be	www.salgarollo.be	014 264 393		•			•
	Willebroek	Mooi Gemaakt	Mooi Gemaakt	2830	info@mooigemaakt.be		O3 336 27 59		•	•		•
	Wilsele	D.Yarns	P.Van Langendoncklaan 17	3012	d_van_nueten@hotmail.com		(016) 20 13 81		•			•
BULGARIA												
	Sofia	**MEZ Crafts Bulgaria EOOD (Distributor)**	**7 Magnaurska Shkola Str., BG-1784**		**office.bg@mezcrafts.com**	**www.mezcrafts.com**	**+359 2 439 24 24**	•	•	•		
CANADA												
North Carolina	**Hickory**	**Sirdar USA Inc (Distributor)**	**406 20th Street SE**	**28602**	**sirdarusa@sirdar.co.uk**		**828 404 3705**	•	•	•	•	•
AB	Canmore	Yarn & Company - AB	#105 717 9th Street	T1W 2V7	yarncanmore@gmail.com		(403) 675-9276		•			•
AB	Calgary	Pudding Yarn - AB	1516 6th Street SW	T2R 0Z8	sschuld@puddingyarn.com		(403) 244-2996		•			•
AB	EDMONTON	River City Yarns, Ltd - AB	16956-111 Ave	T5M 4C9	barb@rivercityyarns.com		(780) 477-9276		•			•
AL	Lethbridge	Knitting Time - AL	1240 2nd Avenue A North	T1H 0E4	sales@knittingtime.com		(403) 320-5648		•			•
BC	Vancouver	Three Bags Full Knit Shop - BC	4458 Main Street	V5V 3R3	francesca@threebagsfull.ca		(604) 874-9665		•			•
BC	Vancouver	Pretty Good Ideas Ltd - BC	2008 Wall Street	V5L 1B1	nicole@prettygoodideas.ca		(604) 807-8865		•			•
BC	Victoria	Beehive Wool Shop - BC	1700 Douglas Street	V8W 2G7	beehivewoolshop@telus.net		(250)385-2727		•			•
BC	Surrey	Valley Yarn Ltd. - BC	#192 6758 188 Street	V4N 6K2	info@valleyyarn.com		(604) 576-4222		•			•
BC	Port Moody	Black Sheep Yarns LTD - BC	88 Grant Street	V3H 0B6	helen@blacksheepyarns.ca		(778) 355-9665		•			•
BC	Vancouver	Urban Yarns Ventures - BC	4437 West 10th Avenue	V6R 2H8	knitting@urbanyarns.com		(604) 228-1122		•			•
BC	Kamloops	Knit 2 Yarns - BC	40-1967 Trans Canada Hwy East	V2C 4A4	contact@knit2yarns.com		(250) 314-0276		•			•
BC	Vernon	A Twist of Yarn - BC	3915 31 Street	V1T 5J7	info@atwistofyarn.com		(250) 549-4200		•			•
BC	Prince George	Top Drawer Yarn Studio - BC	#203 1685 Third Avenue	V2L 3G5	topdraweryarn@yahoo.com		(250) 596-4276		•			•
BC	Comox	Village Yarn Shoppe	103A - 1705 Comox Ave	V9M 3N1	jacquie@villageyarnshoppe.ca		(250) 339-2474		•			•
BC	Vernon	The Twisted Purl - BC	Newport Beach Land Company	V1T 6M6	thetwistedpurlyarnstuido@shaw.ca		(250) 542-7432		•			•
BC	Richmond	Wool & Wicker Sales Ltd - BC	130-12051 Second Ave	V7E 3L6	dianedebray@shaw.ca		(604) 275-1239		•			•
MB	Winnipeg	Wolseley Wool Ltd. - MB	889 Westminster Avenue	R3G 1B4	info@wolseleywool.com		(204) 772-5648		•			•
NB	St. Stephen	The Wool Emporium - NB	170 Milltown Boulevard	E3L 1G8	woolemporium@nb-aibn.com		(506) 465-1418		•			•
NS	Wolfville	Gaspereau Valley Fibres	830 Gaspereau River Rd.	B4P 2N5	brenda@gasperequvalleyfibres.ca		(902) 542-2656		•			•
ON	Orleans	Wool N' Things - ON	1439 Youville Drive	K1C 4M8	gisele@woolnthings.com		(613) 841-8689		•			•
ON	McGregor	Sue2Knits - ON	12045 Ducharme Lane	N0R 1J0	sue2knits@gmail.com		(519) 726-4226		•			•
ON	Port Elgin	Docknits	Box 2140 651 Goderich Street	N0H 2C0	docknits@eastlink.ca		(226) 453-5648		•			•
ON	Carleton Place	The Real Wool Shop - ON	142 Franktown Road	K7C 3P3	woolshop@wool.ca		(613) 257-2714		•			•
ON	Toronto	Eweknit - ON	832 Bloor Street W	M6G 1M2	claudia@eweknit.ca		(416) 530-4438		•			•
ON	Perth	Unraveled - ON	9 Wilson Street E	K7H 1L3	beckie@unraveled.ca		(613) 665-1902		•			•
ON	Lindsay	Aberdeen's Wool Company - ON	228 Kent Street West	K9V 2Z2	heather@aberdeenswool.ca		(705) 928-5417		•			•
ON	Ancaster	The Needle Emporium - ON	420 Wilson Street East	L9G 2C3	julie@needleemporium.com		(905) 648-1994		•			•
ON	Toronto	Romni Wools - ON	658 Queen Street W	M6J 1E5	jonathon@romniwools.com		(416) 703-0202		•			•
ON	Owen Sound	Riverside Yarns - ON	928 2nd Ave E	N4K 2H6	willow@riversideyarns.ca		(519) 371-4311		•			•
QC	Montreal	Espace Tricot Inc - QC	6050 Monkland Avenue	H4A 1H2	info@espacetricot.com		(514) 486-5648		•			•
QC	Sutton	Mont Tricot - QC	20-K Principale North	J0E 2K0	monttricot@gmail.com		(450) 538-8040		•			•
QC	Quebec	Boutique Point Mousse - QC	3146 de Versailles	G1X 1E4	pointmousse.ca@gmail.com		(418) 651-2332		•			•
QC	St. Eustache	Tricotine et cie - QC	112 B Rue St. Laurent	J7P 5T1	bianca@tricotine.ca		(450) 974-1313		•			•
QC	L'Ile Perrot	Marie Mode Tricot - QC	200 Grand Boulevard	J7V 4X1	mariejosee@mariemodetricot.ca		(514) 901-0708		•			•
QC	Gatineau	Magifil - QC	317 Boul St. Joseph	J8Y 3Z1	lorrgab@hotmail.com		(819) 595-3694		•			•
QC	St-Jn-S-Richlieu	Tricolaine - QC	231 Rue Saint-Jacques	J3B 2K6	info@tricolaine.com		(450) 346-0990		•			•
SK	Saskatoon	Prairie Lily Knitting	7-1730 Quebec Avenue	S7K 1V9	prairielilyknitting@saskatool.net		(306)665-2771		•			•
SK	Humboldt	Humboldt Haus of Stitches - SK	626 Main Street	S0K 2A0	haus.stitches@sasktel.net		(306) 682-0772		•			•
CHINA												
China	**Shanghai**	**Shanghai Yujun CO. LTD (Distributor)**	**Room 701 Wangjiao Plaza, No.175 Yan'an Road€**	**200002**	**jessechang@vip.163.com**		**86-21-63739785**		•			•

County	Town / City	Stockist	Address	Postcode	Email	Website	Telephone	Rowan At	Yarn	Fabric	Online	Instore
Germany	Kenzingen	MrVictor Li (Commercial agent)	c/o MEZ GmbH Germany, Kaiserstr. 1	79341	victor.li@mezcrafts.com		+86 13816681825		•			•
China	Shanghai	Good Friend Crafts Store	No.408 Fuzhou Rd	200002	jessechang@vip.163.com		-63739720	•	•			•
				CYPRUS								
	Sofia	***MEZ Crafts Bulgaria EOOD (Distributor)***	***7 Magnaurska Shkola Str., BG-1784***		***office.bg@mezcrafts.com***	***www.mezcrafts.com***	***+359 2 439 24 24***	•	•	•		
				CZECH REPUBLIC								
		Coats Czecho s.r.o. (Distributor)	***Staré Mesto 246***	***569 32***	***galanterie@coats.com***	***www.coatscrafts.cz***		•	•	•		•
	Ceské Budejovice	Tvorivá Ovecka	Obchod Tvorivá Ovecka, Plachého 299/22	370 01	welcome@dextera.cz	www.tvoriva-ovecka.cz	420607949059		•			•
				DENMARK								
	Rødovre	***Carl J. Permin A/S (Distributor)***	***Egegårdsvej 28***	***2610***	***permin@permin.dk***	***www.permin.dk***	***45 36 36 89 89***	•	•			•
	Alborg	Design Vaerkstedet	Boulevarden 9	9000	butik@design-vaerkstedet.dk		45 98 12 07 13	•	•			•
	Arhus	City Stoffer	Park Alle 9	8000	mt@citystoffer.dk	www.citystoffer.dk	45 86 19 03 93	•	•			•
	Arhus	Inger's	Volden 19	8000	design.club@mail.dk	www.design-club.dk	45 86 19 40 44	•	•			•
	Bække	Frü Kamp	Klostergade 18	6622	frukamp@hotmail.com		45 61 70 91 14		•			•
	Blåvand	Ho Strik	Hovej 21	6857	info@hostrik.dk	www.hostrik.dk	45 75 27 54 03	•	•			•
	Ebeltoft	Birn & Bagger	Jernbanegade 7	8400	info@bbgarnstrik.dk		45 86 34 11 51		•			•
	Fanø	Kunstladen	Postvejen 29	6720	kunstladenfano@gmail.com		45 75 16 35 04		•			•
	Frederikshavn	Living By Vanja	H. C. Ørstedsvej 18	9900	info@livingbyvanja.dk	livingbyvanja.dk/by-vanja	4522824737		•			•
	Fur	duddine.dk	Pikhedevej 2	7844	duddine@duddine.dk	www.duddine.dk	45 42 15 83 71		•			•
	Gilleleje	Gilleje Stof og Garn	Stationsvej 1	3250	jschmock@hotmail.com	www.gillelejestofoggarn.dk	45 48 30 31 10		•			•
	Haderslev	Garnache	Nørregade 7 St.	6100	connyboysenfeddersen@gmail.com		45 27 85 87 72		•			•
	Haderslev	Garnache	Nørregade 7 St.	6100	connyboysenfeddersen@gmail.com		45 27 85 87 72		•			•
	Helsingør	Tot og tråd	Rosenkildevej 2	3000			45 49 20 23 00		•			•
	Hornslet	Uldtisken	Tingvej 7B	8543	fischer-filt@mail.dk	www.fischer-filt.dk	45 86 97 51 33		•			•
	Hørsholm	Engle Stof	Usserød Kongevej 10 A	2970	englestof@mail.dk		45 45 86 33 78		•			•
	Kgs. Lyngby	Uldstedet	Gl. Jernbanevej 7	2800	uldstedet@uldstedet.dk	www.uldstedet.dk	45 45 88 10 88	•	•			•
	København K	Sommerfuglen	Vandkunsten 3, Kbh.K	1467	mail@sommerfuglen.dk	www.sommerfuglen.dk	45 33 32 82 90	•	•			•
	København K	Uldstedet	Vendersgade 3	1363	uldstedet@uldstedet.dk	www.uldstedet.dk	45 33 91 17 71	•	•			•
	Kolding	Cashmere Company	Skovløkkevej 11	6000	lisa.renner@post.cybercity.dk		45 20 32 08 95		•			
	Middelfart	Garniture	Østergade 6	5500	garniture@garniture.nu		45 64 41 20 08		•			•
	Ribe	Ribes Broderi & Garn	Dagmarsgade 4	6760	symaskineland@symaskineland.dk	www.symaskineland.dk	45 75 42 16 75		•			•
	Ringsted	S P Garn	Søgade 28	4100	spgarn@hotmail.com		45 57 61 36 37		•			•
	Roskilde	Garnhøkeren	Karen Olsdatterstræde 9	4000	annette@wilsom.dk		45 46 37 20 63	•	•			•
	Sæby Ærø	Fies Strik	Albertslykke 10	5985	bch.tisvilde@mail.dk		45 40 29 16 83		•			•
	Silkeborg	Ønskegarn	Nygade 12	8600	sus.garnstrikken@gmail.com	www.onskegarn.dk	45 86 82 57 07	•	•			•
	Skanderborg	Stof og Sy	Adelgade 123	8660	info@stofogsy.dk	www.stofogsy.dk	45 86 52 02 45	•	•			•
	Slangerup	Paradisets Bamser, Tøj og Brugskunst	Kvinderupvej 17	3550	pia.freck@mail.tele.dk	www.butikparadiset.dk	45 47 33 58 66	•	•			•
	Stege	Sy og Strik	Storegade 70	4780	j.naur@mail.dk		45 55 81 41 31		•			•
				EIRE								
Co Wicklow	Enniskerry	Avoca	Powerscourt House & Garden, Powerscourt Estate			www.avoca.ie			•			•
Co Wicklow	Wicklow	Avoca	The Mill, Avoca Village			www.avoca.ie			•			•
Co. Clare	Tulla	Saolre	Tulla Stables Studio				353876496040		•			•
Co. Dublin	Dublin	Springwools Ltd	The Olde Sawmills, Walkinstown	12	sales@springwools.com	www.springwools.com	353 1 450 9134		•			•
Dublin	Dublin	Avoca	Suffolk Street	2		www.avoca.ie			•			•
				ESTONIA								
Harjumaa		MEZ Crafts Estonia	OÜ Ampri tee 9/4	74001			+372 630 6252		•			•
Harjumaa	Viimsi	Kauplus Piste	Viimsi Kaubanduskeskus, Randvere tee 6	74001	piste@piste.ee	www.piste.ee	3726000443		•			•
				FAROE ISLANDS								
	Klaksvik	Búnin	Nolsoyarpálsgøta 18, Box 282	700	bunin2010@hotmail.com		298 455210	•	•			•
				FINLAND								
	Kerava	***Prym Consumer Finland Oy (Distributor)***	***Huhtimontie 6***	***FI-04200***			***358 9 274871***		•			•
	Espoo	Menita Outlet	Ylakartanontie 26	2360			358 9 2567536		•			•
	Helsinki	Fiinaneule	Simonkatu 12	100		www.fiinaneule.fi	358 9 47890065		•			•
	Helsinki	Oy Menita Ab	Korkeavuorenkatu 20	120	helsinki@menita.fi		358 9 632 844		•			•
	Järvenpää	Lentävä Lapanen	Mannilantie 30	4200	info@lentavalapanen.fi		358 50 434 2374		•			•
	Joensuu	Joensuun Kasityovakka	Kauppakatu 30	80100	myynti@kasityovakka.fi	www.kasityovakka.fi	358 400 602 908		•			•
	Kirkkonummi	Mamman Tupa	Toritie 3	2400			358 45 2311470		•			•
	Kuopio	Kuopion Nauha ja Nappi	Vuorikatu 23	70100			358 17 2165756		•			•
	Oulu	Nappi Kikka Design Ateljeé Oy	Pakkahuoneenkatu 18	90100	nappikikka@gmail.com				•			•
	Päntäne	Tapio E Nevanpää	Oikotie 4	61980	info@tapionkauppa.net	www.lankatalo.net	358400362416		•			•
	Sastamala	Silmu & Solmu	Marttilankatu 16	38200	info@silmusolmu.fi	www.silmusolmu.fi	358 50 407 5758		•			•
				FRANCE								
	Toulouse	***3bcom (Distributor)***	***35 avenue de Larrieu***	***31094***	***Commercial@3b-com.com***		***0033 (0) 562 202 096***					
	Angers	Maison Marot	12 rue Championniere	49100	nosouvrages@free.fr		02 41 88 37 66		•			•
	Azay Le Rideau	Théophile	31 Rue Nationale	37190	theophile37@hotmail.fr		0033 2 34 38 19 80		•			•
	Besançon	La Boîte a Laine	15 Rue Xavier Marnier	25000	contact@laboitealaine-besancon.com		06 07 23 25 37		•			•
	Bordeaux	La Lainerie	22 rue des Ayres	33000	la.lainerie@orange.fr	www.lalainerie.com	05 56 81 43 92	•	•			•
	Briançon	L'Atelier de la laine	2 Rue Pasteur	5100	nathphilip@email.com		04 92 20 45 60		•			•
	Cesson	ABC laines	1068 Route de Lucats	77240	abclaines@orange.fr		06 69 52 11 28	•				•
	Colmar	Ambiance Laine	5 Rue Des Pretres	68000	info@ambiance-laine.fr	www.ambiance-laine.fr	03 89 41 87 71	•	•			•
	Gerardmer	Rosavril	43 rue Charles De Gaulle	88400	rosavril@laposte.net		03 29 41 35 49	•	•			•
	Grenoble	Maille a Part	5 Rue Genissieu	38000	contact@mailleapart.fr		04 80 38 27 41	•	•			•
	Joigny	Lady Laine	47 bis rue Gambetta	89300	ladylaine.joigny@wanadoo.fr	www.ladylaine.fr	03 86 62 21 21	•	•			•
	La Réunion (île de)	ce a mwin	Sainte Clothilde	97490	ciahoareau@orange.fr	www.ceamwin.re	2620692 20 39 08	•				•
	Le Plessis Robinson	La Mercerie Carrée	8 place François Spoerry	92350	contact@la-mercerie-carree.fr	www.la-mercerie-carree.fr	01 46 32 61 74	•	•	•		•
	Levallois-Perret	Laines en Vogue	36 rue Gabriel Peri	923000	contact@millemilliersdemailles.fr	www.millemilliersdemailles.fr	01 47 57 58 64		•			•
	Montpellier	Anne Ouvrages	28 Rue Paul Brousse	34000	anneouvrages@bbox.fr		04 67 92 50 92	•	•			•
	Nancy	2 Aiguilles dans la Cafetière	5 rue Gustave Simon	54000	www.anneouvrages.fr		03 83 39 46 70	•	•			•
	Oyonnax	La roulotte des laines		1100	contact@laroulottedeslaines.fr	www.leslaines.com	06 33 43 32 40	•				
	Parentis en Borne	Sur la rive cote laine	1068 Route de Lucats	40160	robelinvirginie@gmail.com	www.surlarivecotelaine.fr	06 33 43 32 40	•				
	Paris (6)	Le Minor	5 Rue du Sabot	75006	sandra.kremmer@neuf.fr		07 78 69 12 92	•				
	Paris	LIL WEASEL	LIL WEASEL, 1 passage du grand cerf	75002	contact@lilweasel.com	www.lilweasel.com	01 73 71 70 48		•	•		•
	Paris (9)	Le Comptoir	26 rue Cadet	75009		www.lecomptoir.canalblog.com/	01 42 46 20 72		•	•		•
	Ploeren	1000 et 1 mailles	38 Rue des 2 moulins	56880	1000et1mailles@gmail.com	1000et1mailles@gmail.com	09 86 16 10 18	•				
	Poitiers	La Mercerie	9 rue Lebascles	86000	boutiquelecomptoir@gmail.com	www.lapetiteboutiqueducomptoir.com	05 49 52 59 22		•			•
	Rennes	LTM	11 rue Poullain Duparc	35000	ltm.hobby@wanadoo.fr		02 99 78 20 60		•			•
	Sarzeau	Les chemins buissonniers	1 place Marie Le Franc	56370			02 97 48 08 30	•	•			•
	Thonon les Bains	Au vieux rouet	7 rue Ferdinand Dubouloz	74200	auvieuxrouet@orange.fr		04 50 71 07 33		•			•
	Toulouse	Jeu de mailles	18 J. Perrin, Le Chapitre Actisud, Bat	31100	contact@jeudemailles.com	www.jeudemailles.com	05 62 26 42 02	•	•		•	•
	Tours	La Boîte à Laine	37, rue du Grand Marché	37000	laboitealaine@orange.fr	www.laboitealaine.fr	02 47 37 76 47		•			•
		MIHL				http://milh-diy.com/	33631226541	•	•	•	•	•
		Pretty Laine			contact@prettylaine.com	www.prettylaine.com						
				GERMANY								
	Kenzingen	***MEZ GmbH (Distributor)***	***Kaiserstr. 1***	***79341***	***kenzingen.vertrieb@mezcrafts.com***	***www.mezcrafts.com***	***0049 7644 802 222***	•	•	•		
	Aachen	Strickstück	Harscampstraße 81	52062	info@strickstuck.de	www.strickstuck.de	0151-64414900	•	•			•
	Ammersbek	Angelika Lehmann	Schwarzerweg 21	22949	wochenmarktwolle@gmx.de		04532/4641		•			•
	Arnstein	Jutta Heurung	Marktstr. 5	97450			0163/1621785		•			•
	Au a. Inn	Helga Holzner	Steinbach 1	83546	bachmair-helga@t-online.de		08073-916666		•			•
	Augsburg	Augsburger Restehaus	Vorderer Lech 39	86150			0821 - 519019		•	•		•
	Bad Laer	Wollecke Gäbel	Mozartstr. 12	49196			54248939		•			•
	Bad Neuenahr-Ahrweiler	Dat Lädche	Niederhutstr. 17	53474	dat-laedche_adams@t-online.de	www.dat-laedche.de	02641/4464		•			•
	Bad Segeberg	Pawlowski	Kurhausstrasse 33	23795	wollideen@web.de		04551 - 8955348		•			•
	Bamberg	Friedericke Pfund	Promenadestr. 18	96047	wollstudio@fritzi.pfund.de	www.home.t-online.de/home/fritzi.pfund	0951-202173	•	•			•
	Bayreuth	Strickart	Kirchplatz 7	95444	strickwerk@gmx.de	www.strickart-cafe.de	0921/5304870	•	•			•
	Beckum	Doris Dreisewerd	Kirchplatz 7	59269			02521 - 3468		•			
	Berlin	Birgit Küttner	Teltower Damm 34	14169			030-8026500		•			•
	Berlin	Die Wollnerin	Gleditschstraße 45	10781	info@die-wollnerin.de	www.die-wollnerin.de	0151/24035100		•			
	Berlin	Holz & Wolle	Warnemünder Str. 29	14199			030/83222762		•			•
	Berlin	Jolanta Schulze	Aßmannstr. 40	12587	joschulze@versanet.de		030-65484239		•			•
	Berlin	Kerstin Hering	Helene-Weigl-Platz 13	12681	hering.kerstin@gmx.de		030 66 30 80 55		•			•
	Berlin	maKuT	Spitzmühler Straße 6	12685	makut2006@online.de	www.makut.de	0152/05110246		•			
	Berlin	Maren Meier	Teltower Damm 20	14169	mlang@cottonfields-berlin.de		030 80902451		•			•
	Berlin	Wollwind	Brunowstraße 52	13507	mail@wollwind.de	www.wollwind.de	030 55591155		•			
	Berlin	Tanja Lay & Michael Schindler Gbr	Monbijouplatz 9	10178	info@handmadeberlin.com	www.handmadeberlin.com	030/97005515		•			•
	Berlin	Simply Stitch	Dietzgenstraße 88	13156	info@simplystitch.de	www.simplystitch.de	030 47489698		•			
	Biberach	Regina Kreuzer-Krause	Gymnasiumstr. 14	88400	rkk@handarbeitslaedele.de		07351/1889980		•	•		•
	Biebertal-Rodheim	Scherer, Barbara	Hauptstr. 62	35444	info@babs-puppen-und-baerenwelt.de		06409-8080330		•			•
	Bielefeld	Adelheit Stanko	Wikingerstrasse 13	33647			0521 - 444425		•			•
	Bielefeld	Renate Kercan	Friedrich-Ebert-Strasse 2	33602			0521/60296		•			•
	Bielefeld	Wolle am Leineweber	Altstädter Kirchplatz 3	33602			0521 / 32932865		•			•
	Bielefeld	WollZauber	Vilsendorferstr. 45	33739			05206/2992		•			
	Blumenthal	Strickmode und Design	Straße der Einheit 91	16928	info@AJ.Strickmodeunddesign.de	www.aj-strickmodeunddesign.de	033984 71459		•			•
	Bocholt	Neue Masche Schlichte	Nordstrasse 49	46399			02871 - 2373661		•	•		•
	Bochum	Danijela Semmler	Südring 19	44787			0234/8937990		•	•		•
	Braunschweig	Susanne Wenke	Schützenstr. 37	38100	info@stil-bluete.net	www.stil-bluete.net	0531-2191337		•			•
	Bremen	Wollstube A. Heyn	Brüggeweg 40-42	28309			0421/413869		•			
	Bremen	Woolbar	Hindenburgstr. 39	28717	info@woolbar.de		0421 63925133		•			•
	Buchloe	Rosine	Bahnhofstr. 50	86807	info@rosine-stoffe.de		08241-9976033		•	•		•
	Burscheid	Bergische Schnatterhütte	Bürgermeister-Schmidt-Str. 6-8	51399			02174 - 892101		•			•
	Chemnitz	Zwillingsnadel	Neumarkt 2	9111	info@zwillingsnadel.de	www.zwillingsnadel.de	0371-3331866		•	•		•
	Coburg	Kristina Hackert	Judengasse 1 a	96450	kristina.hackert@umgarnt.de		95617958133	•	•			•
	Coburg	umGarnt	Judengasse 1 a, Kristina Hackert	96450	info@umgarnt.de	www.umgarnt.de	09561-7958133	•	•			•
	Creuzburg	Lenhard	Adelbert-Kühmstädt-Straße 2	99831	info@wollmaus-wolle.de		036926-9411		•			•
	Dachau	Cotton Club	Konrad-Adenauer-Str. 20	85221	info@cotton-club-dachau.com	www.cotton-club-dachau.com	08131-736859		•			•
	Dannenberg	Annette Gierow	Lange Str. 32	29451			05861/976050		•			•
	Detmold	Handarbeitsgeschäft Müller	Krummestr. 19	32756	info@handarbeitenmueller.de	www.handarbeitenmueller.de	05231/28216		•			•
	Dinslaken	Quiltzauberei	Hans-Böckler-Str. 10-12	46539	bestellung@quiltzauberei.de	www.quiltzauberei.de	02064 - 827980		•	•		•
	Dornhan	Regina Temelkoski	Roßgartenstr. 14	72175			07455/2785		•			•
	Dresden	Strick und Faden	Rothenburger Str. 14	1099	nachstrickundfaden@web.de		0351/8104086	•	•			•
	Düsseldorf	Woll Duo	Scharnhorststr. 16	40477			0211/467776		•			•
	Emmering	Bodendörfer & Heggberg	Kirchplatz 7	82275	dunja@luise-online.net	www.luise-online.net	08141-3634839		•			•
	Erlangen	Emanuel Keller	Hauptstr. 115	91054	shop@wollkontor-erlangen.de	www.wollkontor-erlangen.de	09131/204327		•			•
	Eschach	Karin Schmid	Vellbach 5	73569	info@schmid-viehhandlung.de		07957-9106170		•			
	Ettenheim	Avoco KG	Austr.4	77955	elke.markstahler@hotmail.de		0175-6922375	•	•			
	Frankfurt	Lana	Große Bockenheimer Str.35	60313	lana.lejeune@gmail.com		069/281758		•			•
	Frankfurt	Wolle-Boutique	Eckenheimer Landstr. 34	60318	k-elflein@web.de		069/59792080		•			•
	Frankfurt am Main	Maschenwerke	Marburger Str. 4	60487	info@maschenwerke.de	www.maschenwerke.de	069-71 58 89 80	•	•			•
	Freiburg	Welt der Handarbeit	Salzstr.37-39	79098	info@welt-der-handarbeit.com		0761/2172135	•	•			•
	Freising	Kirsten Bürgel	Obere Hauptstr. 37	85354	info@kimoco.de	www.kimoco.de	08161-140269		•			•
	Freudenberg	Gabriele Rösler	Mittelstrasse 2	57258	roesler.gabriele@t-online.de		02734/436999		•			•
	Friedrichsdorf	Claudia Hahn	Hugenottenstr. 85a	61381	info@wolleundwolle.de		06172/72498		•			•
	Garmisch-Partenkirchen	Edith Vogel	Ludwigstr. 81	82467			88212200		•			•
	Garwitz	Britta Kremke	Am Kanal 4	19372	info@schmeichelgarne.de	www.schmeichelgarne.de	038722/22722		•		•	•
	Gauting	Bonifaktur	Grubmühlerfeldstr. 25	82131	mgraeb@aol.com	www.bonifaktur.de	089-89357858		•			•
	Geldern	StrickStück	Glockengasse 29	47608	info@strickstueck.de	www.strickstueck.de	0151/64414900	•	•			•
	Gifhorn	Schmedt, Heidelore	Steinweg 60	38518			0537-153260		•			
	Gröbenzell	Kimoco	Kirchenstr. 15	82194	groebenzell@kimoco.de		08142-667111		•			
	Haan	Andrea Schleicher	Turnstrasse 2	42781			02129 - 3797966		•			•
	Hagen	Der Wollwichtel	Im Mühlenwert 20	58135			02331 - 7379433		•			•
	Halfing	Ruth Krumme	Chiemseestr. 8	83128	info@lebenstraum-halfing.de		080/559030300		•			•
	Hamburg	Hand-Werk	Papenhuder Strasse 24	22087	hand-werk.bendixen@web.de		040/2798254		•			•
	Hamburg	Karstadt Warenhaus GmbH	Mönckebergstraße 16	20095				•	•			•
	Hamburg	PurPur-Wolle	Heußweg 41b,	20255	info@purpurwolle.de	www.purpurwolle.de	040/4904579		•			•
	Hamburg	Wollboutique	Wandsbeker Chaussee 315	22089	service@wollboutique.de		040/2007620		•			•
	Hamburg	Wollvik	Ratsmühlendamm 26	22335	wollvik@web.de		040/41543767		•			•
	Hanau	Annette Schnabl	Bangertstr.7	63450	Wollparadies-Hanau@web.de	www.wollparadies-hanau.de	61815072732		•			•
	Hanau	Wollparadies	Bangertstraße 7	63450	Wollparadies-Hanau@web.de		06181-5072732		•			
	Hannover	Zeier-Möller Sophie	Sallstr. 81	30171	info@wollkultur.de		0511/3009622		•			•
	Heilbronn	Wollke	Am Kieselmarkt 2	74072	wollke@t-online.de		07131/629357		•			•
	Hemer	Andrea Telge	Hauptstrasse 156	58675			0172 - 5309690		•			
	Hennef	Buchhandlung am Markt	Adenauerplatz 22	53773	kontakt@buchhandlung-hennef.de		02242-81630		•			•
	Heppenheim	Alpaka	Marktstr. 18	64646	hennes.schaab@web.de		06252/2889		•			•
	Herne	Verstrickt und Zugenäht	Mont-Cenis-Str. 1	44623			02323/9595839		•			
	Herzberg	Ursula Deppe-Krieger	Heidstr. 23	37412			0552 172861		•			•
	Hilden	Ellen Klaft	Worrington Platz 28	40721			02103-298249		•			•
	Hofheim	Clothild Wolf	Hauptstr. 29	65719	clothild.wolf@t-online.de		0172-6827937		•			•
	Hohenpeißenberg	Heidi Fischer	Hauptstr. 43	82383	heidi@wolle-und-sonstno.de		08805-8999729		•			
	Holzgerlingen	Handmadel	Tübinger Str. 31	71088	handmadel@online.de		07031-2044732		•			
	Horn Bad Meinberg	dibadu	Lange Str. 26	32805	barbara@dibadu.de	www.dibadu.de	05234-2061841		•			•
	Hoyerhagen	Waltraud Elsner	Hauptstr. 44	27318	blumenstube-hoyerhagen@gmx.de		0425 13478		•			•
	Ibbenbüren	A mano	Unterer Markt 4	49477			05451/936417		•	•		•
	Ingelheim am Rhein	Wolle-im-Hof	Bingerstraße 6	55218	astridkirch@gmx.de	www.wolle-im-hof.de	0173/6714610		•			•
	Kandel	Sybille Riehm	Waldstr. 10	76870	mail@nadel-adel.de		07275 729064		•			•
	Kappeln	Ulrike Jödecke	Schmiedestr. 14	24376	info@rikes-wollmaus.de	www.rikes-wollmaus.de	04642 / 987766	•	•			•
	Karlsruhe	Machart Anna Maier	Amtshausstr. 2	76227			0721-405310					

County	Town / City	Stockist	Address	Postcode	Email	Website	Telephone	Rowan At	Yarn	Fabric	Online	Instore
	Kassel	Christina Geyer	Friedrich-Ebert-Str. 147	34117	info@fil-garn-wolle.de	www.fil-garn-wolle.de	0561/710029		•			•
	Kempten	Kemptener Wollparadies	Klostersteige 15	87435	Wollparadies-Lutz@t-online.de	www.kemptner-wollparadies.de	0831/5239377		•			•
	Kenzingen	Avoco KG	Hauptstr. 6	79341	elke.markstahler@hotmail.de		0175-6922375	•	•			
	Kiel	Dörte Dietrich	Damaschkeweg 50a	24113	info@wollwerkstatt-kiel.de	www.wollwerkstatt-kiel.de	0431/2405493		•			•
	Kirchheim	Ulrike Beck-Kley	Schuhstr. 5	73230			0702 145275		•			•
	Koblenz	Birgit Reich	An der Liebfrauenkirche 11	56068	dasi-tuepfelchenkoblenz@web.de		0261-9733224		•	•		•
	Köln	Maschenkunst	Christophstr. 9-11	50670	info@maschenkunst.de	www.maschenkunst.de	0221/2783489	•	•			•
	Köln	Rapp	Goltsteinstr. 96	50568			0221-16906088		•			•
	Königstein im Taunus	AR Königstein	Kronenberg Strasse 7	61462	info@ar-koenigstein.com	www.ar-koenigstein.com	61749986547		•			•
	Ladenburg	Jutta Dankworth	Hauptstr. 48	68526	info@zierstichladen.de		06203-6730957		•	•		
	Landsberg am Lech	Maschenwerk	Hinterer Anger 324	86899								
	Landshut	Barbara Zeilhofer	Kirchgasse 247	84028			0871/2764217	•	•			•
	Langen	Die Wollstation	Stresemannring 7	63225	info@diewollstation.de		06103-5093355	•	•		•	
	Langenau	Burmeister u. Steck	Bahnhofstr. 3	89129	wollelangenau@aol.com		07345-5393		•			•
	Langgöns	Patchworkstatt	Breitgasse 12	35428	info@woll-lust-wolle.de	www.patchworkstatt.de	06403/940665		•	•		
	Laupheim	Hobbykunst	Mittelstr. 36	88471	mail@hobbykunst-laupheim.de		07392-9674934		•			•
	Leipzig	WOLLEwelten GmbH	Erich-Zeigner-Allee 64	4229	steffen.koehler@wollewelten.de	www.wollewelten.de	0341 22170440	•	•		•	
	Leutkirch	Brigitta Schwarz-Frehner	Marktstr. 30	88299	info@diezweigstelle.de		07561-9834566		•			•
	Leverkusen	Stoffknirps	Wiesdorfer Platz 10b	51373	info@stoffknirps.de		0214 - 86099109		•	•		•
	Limburgerhof	Fabrizio, Mira	Speyererstr. 111	67117	mirafabrizio@aol.de		06236-428387		•			•
	Lingen	Daniela Feike	Göthestr. 27	49811	info@emslaedchen.de	www.emslaedchen.de	0591/75631		•		•	•
	Lüdenscheid	Viebahn	Kluser Strasse 1a	58511			02351 - 6569602		•			•
	Lüneburg	stricxs	Reichenbachstr. 2	21335	stricxs@gmail.com	www.stricxs.com	41316030731		•			
	Magdeburg	maschinistin	Klosterbergestr. 20	39104	ehses@maschenhaft-wolle.de	www.maschenhaft-wolle.de	0391 582 391 63		•			
	Mainz	Andrea Seufert	Fuststr. 2	55166	wolle-seufert@t-online.de		06131-2407196		•			•
	Mainz	Andrea Seufert	Kirschgarten 27	55116	wolle-seufert@t-online.de		0170-8781351	•	•			
	Marburg	Saskia Krieger	Frauenbergstr. 13	35039	wolle-laedchen@t-online.de		06421-34230		•			•
	Meerane	Zick-Zack	August-Bebel-Straße 95	8393	zickzackroessel@aol.com		0376 43374		•			•
	Meiningen	Stoff- Art	Wettiner Str. 12	98617	info@stoff-art.com	www.stoff-art.com	03693-502916		•	•		•
	Melle	Wolllust	An der Kirche 3	49326			05428/927877		•			•
	Mettmann	Pattberg	Peckhauserstrasse 13	40822			02104 - 802633		•			•
	Metzingen	Godelmann, Günther	Stuttgarter Str. 45	72555	info@guenther-godelmann.de		07123-2232		•			•
	München	Die Mercerie	Nymphenburger Str. 96	80636	info@diemercerie.com	www.diemercerie.com	491624358885		•	•		•
	München	Wolle und Schönes	Wasserburger Landstraße 250	81827	wolleundschoenes@t-online.de		0894-308744		•			
	Münster	Maschenrausch Lacatus	Hörster Strasse 56	48143	info@maschenrausch.com		0049521/3846293		•			•
	Norderney	Patchwork-Stübchen	Jann-Berghaus-Str.13	26548			04932/927160		•			•
	Nürnberg	Anita Hammel	Weinmarkt 10	90403	mail@tollewolle.de	www.tollewolle.de	0911-209497		•			•
	Nürnberg	Katharina Stumpf	Zerzabelshofer Hauptstr. 4	90480	kontakt@wollwerkstatt-woll-lust.de		0177-4973353		•			•
	Oberursel	Daniela Queißer	Rathausplatz 6	61440	info@wolllaus.de		06171/586555		•	•		•
	Offenbach	Maschenwahn - In der Etagerie	Taunusstr. 1	63067	maschenwahn@posteo.de		069-87202153	•	•			
	Oldenburg	Simone Wörl	Lindenallee 56	26122			0441/39021818	•	•			•
	Osnabrück	Woll-Perle	Hakenstr. 3	49074			0541/258561		•			•
	Paderborn	handgewirk	Rathausplatz 6	33098			05251 - 8769157		•			•
	Paderborn	Kersek - Meilwes	Kürassierweg 8	33104			05254 - 10126		•			•
	Pirmasens	Wollkörbchen	Tirolerstraße 51	66954					•			
	Plauen	Heike Bromnitz	Stresemannstr. 6	8523	info@kurzwaren-profi.de	www.naehstuebl-bromnitz.de	03741 221316		•			•
	Potsdam	Garn Atelier	Benkertstr. 11	14467	info@garnatelier.de	www.garnatelier.de	0179/2924132		•			
	Prien a. Chiemsee	Susanne Julinek	Geigelsteinstrasse 8 a	83209	susanne@made-am-chiemsee.de	www.made-am-chiemsee.de	08051-6014420		•			
	Ratingen	Wollkörbchen	Turmstr. 30	40878			02102 - 5533797		•			•
	Recklinghausen	Christine Willuda	Am alten Kirchplatz 1	45665					•			
	Regensburg	Birgit Birner	Fröhliche Türkenstr. 5	93047	Strickeria@gmx.net	www.strickeria.net	0941-58612300		•			•
	Reutlingen	Wolle und Mehr	Metzgerstr. 64	72764			07121/310488		•			•
	Rheinberg	Die Strickleiter	Kamper Strasse 37	47495			02843 - 9595335		•			•
	Riedlingen	Kaufmanns WarenWelt	Gammertingerstr. 33	88499	h.goenner@kaufmannswarenwelt.de	www.garnwelt.de	07371-9296212	•	•			
	Röthenbach	L.A. Lana	Erlenplatz 8	90552	L.A.Lana.@ t-online.de		0911-54044695		•			•
	Salzhausen	Wollart Ute Rudat	Eyendorfer Str. 3	21376	info@wollart.de	www.wollart.de	04172-969123		•			•
	Schorndorf	Isy's Kreativinsel	Gottlieb-Daimler-Straße 32	73614	info@kreativinsel-schorndorf.de		07181/480917-0		•			
	Schönstedt	Heike Hüttenroth	Siedlung 4	99947	heike.goerlitz@t-online.de		036022/18935		•			•
	Schwandorf	Wollwerkstatt	Pflegholstufen 2	92421	wollwerkstatt@wolle-kreatives.de		09431-7547845		•			•
	Schwelm	Kunsthandwerk Kolb	Hauptstrasse 88	58332	nokolb@t-online.de		02336 - 4085030		•			•
	Siebnen	Strick and Style	Glarnerstraße 38	8854	strick_and_style@bluewin.ch	www.strickandstyle.ch/de/	0041 55 440 38 01		•			
	Siegen	Stecknadel	Rathausser. 2	57078	creativ@stecknadel.info	http://www.stecknadel.info	27189002667		•			•
	Schwieberdingen	Ulrike Schneider	Stuttgarter Str. 27	71701	stapfreschneiderle@web.de	www.stapfreschneiderle.com	07150-9529289		•	•		
	Soest	Der Faden	Potsdamer Platz 1	59494			02921/3192277	•	•			•
	Solingen	DYO	Ufergarten 25	42651	info@dyostyle.de	www.dyostyle.de	0212 - 64591949		•	•		
	Solingen	Wollfühloase Koch	Ohligser Markt 9	42697			0212 - 66884		•			•
	Stadtlohn	Wolle und Design	Benzstrasse 1	48703	info@wolleunddesign.de	www.wolleunddesign.de	02563/98208	•	•	•		•
	Steinhude	Schönwerk	Vor dem Tore 1	31515	info@schoenwerk-steinhude.de	www.schoenwerk-steinhude.de	05033 9965071		•			•
	Stuttgart	Isabelle Roche	Sophienstr. 24	70178			0711 2265758		•			•
	Suhl	Steffi Hengelhaupt	Friedrich-König-Str. 5	98527	info@stoff-art.com		03681-723704		•			•
	Sulzbach a.d.Murr	Flour-Bretschneider Schettler	Haller Str. 1	71560	m.schetter-flour@vonhand.info	www.vorhand.info	07193-6492		•			•
	Thalmässing	Sabine Hauke	Blumenstr. 22	91177	haukes-stuebchen@gmx.de	www.haukes-stuebchen.de	0917 - 37 89 73		•			•
	Titisee-Neustadt	Jürgen Steiert	Scheuerlenstr. 24	79822			07651/7218		•			•
	Ulm	Wolle & Ideen	Kornhausgasse 6	89073	Heike@Redlinghaus.de	www.wolleundideen.de	0731/619491	•	•	•		•
	Undorf	Roswitha Baierl	Hofmarkstr. 38	93152	rosis_wollstube@yahoo.de		09404-6410341		•			•
	Vincenzbronn	Anita Krehn	Vincenzbronner Hauptstr. 26	90613	georg.krehn@gmx.net		0910 - 59 31 9		•	•		•
	Waren	Silke's Kreativatelier	Große Wasserstraße 34	17192	mondschein31@freenet.de	www.silkes-kreativatelier.de	0162/9254505		•			
	Weimar	Steffi Hengelhaupt	Eisfeld 3	99423	info@stoff-art.com		03643/901748		•			•
	Weißenburg	Karin Schärtel	Unt. Stadtmühlgasse 3	91781			09141-3873		•			•
	Weißenhorn	Susanne Peranovic	Hauptstr. 23	89264	susanne.peranovic@gmail.com		07309-9290540		•			•
	Wendlingen	Frieda Gerhard	Lindengasse 6	73240	info@zaungucker.com		07725-919915		•			•
	Wettstetten	Brigitte Boxleitner	Lange Gasse 16 a	85139	brigitte-boxleitner@t-online.de		0841-9535384		•			
	Wiesbaden	Fil à Fil Der Woll-Laden	Rathausstr. 61	65203	woll-laden@web.de		0611-66969	•	•			
	Winsen/ Aller	Markus Schröter	Celler Str. 11	29308	schroeter-winsenaller@t-online.de		0514 35336		•			
	Zetel	Marion Schäfer	Feldhörn 70	26340			04453 - 3971		•			•
				GREECE								
	Sofia	***MEZ Crafts Bulgaria EOOD (Distributor)***	***7 Magnaurska Shkola Str., BG-1784***		***office.bg@mezcrafts.com***	***www.mezcrafts.com***	***+359 2 439 24 24***	•	•	•		
				HOLLAND								
	Wilnis	***Brouwer & Zn B.V (Distributor)***	***Oudhuijzerweg 69,***	***3648 AB,***	***info@gbrouwer.nl***		***0031 (0) 297-281 557***		•			•
	Alblasserdam	Koperdraadje	Scheldeplein 15	2953 EV	info@koperdraadje.nl	www.koperdraadje.nl			•			
	Ambt Delden	Het Haakwinkeltje	Werninksweg 2	7495 TA	info@hethaakwinkeltje.nl	www.hethaakwinkeltje.nl	074 3765195		•			•
	Amsterdam	de Afstap (Lonnie Bussink)	Oude Leliestraat 12	1015 AW	info@afstap.nl	www.afstap.nl	020-6231445	•	•			•
	Arnemuiden	Atelier Jaffari	Markt 1	4341 EG	jaffari@zeelandnet.nl	www.jaffari.nl	0118 604031		•			•
	Barneveld	Woolfactory	Jan van Schaffelaarstraat 15	3771 BR	info@woolfactory.nl	www.woolfactory.nl	06-20321327		•			•
	Bergen	Finlandia	Kleine Dorpsstraat 26	1861 KN	info@finlandia.nl	www.finlandiaimport.nl	0725 894642	•	•			•
	Den Ham	De Wolboutique	Dorpstraat 44	7683BK	info@dewolboutique.nl	www.dewolboutique.nl	0546-672271	•				
	Driebergen	Trollenwol	Traay 7	3971 GB	info@trollenwol.nl	www.trollenwol.nl	0343-750700		•			•
	Eindhoven	Breimode Brigitte	Ouverture 212	5629 PX	info@brigitte-handwerken.nl	www.brigitte-handwerken.nl	040-2435576	•	•			•
	Etten-Leur	De Wolboetiek	Bisschopsmolenstraat 169	4876 AL		www.wolboetiek.nl	076-5022597		•			•
	Haarlem	WOL!	Barrevoetestraat 9	2011 WN	barte892@planet.nl	www.wol-online.nl	063 1780100	•	•			•
	Heerlen	Ut Bolke	Benzenraderweg 92	6417 SV	info@utbolke.nl	www.utbolke.nl	045 /571 64 51		•			•
	Huizen	De Pauw	Voorbaan 25	1271RR	info@handwerkzaakdepauw.nl	www.handwerkzaakdepauw.nl	035 525 1212		•			•
	Joure	Ajoure	Pastorielaan 2	8501 EZ	info@ajoure.nl	www.ajoure.nl	051/3413344		•			•
	Kampen	Pingouin wol & handwerken	Oudestraat 20	8261 CP	pingouinkampen@uwnet.nl		038-3322811		•			•
	Koewacht	Wolboerderij Blij Bezuiden	Het Zand 61	4576 CB	info@wolboerderij.nl	www.wolboerderij.nl	114361402		•			•
	Leiden	Ribbels	Pieterskerk-Choorsteeg 18	2311 TR	annelies.danton@ribbels.nl	www.ribbels.nl	071 5133126	•	•			•
	Oldenzaal	Lohuis	Steenstraat 26	7571 BK	t.lohuis@planet.nl	www.lohuis-tijhuis.nl	05415-12626		•	•		•
	Rijssen	Het Wolhuis	Haarstraat 148	7462 AV	info@hetwolhuis.nl	www.hetwolhuis.nl	0031 548 78 52 75		•			•
	Sittard	Wollstreet	Rijksweg Noord 61	6131 CJ	info@wollstreet.nl	www.wollstreet.nl	0464-586330		•			•
	Utrecht	Modilaine	Lijnmarkt 22	3511 KH	info@modilaine.nl	www.modilaine.nl	030-2328911	•	•			•
	Voorburg	Wollig	Herenstraat 95	2271 CC	info@wollig-online.nl	www.wollig-online.nl			•			
	Workum	It Nifelhoekje	it Sud 81	8711CT	info@itnifelhoekje.nl	www.itnifelhoekje.nl	0515 542501		•			•
	Zaandam	Zaans Geluk	Kleine tocht 7L	1507 CB	info@zaansgeluk.nl	www.zaansgeluk.nl	075-6124024		•			•
	Zuidlaren	Ryahuis	Telefoonstraat 26	9471 EN	info@ryahuis.nl	www.ryahuis.nl	050-4092618	•	•			•
				HONG KONG								
		East Unity Company Ltd. (Distributor)	***Unit B2, 7/F., Block B, Kailey Industrial Centre, 12 Fung Yip Street, Chai Wan***		***eastunityco@yahoo.com.hk***		***(852)2869 7110***		•			•
				HUNGARY								
Pest	Budapest	ECOSOL KFT.	KERÉNYI FRIGYES KÖZ 7/B	1028	anna.pap@xapt.com		06-20-296-8480	•	•			•
				ICELAND								
	Rødovre	***Carl J. Permin A/S (Distributor)***	***Egegårdsvej 28***	***2610***	***permin@permin.dk***	***www.permin.dk***	***45 36 36 89 89***	•	•			•
				ITALY								
MI	***MILANO***	***Mez Cucirini (Distributor)***	***Viale Sarca, 223***	***20126***	***servizio.clienti@mezcrafts.com***	***www.mezcucirini.it***	***0039 0264109080***		•			•
AN	SENIGALLIA	GIRALDI MERCERIE	CSO 2 GIUGNO 80	60019			+39 07163831		•			•
AR	SAN GIOVANNI VALDARNO	AGO E SVAGO DI REDAELLI SIMONETTA	VIA PIAVE 58	52027	simonettaredaelli@live.it		+39 0555275984		•			•
AT	ASTI	LA BOTTEGA DI EVELINA	VIA GIOVANNI GIOBERT 62	14100			+39 0141595579		•			•
BA	BARI	CREATTIVA SRL DI MANCINO SECCIA	VIA PASUBIO 43	70125	creattiva.srl@gmail.com		+39 0809678609		•			•
BG	SUISIO	GOGIANDO di A.B.	PIAZZA MARTIRI DI VIA FANI 1/B	24050	gogiando@gogiando.com		+39 3662704081		•			•
BG	BERGAMO	SAVOIR FAIRE di SECOMANDI UGO	VIA CORRIDONI 28/E	24124	ambra.lupini@alice.it		+39 3358075069		•	•		•
BL	TAIBoN AGORDINO	EL GEM DA TIZIANA di DAI PRA	VIA COMEDON 15	32027	elgem.tiziana@libero.it		+39 043765259		•			•
BL	BELLUNO	GOMITOLO D'ORO DI ZAMPIERI RENATA	VIA 30 APRILE 1	32100			+39 0437940516		•			•
BL	CORTINA D'AMPEZZO	LA COOPERATIVA DI CORTINA S.C.	CORSO ITALIA 40	32043	info@coopcortina.com	www.coopcortina.com	+39 0436861245		•			•
BO	S.GIOVANNI IN PERSICETO	AGOFILO di FRASCARI CLAUDIO	VIA MODENA 40	40017	claudio.frascari@agofilo.com	www.agofilo.com	+39 051 822002		•			•
BO	BOLOGNA	ATELIER DELLA LANA DI NINETTA	VIA RIALTO 19/C	40124	nbadile@gmail.com	www.atelierdellalana.it/	+39 051238268		•			•
BO	BOLOGNA	CASA DELLA LANA	VIA AUGUSTO RIGHI 19	40126	monica@cinius.com		+39 051227731		•			•
BO	SAN LAZZARO DI SAVENA	CUCILANDIA BOLOGNA	VIA CARLO JUSSI 71	40068	info@cucilandiabologna.it	www.cucilandiabologna.it	+39 0516271610		•			•
BO	IMOLA	DRITTO FILO DI BARBIERI STEFANIA E PRESTA ILARIA S	VIA PISACANE 43	40026	ilaria.presta71@gmail.com				•			•
BO	CREVALCORE	FILIVARI LA BOTTEGA DEL FILO	VIA MATTEOTTI 247	40014	filivari.bottegadelfilo@gmail.com		+39 3311881062		•			•
BO	BOLOGNA	IL MONDO DI ALICE di EMANUELA BONOR	VIA CASTIGLIONE 58/A	40124	ilmondodialicesnc@libero.it		+39 051744835		•			•
BO	CASTEL SAN PIETRO	MOLINARI DI RAGGI ROBERTA & C. SNC	VIA MATTEOTTI 116	40024	raggiroberta64@gmail.com		+39 051 6958688		•			•
BR	BRINDISI	ARTEMAGLIA DI D'ADDARIO ANTONELLA	VIA APPIA 136	72100	artemaglia@alice.it	www.artemagliacreazioni.it	+39 346 3025490		•			•
BS	DESENZANO DEL GARDA	AMARENGO SRL	VIA BRESCIA 56	25015	amarengo2015@gmail.com		+39 3806371589		•			•
BS	CHIARI	CASA DEL TENDAGGIO	VIA S.MARTINO DELLA BATTAGLIA 13	25032	alessia.vago@alice.it	www.casadeltendaggiomorsia.com	+39 030712022		•			•
BS	CASTENEDOLO	CDB MERCERIE di CASAROTTI A.	VIA BRESCIA 65/67 c/o CITYPER	25014	info@casadelbottone.com		+39 030 2131204		•			•
BS	PROVAGLIO D'ISEO	L'AGORAIO	VIA FIUME 8	25050	info@agoraio.it	www.agoraio.it	+39 0305057946		•			•
BS	BRESCIA	LE FORBICI D'ORO S.R.L.	VIA DELLE BATTAGLIE 8	25122	leforbicidoro@gmail.com		+39 03044203		•			•
BS	BRESCIA	LILLA E LAVANDA DI BONETTI	VIA CAVOUR 28	25122	lillaelavanda@libero.it		+39 3892854758		•			•
BS	MONTICHIARI	SOTTOPUNTO di PIRAS ILARIA	VIA CESARE BATTISTI 8	25018	sottopunto.ilaria@hotmail.it	www.sottopunto.altervista.org	+39 3401578197		•			•
BZ	MERANO	AMALALANA di ISOARDI PAOLA	VIA PORTICI 170	39012	paolaisoardi@gmail.com	www.amalalana.it	+39 3393377936		•			•
CN	BRA	ATTISANI VITTORIA	VIA PIUMATTI 76	12042			+39 017244769		•			•
CN	BORGO SAN DALMAZZO	BRICIOLE DI FANTASIA	VIA LOVERA 31	12011	patdif@libero.it		+39 3495315516		•			•
CO	SORICO	BLANCHE	VIA BOSCHETTO 45	22010	info@blanche-atelier.com		+39 335 6219732		•			•
CR	CREMONA	GOMITOLI di MANGIAROTTI MONICA	CORSO MATTEOTTI 90	26100	monimoni64@gmail.com	gomitolicremona.altervista.org	+39 338 2802699		•			•
CT	MISTERBIANCO	SCUDERI ROSALINDA	VIA DEI VESPRI 236	95045	info@perfilopersegno.it	www.perfilopersegno.it	+39 347 5539876		•			•
FC	CESENA	JOLLY CASA DI DEGLI ANGELI SILVIA	FIORENZUOLA 193	47023	jolly_casa@libero.it	www.jollycasahobbistica.it	+39 0547303026		•			•
FC	CESENA	L'AGO E IL DITALE DI CANTONI LUGHI	VIA STRINATI 6	47521	manuela.cantonilughi@alice.it	www.lagoeilditale.it	+39 0547610296		•			•
FC	FORLI'	PUNTI E SPILLI di MORELLI	PIAZZETTA DELLA GRATA 1	47121	info@puntiespilli.it	www.puntiespilli.it	+39 3667200509		•			•
FI	FIRENZE	LA MERCERIA DEL 900 DI RUSSI STEFAN	VIA DEL POLLAIOLO 108 ROSSO	50142	lamerceriadel900@gmail.com		+39 339 5315731		•			•
FI	TAVARNUZZE	PUNTO SU PUNTO DI MANCINI MARTINA E MANCINI AMMA S	VIA MONTEBUONI 194	50029	info@puntosupunto.it		+39 3409387371		•			•
GE	GENOVA	FONTE DELLA LANA	GALATA 27 R	16121	rita.rollino@gmail.com		+39 010562594		•			•
GE	GENOVA	IL SALOTTO DELLA MADDA SNC DI CINZIA NIVES DE BONI	VIA DELLA MADDALENA 28/30 R	16124	nivesdb@libero.it		+39 010 2091782		•			•
GE	GENOVA	TASSAROLO ANGELA	VIA GIANELLI 91 R	16166	mariangelapontenani@gmail.com		+39 0103725221		•			•
GE	RONCO SCRIVIA	ZIG ZAG DI BARBARINO GIULIA CRISTINA	VIA ROMA 57	16019	zigzag1963@libero.it		+39 3405249077		•			•
GR	GROSSETO	CASA DEL BOTTONE SNC F.LLI SANTINI	VIA PAGLIALUNGA 8	58100	mariapiasantini@virgilio.it		+39 056 423971		•			•
IM	DIANO MARINA	BOTTERO MAURA	CORSO ROMA 153	18013	botteromaura@gmail.com		+39 0183 498671		•			•
IS	ISERNIA	BRUSCO ROSARIA	CORSO GARIBALDI 195	86170			+39 086550648		•			•
LE	TRICASE	ANTICA MERCERIA SAS DI CITO IMMACOLATA & C.	VIA L. CADORNA 127	73039	antica-merceria@libero.it		+39 0833543011		•			•
LE	CUTROFIANO	GATTAMATTA SRL	VIA VINCENZO COLI 25	73020	gattamattamaglie@alice.it		+39 0836427805		•			•
LE	CASARANO	IL FILO DI MARIANNA DI PRETE MARIANNA	CORSO XX SETTEMBRE 133	73042	mariannaprete@libero.it		+39 3336784948		•			•
LE	CARMIANO	LA MATASSA DI BENEGIAMO MARIA	VIA REGINA ELENA N.3	73041	mariaritabenegiamo@libero.it		+39 3297859440		•			•
LE	TREPUZZI	PEZZUTO MARIA ANGELA	VIA MONTALE 1	73019	mary1288@live.it		+39 3404957321		•			•
LI	COLLESALVETTI	LA MIA IMPRONTA DI STEFANIA SOZZI	VIA ROMA 236	57014	stefania.sozzi@gmail.com		+39 3476970362		•			•
MI	MILANO	DO KNIT SRL	VIA MOSCATI 20-ANG.VIA CANONICA	20154	do-knit@libero.it	www.do-knit.it	+39 3391242881		•			•
LO	SANGELO LODIGIANO	LA BOTTEGA DELLO SCAMPOLO	VIA CESARE BATTISTI 8	26866	Elena.dioli@yahoo.it		+39 037192584		•			•
LO	LODI	LA VIA LATTEA SRL	CORSO ARCHINTI 33	26900	info@penelopeknit.it		+39 3925670758		•			•
LT	CISTERNA DI LATINA	CREIAMO INSIEME	VIA LEONARDO DA VINCI 35	04012	luciadiantonella@virgilio.it		+39 347 8608525		•			•
LU	LUCCA	L'ARCOLAIO DI PASQUINELLI E RAGONE	PIAZZA CITTADELLA 11	55100			+39 0583580248		•			•
LU	PIETRASANTA	LE COSE DI STEFANIA DI VEZZONI STEFANIA	VIA DEL MARZOCCO 128	55045	info@lecosedistefania.it	www.lecosedistefania.it	+39 0584793647		•			•
MB	SEREGNO	I FILATI INCANTATI di ALTOMONTE FRA	VIA MEDICI DA SEREGNO 14	20831	afrancesca590@gmail.com		+39 3381842937		•			•
MC	MACERATA	MENICHELLI - RAMBOZZI DI L.B. & C.	PIAZZA C. BATTISTI 14	62100	merceriamenichelli@libero.it		+39 0733232628		•			•
MI	VIMERCATE	IL BOTTONE di FENAROLI MARIA TERESA	VIA DE CASTILLIA 14	20059	mt.fenaroli@gmail.com		+39 039660890		•			•
MI	MILANO	PLANA MERCERIA	VIA PLANA 43	20155	merceriaplana@gmail.com		+39 02 33002241		•			•
MI	MILANO	STIM ITALIA SRL	VIA TROYA 7	20144	info@stim-italia.com	www.stim-italia.com	+39 3929236898		•			•
MI	MILANO	TRICOTS DI GUIRTI CHIARA	PIAZZA SIENA 8	20146	chiarastella.guirti@fastwebnet.it	www.tricots.it	+39 024075777		•			•
MN	MANTOVA	IL FILO DI USVARDI FRANCA	VIA ALDO MORO 10	46100			+39 0376321637		•			•

County	Town / City	Stockist	Address	Postcode	Email	Website	Telephone	Rowan At	Yarn	Fabric	Online	Instore
MN	CASTIGLIONE DELLE STIVIERE	PUNTI & SPUNTI di MENTA E. e A. SNC	VIA MAZZINI 14	46043	elena.menta@libero.it		+39 340 2978508		•	•		•
MO	MODENA	DRITTO E ROVESCIO	LARGO S. FRANCESCO 144	41121	tizianasoncini@tiscali.it		+39 059 4555316		•			•
MO	FORMIGINE DI MODENA	ZA-MA S.N.C.	VIA DON MINZONI 1/B	41043	marisazampieri@hotmail.it		+39 059 571364		•			•
NA	NAPOLI	CUCISHOP DI PAOLA DORA	GALLERIA VANVITELLI 13 VOMERO	80129	info@cucishop.it	www.cucishop.it	+39 0815584007		•			•
PD	PADOVA	BIASIOLI DONATELLA	GALLERIA S. CARLO 10	35133			+39 049600498		•			•
PD	NOVENTA PADOVANA	CELIN MARILENA "PRIMO LABORATORI	VIA VALMARANA 49/C	35027	primo.laboratorio@libero.it		+39 0498959126		•	•		•
PD	PADOVA	LANE NUOVE DI BARCELLAN MARINA	VIA BARBARIGO 6	35141	barcellan.marina@libero.it		+39 3477109016		•			•
PG	SPOLETO	CIMARELLI AGOSTINA	VIA PASQUALE LAURETI 15	06049			+39 074349450		•			•
PG	CASTIGLIONE DEL LAGO	LANDI SIMONETTA	VIA SESTINO 12 -LOC.BADIACCIA	06061	lslucianosimonetta@gmail.com		+39 0758230220		•			•
PG	TODI	PAZZAGLIA ELISABETTA	VIA S.AGOSTINO 5	06059	gervasi_alessandro@alice.it		+39 0758942580		•			•
PI	PISA	CASA DELLA MERCERIA DI TARABELLA MARZIA	VIA D'AZEGLIO 15	56100	marziatarabella@alice.it		+39 3355956139		•			•
PO	PRATO	PERLE DI ALESSANDRA GHERI	VIA F. FERRUCCI 339/3	59100	perle.ale@libero.it	www.merceriaperle.it	+39 0574575144		•			•
PR	PARMA	DALL'ARGINE - dett	PIAZZA GHIAIA 5	43100	info@dallargine.it		+39 0521607989		•			•
PT	PISTOIA	BORSELLI FILATI	VIA CAN BIANCO 9	51100	nestbor61@gmail.com		+39 0573 26101		•			•
PV	PAVIA	BOUTIQUE LANA CIOTTI DONATELLA	VIA MASCHERONI 18	27100			+39 038223675		•			•
PZ	LAURIA SUPERIORE	L'ALBERO DELLE IDEE S.R.L. ARTIGIANTATO E DESIGN	VIA ROCCO SCOTELLARO 139	85044	marialongo70@gmail.com		+39 3293933769		•			•
RA	FAENZA	IL GOMITOLO DIETRO L'ANGOLO	VIA TORRICELLI 23/A	48018	elisaemiliani@ymail.com	www.ilgomitolodietrolangolo.com	+39 328 6693475		•			•
RA	LUGO DI ROMAGNA	SCARDOVI SNC - SCARDOVI STEFANO & C	VIA MENTANA 71	48022	info@scardovi.com		+39 054526997		•			•
RE	SCANDIANO	IL FILO DI ARIANNA DI GRISENDI ROBE	VIA GARIBALDI 9/C	42019			+39 0522984736		•			•
RE	MONTECCHIO EMILIA	MONTEPIETRA MERCERIA	PIAZZALE CAVOUR 3	42027	merceria_montepietra@libero.it	www.merceriamontepietra.it	+39 0522865658		•	•		•
RM	ROMA	CA.FI.LAN S.R.L.	VIA U. BIANCAMANO 7	00185	info@cafilan.com	www.lanaefilati.com	+39 067000503		•			•
RM	ROMA	CAPUANI MARIANTONIETTA	PIAZZA DELLA TORRETTA 22	00186	mc.capuani@gmail.com		+39 06 6871215		•			•
RM	ROMA	CIOTTI BARBARA	VIA DELLO STATUTO 70	00185	barbaraciotti@inwind.it	www.centrocucitocreativo.com	+39 064872814		•			•
RM	GUIDONIA	CREANDO CON AZZURRA DI AZZURRA MARINO	VIA DEI GIRASOLI 45	00012	info@creandoconazzurra.com	www.creandoconazzurra.com	+39 0774304006		•			•
RM	ROMA	ELLA SAS DI CASPONI MIRELLA	VIA VINCENZO TIERI 215	00123	ella_arte@hotmail.com		+39 0630894351		•			•
RM	ROMA	GENOVESI MIRELLA	L.GO S. EUFRASIA PETTETIER 13	00151	cgenovesi@toy-roma.net		+39 06-58232305		•			•
RM	ROMA	GOMITOLANDO S.R.L.	VIA IGNAZIO GIORGI, 42/44	00162	info@gomitolando.it	www.gomitolando.it	+39 06 45428653		•			•
RM	ROMA	IL TRIANGOLO DI NUNZIATA CRISTINA	VIA DEGLI ORAFI 79	00133	merceriailtriangolo@gmail.com		+39 062023299		•			•
RM	ROMA	LA CARTARECCIA SRLS	VIA DOMENICO PURIFICATO 170	00125	info@lacartareccia.com	www.lacartareccia.com	+39 0652351018		•			•
RM	FIUMICINO	L'ANGOLO DELLE IDEE DI TIZIANA GIAMBARTOLOMEI & C S	VIA TRINCEA DELLE FRASCHE 168/172	00054	s.angolodelleidee@gmail.com		+39 06 65024516		•	•		•
RM	MONTEROTONDO	PERFETT'ARMONIA SNC DI TIZIANA SANTINI E C	VIA EDMONDO RIVA 17	00015	perfettarmonia@gmail.com		+39 0662286823		•			•
RM	ROMA	TUTTO CASA SNC	VIA DI CASALOTTI 103	00166	lorenzodigianni@yahoo.it		+39 0661550920		•			•
RN	RIMINI	BENVENUTI MERC. ADRIATICA	VIA CLEMENTINI 31	47921	mail.signorile@gmail.com		+39 0541 29400		•			•
RO	OCCHIOBELLO LOCALITA' S.MARIA MADDALENA	WOOLOVE DI COLOGNESI MONIA	VIA ERIDANIA 243	45030	monia.colognesi@gmail.com		+39 3921650412		•			•
SI	SARTEANO	IL MONDO DI FRANCESCA DI FRANCESCA GIULIACCI	P.ZZA BARGAGLI 16	53047			+39 347 905 4544		•			•
SI	SIENA	RAFFAELLA di RAFFAELLA CHELLINI	VIA CAMOLLIA 148	53100	studioguerrini@infinito.it		+39 057741161		•			•
SI	POGGIBONSI	SUL FILO DI LANA SNC	VIA SENESE 85	53036		www.sulfilodilana.it	+39 0577 982110		•			•
SP	LA SPEZIA	CERRETTI E C. SNC	CORSO CAVOUR 178	19121	info@cerrettisnc.com	www.cerrettisnc.com	+39 0187735108		•	•		•
SV	CAIRO MONTENOTTE	BRUZZONE P&C SAS	VIA ROMA 91	17014	patriziabruzzone@gmail.com		+39 019503664		•			•
SV	ALBISOLA SUPERIORE	MERCERIA E BIANCHERIA DEL CORSO DI GIANNELLI ANTON	CORSO FERRARI 121	17011	merceriadelcorso@libero.it		+39 0197700510		•			•
TA	MANDURIA	ANRY TUTTO CREA DI DISTRATIS ANTONIO	VIA BELL'ACQUA 3	74024	valeriodistratis@hotmail.it		+39 3391291430		•			•
TA	MARTINA FRANCA	PRETTY MODA DI LEO MARIA	VIA ELIO VITTORINI, 70-72	74015	mariaitleo@alice.it		+39 328 7158227		•			•
TE	GIULIANOVA LIDO	CHIOVI CLAUDIO	VIA NAZARIO SAURO 78	64021			+39 0858004668		•			•
TN	ROVERETO	INCANTESIMO di STEFANO GIOS	VIA RIALTO 58 / 1	38068	incantesimosg@teletu.it		+39 0464 435776		•			•
TN	PINZOLO	MARGIT MATURI	VIA FUCINE 79	38086	atelier@margitmaturi.com	www.margitmaturi.com	+39 3349397955		•			•
TO	LEINI'	FILOFILA' di QUARANTOTTO FABIO	VIALE EUROPA 38/B	10040	fabio.filofila@gmail.com		+39 0112762097		•			•
TO	PINEROLO	FILOSOFIA DI ANTONELLA MELONI	VIA BUNIVA 23	10064	antonella.meloni@gmail.com		+39 3406491860		•			•
TO	TORINO	LA COMPAGNIA DEL COTONE DI DANIELA BASSO & C.	VIA MAZZINI 44	10123	lacompagniadelcotone@tiscali.it		+39 0118178381		•	•		•
TO	IVREA	MERCERIA CRISTINA DI VAIO CRISTINA	VIA CIRCONVALLAZIONE 34	10015	yaiocri@hotmail.it		+39 340 4760973		•			•
TO	TORINO	WOOL CROSSING di GIUDICE FEDERICA	VIA BOCCACCIO 58	10132	federica@woolcrossing.it	woolcrossing.it	+39 3482905189		•			•
TS	TRIESTE	FONDA SILVA SAS	VIA DELLE TORRI 2	34122	roberta.zu.ars@gmail.com		+39 040771717		•			•
TV	VEDELAGO	BARICHELLO SAS DI BARICHELLO PRIMO	VIA VICENZA 20	31050	barichellosas@tiscali.it	www.bottegabarichello.com	+39 0423 700167		•			•
TV	TREVISO	LA MERCERIA PREZZEMOLO	VIA CAMPANA 9	31100	eugenia.dapolito@alice.it		+39 0422 412898		•			•
UD	UDINE	ELISA CESSELLI DI FOI CATERINA	VIA SAVORGNANA 18	33100	caterina.foi@libero.itc		+39 0432 295633		•			•
VI	SAN GIUSEPPE CASSOLA	SIMONCELLO PATRICK	VIA ROSSINI 3	36022					•			•
VR	VERONA Loc. PARONA	FALCETTO S.N.C. DI RIGHETTI LAURA E	VIA DEGLI ARUSNATI 3	37025	info@falcetto.it		+39 045941091		•	•		•
				JAPAN								
Tokyo	Tokyo	Hobbyra Hobbyre Corporation (Distributor)	23-37, 5-Chome, Higashi-Ohi, Shinagawa-Ku	1400011			81334721104					
Chiyoda-ku	Tokyo	Daidoh International Ltd.	Sotokanda 3-chome, PUPPY Div. / 1-16	101-8619			0081-3-3257-7135		•			•
Hiroshima	Hiroshima	Puppy Hiroshima	8-16 kamihacchoubori, nakaku	730-0012			81-082-222-0537	•	•			•
Hukuoka	Kitakyusyu	Izutsuya Department Store	2-4 igashiko, Kokurakitaku	803-0802			81-093-522-2729	•	•			•
Hyogo	Kobe	Union Wool	1-30-22 Kitanagasadori, Chuouku	650-0012	union@smile.ocn.ne.jp		81-078-331-8854		•			•
Osaka	Osaka	Hankyu Department Store	8-7 kakudacho, Kitaku	530-8350			81-06-6313-8938	•	•			•
Osaka	Osaka	Masuzakiya	4-5-4 Kawaramachi, Chuouku	541-0048			81-06-6222-1110	•	•			•
Osaka	Osaka	Room Amie	3-11-8-109Yamate-cho, Suita-city	564-0073	info@roomamie.jp	http://roomamie.jp	81-06-6821-3717		•			•
Shinagawa-Ku	Tokyo	Hobbyra Hobbyre Corporation	23-37, 5-Chome, Higashi-Ohi	1400011			0081-33472-1104		•			•
Tokyo	Tokyo	Mitsubaya	1-1-1 Minamiaoyama, Minatoku	107-0062			81-03-3404-1677	•	•			•
Tokyo	Tokyo	Mitsukoshi Department Store	Hobby & Craft Salon 8F Mitsukoshi New Bild., 1-4-1 Nihonbashi Chuouku	103-8001			81-03-3273-6500		•			•
Tokyo	Tokyo	Puppy Shimokitazawa	2-26-4 Kitazawa, Setagayaku	155-0031			81-03-3468-0581	•	•			•
Tokyo	Tokyo	Seibu Department Store	100 idee 7F Seibu Ikebukuro, 1-28-1 Minami-Ikebukuro Toshima-ku				81-03-3983-5433	•	•			•
		Rowan-Jaeger				www.rowan-jaeger.com			•		•	•
				KOREA								
Seoul	Jongno-Gu	My Knit Studio (Distributor)	3F, 144 Gwanhun-Dong	110-300	myknit@mykint.com	www.myknit.com	82-2-722-0006		•			•
Seoul	Jongno-Gu	Danju	1F, 65-4 Samcheong-Ro	110-200	jade@danju.co.kr	www.danju.co.kr	82-2-720-1127		•			•
				LATVIA								
	J⊠rmala	latvian Crafts	12-2, Jur⊠u street	LV-2011	vjelkins@latviancrafts.lv	www.latviancrafts.lv	37126326825	•	•	•	•	
				LEBANON								
	Beirut	y.knot (Distributor)	Saifi Village, Mkhalissiya Street 162		y.knot@cyberia.net.lb		(961) 1 992211		•			•
				LITHUANIA								
	Vilnius	MEZ Crafts Lithuania UAB (Distributor)	A. Juozapaviciaus str. 6/2,	LT 09310	info.lt@mezcrafts.com		+370 527 30971					
	Kaunas	www.kaSiulai.lt	Parduotuve "Siulai", Savanoriu pr. 192C	LT44151	parduotuve@kasiulai.lt	www.kasiulai.lt	37068227187	•	•	•		•
	Kaunas	Karaliska Vilna	Nemuno str. 45	LT44288	karaliskavilna@gmail.com	www.karaliskavilna.com	37069966699	•	•			•
	Kaunas	Si⊠lo galas	Kestucio str. 80-9	LT44297	info@siulogalas.lt	www.siulogalas.lt	'+370 682 47 334	•	•			•
	Siauliai	Casa Lana	Vilniaus g. 255	76343	g_mazze@yahoo.com		868502795		•			•
	Vilnius	kaSiulai	Ladygos g. 5, Žukausko g. 36	LT8235	parduotuve@kasiulai.lt	www.kasiulai.lt	37068231492		•	•		•
	Vilnius	Mezgimo zona	Parduotuve, K. Ladygos str. 5/S. Žukausko str. 36	LT01136	parduotuve@kasiulai.lt	www.kasiulai.lt	37068231492	•	•	•		•
	Vilnius	Si⊠l⊠ r⊠sys	UAB "RE Stilius", R⊠dnink⊠ str. 18	LT01106	siulurusys@gmail.com	www.siulurusys.lt	00370 6 1060422		•			
	Siauliai	Siuludama	Sved⊠s g. 41, Gink⊠n⊠ km.	LT-81491	info@siuludama.lt	www.siuludama.lt	37067338583	•	•		•	
				LUXEMBOURG								
	Kenzingen	MEZ GmbH (Distributor)	Kaiserstr. 1	79341	kenzingen.vertrieb@mezcrafts.com	www.mezcrafts.com	0049 7644 802 222	•	•	•		
Luxembourg	ESCH s/ALZETTE	Ouvrages Elisabeth	Rue S. Bolivar 29	4037	hansen_elisabeth@yahoo.de		00352 26 53 27 86		•			
Luxembourg	KAHLER	WICKED WOOL	74, RUE PRINCIPALE	8376				•				•
Luxembourg	Luxembourg	Bastel Kiste	Rue Du Fort Elisabeth 17-19	1463	mail@bastelkiste.lu	www.wollzauber.com	00352/40 05 06		•	•	•	
				MEXICO								
Mexico	Santa Catarina, NL	Estambres Crochet SA de CV (Distributor)	Calle 1° de Mayo # 230 Interior 8, Col. Trabajadores	64650	abremer@redmundial.com.mx		+52 (81) 8335-3870		•			•
Mexico City	Cd. Satelite	Crochet Satelite	Pafnuncio Padilla 47				+52 (55) 5374-3167		•			•
Mexico City	Col. Jardines del Pedregal	Crochet Pedregal	Plaza Santa Teresa, Periferico Sur	4020			+52 (55) 5652-0694		•			•
Mexico City	Col. Polanco	Crochet Masaryk	Pasaje Polanco, Masaryk	360			+52 (55) 5280-5385		•			•
Monterrey	Col. Cumbres	Crochet Cumbres	Plaza Milenium, Paseo de los Leones	2968			+52 (81) 1167-0992		•			•
Monterrey	Col. Del Valle	Crochet Valle	Plaza Las Palmas, Gomez Morin	911-7			+52 (81) 8335-2980		•			
				NEW ZEALAND								
Christchurch	Northwood	ACS New Zealand (Distributor)	P.O Box 76199		lynn@impactmg.co.nz		64-3-323-6665		•			•
Auckland		Alterknitives	PO Box 47961				(64 9) 376 0337		•			•
Aukland	Devonport	Wild and Woolly Yarns	10 Victoria Road		wildandwoollyyarns@gmail.com	www.wildandwoollyyarns@gmail.com	09 445 3255		•			•
Christchurch		Knit World	189 Peterborough St				03 379 2300		•			•
Nelson		Creations Unlimited	118 Hardy Street		creations@jasnelson.co.nz		03 548 4297		•			•
Northland	Kaiwaka	The Apple Basket	1914 State Highway 1		applebasketquilts@xtra.co.nz		09 4312 443		•			•
Northland	Warkworth	Robyn Egge Yarns	15 Elizabeth Street	910	info@robyneggeyarns.co.nz		09 425 7246	•	•			•
Northland		Twinset and Pearls	Elizabeth Street		twinsetandpearls@clear.net.nz		09 425 7246		•			•
Taupo		Fabryx	Unit 5a, 29 Totara Street				07 376 7494		•			•
Tauranga		Tauranga Knitting Centre	8/152 11th Avenue		tgaknitcentre@hotmail.com		07 571 8892		•			•
Wellington	Cuba Mall	Knit World	Shop 210b, Left Bank				04 385 1918		•			•
		Knit World Mail Order	PO Box 30 645		info@knitting.co.nz,	www.knitworldstudio.co.nz	04 586 4530		•		•	
				NORWAY								
	Rødovre	Carl J. Permin A/S (Distributor)	Selma Ellefsensvei 6	2610	permin@permin.dk	www.permin.dk	45 36 36 89 89	•	•			•
	Asgårdstrand	Leo Design	Grev Vedels gate 46	3167	leoellen@online.no		33082779		•			•
	Bergen	Norwegian Spirit	Seiersbjerget 4	5022	anne@norwegian-spirit.com	www.norwegian-spirit.com	48123799	•	•			•
	Bergen	Strikkelykke AS	STRANDGATEN 76	5004	siljecy@gmail.com		92080231		•			•
	Drammen	Ulla Garn & Broderi	Sankt Olavsgate 2	3018	butikk@ullgarn.no	www.ullagarn.no	32 89 00 58		•			•
	Evje	Garn & Lysstua A/S	Nils Hegelandsveg	4735	marianne@garnoglysstua.no		97 54 21 00		•			•
	Gresvik	FLAMINGO GARN OG HOBBY	STORVEIEN 3	1621	angel-an@online.no		69353417		•			•
	Grimstad	Broderihjørnet Huslidstua	Storgata 32	4876	Husflidstua@live.no		37 04 89 14		•			•
	HØNEFOSS	STRIKKEGRY AS	STORGT. 1	3510	gry@strikkegry.no		99259708		•			•
	Inderøy	1 Stopp Et Skattekammer	Stasjonsvn. 24, Røra Stasjon	7670	stopp@etskattekammer.no		41245050		•			•
	Kongsberg	Strikkestua	Kirkegt. 7	3616	strikkestua@online.no		32731899		•			•
	Kristiansand	Langfeldt Garn	H.Wergwlandsgt. 21-23	4612			38 02 20 29	•	•			•
	Kristiansund	Corianders Hus	Batterivn. 28	6508	coriandershus@hotmail.no		48039831		•			•
	Laksevåg	Pinsvin Design	Lyngboveien 160	5164	kontakt@pinnsvinsdesign.no	www.pinnsvindesign.no	92370912		•			•
	Moss	Hobbymakeren A/S	Carlbergveien 2, Rygge storsenter	1521	wenche@hobbymakern.no		92435800		•			•
	Moss	Norsk Flid Husfliden Moss A/S	Dronningensgate 4	1530	moss@norskflid.no		69255236		•			•
	Moss	Strikkedilla Moss a/s	Th.Petersonsgate 12	1530	kontakt@strikkedilla-moss.no		69255282		•			•
	NAMNÅ	GARNRIKE SISSEL LAUTEN	SVARTMOBAKKEN 4	2265			92018102		•			•
	Oslo	Carl Permin A/S	Lørenveien 42	585	norge@permin.dk	www.permin.dk/no	23 16 35 30	•	•			•
	Oslo	Nøstet Mitt	Lambertseter Senter	1150			23 38 22 20		•			•
	Oslo	Nøstet Mitt	Storo Senter	485	henille@gmail.no		48 06 66 63	•	•			•
	Oslo	Nye Sømsenteret A/S	Akersgt. 8	158	oslo@somsenteret.no		22 41 35 69	•	•			•
	Oslo	Tjorven Garn og Gaver	Valkyriegt. 17	366	tina@tjorven.no	www.tjorven.no	22 69 33 60	•	•			•
	Sandvika	Stofthjørnet	Engervannsveien 39	1337	maia__55@hotmail.com		40241556	•	•			•
	SANNIDAL	STRIKK INNOM!	Kjølebrøndsveien 9	3766	POST@STRIKKINNOM.NO		93061060		•			•
	SORTLAND	DEN BLÅ TRÅD AS	STRANDGT. 18	8400	heidi.johansen@vkbb.no		76123339		•			•
	Stord	Kvist og Kvast A/S	Borggata 20	5411			92858797	•	•			•
	Tromsø	Bundingen	Heiløvn 4	9015	bundingen@bundingen.no		95835525	•	•			•
	Vestby	Bryggerhuset	Nordbyvn 2	1540	eombudstvedt@gmail.com		64950857		•			
				POLAND								
	Brzoza	Motkolandia	Brzozowa 5	86-061	sklep@motkolandia.pl	www.motkolandia.pl	48605288117	•	•		•	
	Kraków	ART-BIJOU	os. Krakowiaków 5/31	31-962	kontakt@art-bijou.com	www.art-bijou.com	48602316541	•	•		•	
				PORTUGAL								
Portugal	Gaia	Mez Crafts Portugal, Lda (Distributor)	Av. Vasco da Gama, 774	4431-059 V.N,	sales.iberia@mezcrafts.com		223770700		•			•
Portugal	Funchal	Eduardo G. Luiz & Fº (Coats & Clark agent in Madeira)	Av. De Zarco, 22, Cx. Postal 155	9002			291201990		•			•
Portugal	Ponta Delgada	Eduardo J. Moura (Coats & Clark agent in Azores)	R. Arcanjo Lar, Cave, Apartado 182	9500			296284341		•			•
Portugal	Porto	Ovelha Negra	Rua da Conceição, 100	4050-214		www.ovelha-negra.com	+351 220935847		•			
				RUSSIA								
	Moscow	Family Hobby (Distributor)	Zelenograd, Haus, 1505, Ramu III	124683	ty@fhobby.ru		007 (499) 2703247	•	•	•		•
Moscow	Zelenograd	YA SAMA	Haus 1505, office III	124683	tv@fhobby.ru		007 (499) 270-32-47		•			•
Moscow		YA SAMA - PRYAZA	Pyatnitskoye shosse, 36/1		tv@fhobby.ru		007 (495) 754-67-93		•			•
Moscow	Zelenograd	YA SAMA	Central'nyi prospekt, 401		tv@fhobby.ru		007 (499) 762-36-31		•			•
Moscow	Zelenograd	YA SAMA	Privokzal'naya ploshhad', 1/4		tv@fhobby.ru		007 (499) 738-61-31		•			•
Moscow	Reutov	YA SAMA	shopping center "Reutov Park", 45, 4th floor, Nosovikhiskoye shosse, 45, 4th floor		tv@fhobby.ru		007 (499) 995-17-06		•			•
	Moscow	Cityarn	Shopping Center "Roll Holl" office 312a, Holodilny per., 3	115191	info@cityarn.ru		007 (495) 933-87-98		•			•
	Moscow	ili-ili	Territory of design plant "Flakon", ul. Bolshaya Nododmitrovskaya 36/4, строение 2	127015	welcome@ili-ili.net		007 (495) 969-71-12		•			•
	Kaliningrad	Klubok	ul. Teatralnaya 21	236006			007 (911) 464-60-54		•			•
	Vladivostok	Mir pryazi	ul. Semenovskaya, 10	690091			007 (4232) 22-06-40		•			•
Moscow region	Korolyov	ili-ili	Shopping mall "Sigma", 3-rd floor, ul.Kalinina 6B	141070			007 (985) 385-36-36		•			•
	Irkutsk	Tanza knit	per. Kooperativnyiy 2	664011	tanza-knit@mail.ru		007 (3952) 72-13-02		•			•
	Moscow	Motochki	ul. 3 ya Tverskaya Yamskaya 11	125047			007 (495) 766-57-17		•			•
	Moscow	Triskeli	Shopping mall "Ostankino Krasniy", 2nd floor, pav. Ж 24 25 26 27, ul. 1 ya Ostankinskaya 53	129515	triskeli@triskeli.ru		007 (495) 926-88-64		•			•
	Moscow	Triskeli	ul. Prospekt Mira 91 hous. 3	129085	triskeli@triskeli.ru		007 (926) 779-96-70		•			•
	Novokuznetsk	Uzelok	ul. Metallurgov 15	654079			007 (905) 961-58-19		•			•
	Moscow	Elite Style	Shopping mall "UniverCity", 1-st floor, pav. 37, Jawaharlal Nehru Sq. 1	119311	zakaz@elstl.ru		007 (926) 106 67-75		•			•
Moscow region	Dzerzhinskij	Ruchnye shtuchki	ul. Lesnaya 17a	140093			007 (903) 155 56-07		•			•
Moscow region	Shhelkovo	Premiere	Shopping mall "Premiere", ul. Tsentralnaya 17	141108			007 (496) 250 95-05		•			•
	Saint Petersburg	Magia pryazi	ul. Komsomola 51	195009	magiap@mail.ru		007 (812) 541 81-92		•			•
	Saint Petersburg	Magia pryazi	pr t Kolomyazhskiy 15, hous. 2	197348	magiap@mail.ru		007 (812) 921 21-07		•			•
	Saint Petersburg	Kardigan	Shopping mall "Kosmos", pav. 242	196211			007 (931) 291 32-93		•			•
	Angarsk	Tanza knit	Shopping mall "Barguzin", 2-nd floor pav. 61, ul. Tipanova 27/39	665816	tanza knit@mail.ru		007 (902) 542 66-05		•			•
	Voronezh		ul. Tsyurupyi 36	394036			007 (473) 228 78-30		•			•
	Kasan	Pryazha ot Alyony	ul. Ostrovskogo 1/6	420111			007 (917) 865 27-44		•			•
	Krasnodar	Rukodelie	ul. Gorkogo 119	350000			007 (918) 251 52-54		•			•
	Krasnoyarsk	Izumrudnyiy gorod	Shopping mall "Izumrudnyiy gorod", ul. Televizornaya 1	660028			007 (908) 011 97-63		•			•
	Mahachkala		ul. Yaragskogo 60	367015			007 (903) 423 81-23		•			•

County	Town / City	Stockist	Address	Postcode	Email	Website	Telephone	Rowan At	Yarn	Fabric	Online	Instore
	Novj Urengoj	Dom knigi	"Dom knigi", ul. Molodezhnaya 3	629306			007 (3494) 94 75-78		•			•
	Orsk	MIX	"MIX" shop, ul. Prospekt Mira 15	462419			007 (3537) 317-073		•			•
	Severodvinsk	Raduga	"Raduga" department store, ul. Sovetskaya 56	164501			007 (911) 599 73-84		•			•
	Temryuk	Dekor	ul.Lenina 40	353500			007 (861) 485 45-54		•			•
	Ussurijsk	Farvater	Shopping mall "Farvater", 3-rd floor, ul. Chicherina 68	692500			007 (924) 261 90-08		•			•
	Zhukovskij	Pryazha v Zhukovskom	"Pryazha v Zhukovskom", ul.bazhenova 11, supermarket spar, 2 floor				007 (917) 580-83-18		•			•
	Dubna	Klubochek	Salon rukodeliya "Klubochek"				007 (916) 302-42-96		•			•
	Novokuznetsk	Domashnee rukodelie	Magazin "Domashnee rukodelie"		domashnee-rukodelie@yandex.ru		007 (3843)74-76-83		•			•
	Moscow	Damskoe rukodelie	Damskoe rukodelie, ul. Rozhdestvenka, 5/7, str 2				007 (499) 714-22-66		•			•
	Sergiev Posad	Metelica	Shopping Center "Trikotazhka", store "Metelica", Pozharnyj pereulok				007 (903) 101-03-89		•			•
	Arhangelsk		Novgorodskij prospekt 153	163061			007 (960) 012-99-32		•			•
	Ekaterinburg	Masterskaya vyazaniya	ul.vajnera 19, "Masterskaya vyazaniya", butik 311				007 (343) 287-87-83		•			•
	Habarovsk	Pryazha dlya vas	ul.pushkina 54, "Pryazha dlya vas"				007 (914) 547-71-12		•			•
	Moscow	Mir pryazhi	32-j km.mkad, shopping center "Shelkovyj put"				007 (915) 407-57-37		•			•
				SINGAPORE								
Singapore		Golden Dragon Store (Distributor)	101 Upper Cross St. #02-51, People's Park Centre	58357	gdscraft@hotmail.com		(65) 65358454 / 65358234		•			
				SLOVAKIA								
	Bratislava	MEZ Crafts Slovakia	s.r.o. Seberíniho 1	821 03	galanteria@mezcrafts.com	www.mezcrafts.com	(421) 2 3230 3119	•	•	•		
				SOUTH AFRICA								
South Africa	Johannesburg	Arthur Bales Ltd (Distributor)	62 Fourth Avenue, Linden	2195	info@arthurbales.co.za	www.arthurbales.co.za	(27) 118 882 401		•			
				SPAIN								
Barcelona	Barcelona	MEZ Fabra Spain S.A (Distributor)	Avda Meridiana 350, pta 13 D	8027	atencion.clientes@mezcrafts.com	www.mezcrafts.com	932908400		•			•
ALBACETE	ALBACETE	Tejeadictos	C/ PEDRO COCA, 7 DERECHA	02006	pilarcallejasg@gmail.com		667 338 270		•			•
MADRID	ALCORCON	La Tijera y el Dedal	CARBALLINO 19	28925	latijerayeldedalalcorcon@yahoo.es		916106774		•			•
ALAVA	AMURRIO (ALAVA)	Entre Punto y Puntada	C/ LANDAKO 6	01470	info@entrepuntoypuntada.com		945 891 101		•			•
BARCELONA	BADALONA (BARCELONA)	Mohair	CL MARIA CRISTINA, 11	08910	montsemohair@gmail.com		625138345		•			•
BARCELONA	BARCELONA	El Corte Inglés Pça Catalunya	PLAZA CATALUNYA, 14	08002			93 3063800		•			•
BARCELONA	BARCELONA	El Corte Inglés Diagonal	EUROPA, S/N	08029			93 3667100		•			•
BARCELONA	BARCELONA	El Almacen de las Lanas	PROVIDENCIA,130-132	08024			661741261		•			•
BARCELONA	BARCELONA	Milana Bonita	CAMP 87	08022			670 294 671		•			•
BARCELONA	BARCELONA	Traça	C/MAJOR DE SARRIÀ, 150 BOTIGA	08017			626 082 117		•			•
BARCELONA	BARCELONA	Oyambre	ROGER DE LLURIA 92	08009	info@oyambreonline.com		934872672		•			•
BARCELONA	BARCELONA	Fil - oh! - Mena	C/ JUAN GUELL 44-48	08028			666 875 155		•			•
BARCELONA	BARCELONA	El Club de la Aguja	VIA AUGUSTA, 100	08006	info@clubdelaaguja.com		934143815		•			•
VIZCAYA	BILBAO	El Corte Inglés Gran Via	GRAN VIA, 9	48001			944253500		•			•
VIZCAYA	BILBAO	El Punto Bobo	ALAMEDA URKIJO, 20	48008	dams@elpuntobobo.com	www.elpuntobobo.com	946855612		•			•
BARCELONA	CORNELLA DE LLOBREGAT	Nilo & Dana	C/ BURI 11	08940			659 247 426		•			•
GIPUZCOA	EIBAR	Artile	C/. BIDEBARRIETA, 18	20600		www.artile.net	943 207227		•		•	•
ALICANTE	ELCHE	Fenosan	REINA VICTORIA 51 1	03201			965448231		•			•
ALICANTE	ELCHE	Las Tijeras Mágicas	C/ CAPITAN ANTONIO MENA, 150	03204	info@lastijerasmagicas.com	www.lastijerasmagicas.com	966 65 64 52		•		•	•
ASTURIAS	GIJON	Lanas Mayalan	DONATO ARGUELLES 16 BJO	33206			985341549		•			•
BARCELONA	GRANOLLERS	Punt Deu	APEL-LES MESTRES, 4 BLOC B LOC 1	08401	PUNTDEU@GMAILCOM		938491151		•			•
A CORUÑA	A CORUÑA	El Corte Inglés Ramón y Cajal	RAMON Y CAJAL, S/N	15006			981 189400		•			•
GRAN CANARIA	LAS PALMAS	El Corte Inglés Mesa López	MESA LOPEZ, 18 S12 D18	35007			928263000		•			•
GRAN CANARIA	LAS PALMAS	El Corte Inglés Siete Palmas	AV.SIETE PALMAS	35018			928423000		•			•
MADRID	LAS ROZAS	La Tertulia del Patch	C/ PRAGA Nº 15	28232	fouparlabores@gmail.com		917104258		•			•
LA RIOJA	LOGROÑO	Al Solecito	DOCTORES CASTROVIEJO, 42	26003	alsolecito@alsolecito.com		679812463		•			•
MADRID	MADRID	Inke Labores	DON RAMON DE LA CRUZ 47	28001	Inke@Inkelabores.com		915762847		•			•
MADRID	MADRID	El Club de Labores	C/ INFANTA MARIA TERESA, nº 11	28016	cmessat@gmail.com		3441068		•			•
MADRID	MADRID	El Corte Inglés Callao	PLAZA DE CALLAO, 2	28013			91 3798000		•			•
MADRID	MADRID	El Corte Inglés Goya	GOYA, 76	28009			914329300		•			•
MADRID	MADRID	El Corte Inglés Princesa	PRINCESA, 56	28008			914546000		•			•
MADRID	MADRID	El Corte Inglés Castellana	RAIMUNDO F.VILLAVERDE, 79	28003			91 4188800		•			•
MADRID	MADRID	El Corte Inglés Sanchinarro	MARGARITA PARMA, 1	28050			650 708881		•			•
MADRID	MADRID	Cañamazo	FERNANDEZ DE LOS RIOS 66	28015	patchmadrid@gmail.com		915449772		•			•
MADRID	MADRID	El Punto Madrid	MELENDEZ VALDES, 68	28015	elpunto@elpuntomadrid.com	www.elpuntomadrid.com	651922777		•			•
MADRID	MADRID	Sweet Sixteen	C/ PADRE DAMIAN Nº 31	28036	sweetsixteencraft@gmail.com		911 427 926		•			•
MADRID	MADRID	El Corte Inglés Campo Naciones	AVDA DE LOS ANDES, 50	28042			913248800		•			•
MADRID	MADRID	Lanas Madrid	CALLE RODRIGUEZ SANPEDRO, 20	28015	info@lanasmadrid.com		915 438 549		•			•
MADRID	MADRID	La Laborteca de Opera	C/ MESON DE PAÑOS Nº 2	28013		www.laborteca-tienda-taller.es	917583106		•			•
MADRID	MADRID	Mamamadejas	C/ MONASTERIO DE OSERIA, 9	28049	info@mamamadejas.com	www.mamamadejas.com	696412761		•			
MADRID	MADRID	Manos Maravillosas - online store		28041		www.manosmaravillosas.com	913180762		•		•	•
LLEIDA	MOLLERUSSA	Repunts	AVDA. BEETHOVEN 3	25230	repuntsmollerussa@gmail.com		636 924 848		•			•
MURCIA	MURCIA	El Corte Inglés Murcia	AVDA.DE LA LIBERTAD, 1	30009			968 298050		•			•
MURCIA	MURCIA	Labores y por qué no	C/ DE LA AURORA 10	30001	laboresyporqueno@gmail.com		968201645		•			•
ALICANTE	ORIHUELA	Lanas Cristina	C/ CATEDRATICO J GUILLEN GARCIA 1	03300	info@femasa.net		633484882		•			•
ISLAS BALEARES	PALMA DE MALLORCA	El Corte Inglés Avenidas	ALEXANDRE ROSELLO	07002			971 770177		•			•
NAVARRA	PAMPLONA	La chica de las lanas	C/ POZOBLANCO 17	31001	lachicadelaslanas@hotmail.com	www.lachicadelaslanas.com	948221684		•			•
MADRID	POZUELO ALARCON-MADRID-	El Corte Inglés Pozuelo	CT.CORUÑA 12,500 CERRO GAMOS	28023			91 7089200		•			•
MADRID	POZUELO DE ALARCON	El mundo de Marieta	AVDA DE EUROPA, 18	28224	elmundodemarieta@yahoo.es		911731900		•			
VALLADOLID	RENEDO DE ESGUEVA	Tira del Ovillos - online store		47170		www.tiradelovillo.com	686361083		•		•	•
TARRAGONA	REUS	Fet amb	AMARGURA Nº 11	43201			670930258		•			•
BARCELONA	SABADELL	El Corte Inglés Sabadell	FRANCESC MACIA, 58-60	08206			93 7284800		•			•
BARCELONA	SABADELL	Lanas Genesca	RAMBLA, 146	08201			937261745		•			•
MADRID	SAN LORENZO DEL ESCORIAL	Merino Feroz	FLORIDABLANCA, 30	28200	fernando@merinoferoz.com		636 612 552		•			•
GIPUZCOA	SAN SEBASTIAN	Casa de Labores - Eskulanen Etxea	ELKANO, 5	20004	eskulanenetxea@gmail.com		943 420205		•			•
BARCELONA	SANT CUGAT DEL VALLES	Llanes del Mon	C/ ENRIC GRANADOS Nº15	08172	llanesdelmon@gmail.com		935 878 110		•			•
TENERIFE	SANTA CRUZ DE TENERIFE	El Corte Inglés Tenerife	AVDA.TRES DE MAYO 7	38003			922849400		•			•
CANTABRIA	SANTANDER	Zulan	C/ SANTA CLARA Nº6 BAJO	39001			942 229 698		•			•
SEVILLA	SEVILLA	El Corte Inglés Duque	PZA.DUQUE DE LA VICTORIA 10	41006			954-222-991		•			•
SEVILLA	SEVILLA	El Corte Inglés Nervión	LUIS MONTOTO, 122-128	41006			954 571440		•			•
SEVILLA	SEVILLA	Devanalana	C/ CUNA, Nº 46 1º PUERTA 3	41002	beatriz@devanalana.com		603-510-309		•			•
VALENCIA	VALENCIA	El Corte Inglés Sorolla	COLON, 27	46004			96 3159500		•			•
VALENCIA	VALENCIA	El Corte Inglés Nuevo Centro	MENENDEZ PIDAL, 15 EDF A	46009			96 3175700		•			•
VALENCIA	VALENCIA	La tia Pepa	C/ FELIZ PIZCUETA 23 bj Izq	46004	latiapepa@latiapepa.es		963 510 199		•			•
VALENCIA	VALENCIA	Lanas Tatino	Avª MALVARROSA, 116	46011	ampariguesmc@hotmail.es		961 477 669		•			•
VALENCIA	VALENCIA	Derecho y Revés	MUSICO PADILLA 4	46005	asuncionchaves@gmail.com		618778072		•			•
VALLADOLID	VALLADOLID	Mi Marinita	C/ NUÑEZ DE ARCE, 14 BAJO	47002	luzmarina@hotmail.com	www.mimarinita.com	637 536 191		•		•	•
ALAVA	VITORIA	Log Cabin	PL DEL CARMEN/MANUEL IRADIER	01005	logcabin.vitoria@gmail.com		945142430		•			•
ZARAGOZA	ZARAGOZA	El Corte Inglés P. Sagasta	Pº.SAGASTA, 3	50008			976 211121		•			•
ZARAGOZA	ZARAGOZA	Entre algodones	C/ SAN MIGUEL, 29 bjo DERECHA	50001	entrealgodonesther@gmail.com		669974949		•			•
ZARAGOZA	ZARAGOZA	Telas de Luna	C/ GIL DE JASA Nº 12 LOCAL	50006	info@telasdeluna.com	www.telasdeluna.com	976 229 130		•		•	•
	A CORUÑA	Picknits	C/Manuel Azaña 41, 3ºA	15001	Veronicaoliveros@gmail.com	www.picknit.es	0034 607 402 528		•			
				SWEDEN								
	Rødovre	Carl J. Permin A/S (Distributor)	Skaraborgsvägen 35C, 3tr	50 630	permin@permin.dk	www.permin.dk	45 36 36 89 89	•	•			•
	Ahus	PP CO i Ahus	Gamla Skeppsbron 10	296 31	kristina@ppco.se		044-240521		•			
	ALINGSÅS	STICK-GALLERIET I ALINGSÅS	KUNGSGATAN 40 A	441 31	birgitta.we@gmail.com		0322 633010		•			•
	AMAL	Widedals Interiør AB	Mellanbrogatan 6	66231	info@widedals.se		0532-10156		•			•
	Borås	Carl Permin AB	Alingsåsv 9	501 10	sverige@permin.dk		033 12 77 10					•
	Borås	Stickat och Klart EF	Hallbergsgatan 2	503 30	kristina.karlson@hotmail.com		(033) 10 32 38		•			•
	Borås	Distributor: Carl Permin AB	Alingsåsv. 9	501 10	sverige@permin.dk	www.permin.dk/se	0033 12 77 10	•	•			
	FALKØPING	Min Stickbutik	Flygaresgrænd 1	52142	snobjorn@outlook.com		0515-10355		•			•
	Goteborg	Garn & Design	Skiljemyntsgatan 18 A	41480	info@maritarolin.se		0707-528210		•			•
	Göteborg	Garnfabriken	Linnegatan 3	413 04	johansson-ingalill@hotmail.com		0704-802772		•			•
	GRÆSTORP	Garn & Mera	Tengene plan 10	46792	info@garnomera.se		731598577		•			•
	Haljarp	Hedenskougs Garnhorna	Olofstorpsvagen 25	261 72			(0418) 430485		•			
	HØRBY	Garnverandan	Gamla Torg 5	24231	info@garnverandan.se		0415-311300		•			•
	JONKOPING	MADAME KREATIV AB	KLOSTERGATAN 64	553 35	astrid@astridknitting.se		0735 200485	•	•			
	LIDKOPING	HEMSLØJDEN I LIDKØPING	SOLBACKEN	531 98	info@hemslojden.se		0510 22635	•	•			
	Lund	SLANDAN I LUND AB	Lilla Fiskaregatan 1	222 22	slandan@telia.com	www.slandaninlund.se	046 128077		•			
	NAMNÅ	GARNRIKE SISSEL LAUTEN	SVARTMOBAKKEN 4	2265			92018102		•			•
	NOSSEBRO	Garnboden	Fræmmestad Laggebo 206	46598	Lindblad@gamlegaarden.SE		0322-46043		•			•
	Stockholm	Sticka by Marie Viktoria	Osterlanggatan 20	111 31	marievictoria@gmail.com	www.knitting.se	(08)21 18 31		•			•
	Stockholm	Wincentgarner	Norrtullsgatan 27	113 27	wincent@gmail.com	www.wincentgarner.se	(08) 33 70 60	•	•			•
	Sundsvall	GARNKORGEN HANDARBETEN	Klackvägen 17	856 53	info@garnkorgen.se	www.garnkorgen.se	(060) 124 501		•			•
	Taby	Trasselgarn & Broderi	Stationsvagen 16	187 30	info@trassel.se	www.trassel.se	(08) 638 00 59		•			
	Vadstena	Vadstena Ull & Garn	Krigsberga 106	592 91	butiken@ullochgarn.se		0143-20149		•			
	Värnamo	C-Knit	Malmstensgatan 16A	331 31	info@c-knit.com	www.c-knit.com	703131949	•	•			•
	Växjö	Umbra Stickspår	Sandgärdsgatan 12b	352 30	info@umbra.nu		0470-777901		•			•
	Vellinge	Vellinge Garnhörna	Östergatan 4	235 33	info@garnhornan.com		040-42 44 05		•			
				SWITZERLAND								
	Zürich	MEZ Crafts Switzerland GmbH (Distributor)	c/o Puplicitas AG, Mürtenstrasse 39	8048		www.mezcrafts.com			•			•
	Aarberg	Wolle Aarberg	Ursula Kaiser, Lyssstrasse 1	3270	ursula-kaiser@bluewin.ch		032 392 41 41		•			•
	Appenzell	Innauen Katrin	Kronengarten 9	9050	wollelade-appenzell@gmx.ch		004171 787 11 16		•			•
	Arlesheim	Lana Moda	V.Tschanz, Obere Holle 25	4144	tschanz.verena@intergga.ch		0041/61 703 92 59		•			•
	Basel	Zum Roten Faden	Steinenrin	4051		1			•			•
	Bern	WollWirrWare	Astrid Balli, Wylestrasse 53	3014	info@wollwirrware.ch	www.wollwirrware.ch	0041/31332 06 33	•	•			•
	Biel	Tasche & Masche	Ariane Fischer, Schmiedengasse 13	2502	tasche@tascheundmasche.ch		032 322 26 12		•			•
	Buchs	Wollig-Anstalt	Ingrid Näscher, Grünaustr. 17	9470			081/ 756 36 19		•			
	Chur	AHA-Mode	Kreuzgasse 1	7000	info@aha-mode.ch		081 650 25 30		•	•		
	Duebendorf	Sarah Gaffuri	Oberdorfstrasse 12	8600	info@mondolana.ch				•			
	Fislisbach	Lana Versum	Badenerstraße 15	5442	info@lanaversum.ch		056 470 90 00		•			•
	Geneve 28	Elna SA Centre Balexert	Av. Louis-Casai 27	1211			022 884 86 66		•			•
	Heiden	Bettina Gantenbein	Vorderbrenden 365, Poststr. 9	9410	be.gantenbein@bluewin.ch				•			•
	Hölstein	Wullestübli Hölstein	Dora Huber, Hauptstr. 19	4434	dora.huber@bluewin.ch		061 951 19 53		•			•
	Interlaken	Woll-Boutique	P. Schoch, Unionsgasse 10	3800			033 822 15 88		•			•
	Lausanne	Carole Jaques	Av. d'Echallens 4a	1004	info@tricot-the.ch		021 62 51 81 0		•			•
	Luzern	Naturel	Müller A., Habsburgerstr. 33	6003			041/210 65 41		•			
	Maienfeld	Bacchini	Schellenbergstraße 8	7304	ambubac@bluewin.ch		0041 78 853 31 88		•			•
	Martigny	Le Monde de Laines	rue du Grand-Verger 11, Isabelle Arlettaz	1920	info@lemondesdeslaines.ch	www.lemondedeslaines.ch	027 722 10 35		•			
	Muri	Stoff-und Wullehuesli	H. Keller, Marktstr. 17	5630	wullehuesli@bluewin.ch		056 664 41 20		•			•
	Orbe	Il était une fois	Mireille Deriaz, Terreaux 19	1350			024 441 24 19		•			•
	Pratteln	Zur Masche	M. Brunner, Burggartenstr. 3	4133			061 821 51 11		•			•
	Richterswil	Rosa Träume	Bachtelstraße 32	8805	rosa.traeume@bluewin.ch	www.rosa-traeume.ch	0041 79 883 17 77		•			•
	Romanshorn	Strick-IN	Aleestrasse 44	8590			071 463 68 18		•			•
	Schoeftland	Mercerie	Vontobel Maya, Dorfstrasse 19	5040			062 721 00 80		•			•
	Siebnen	Strick and Style	Glarnerstraße 38	8854	strick_and_style@bluewin.ch	www.strickandstyle.ch/de/	0041 55 440 38 01		•			•
	Signy-Centre	Passé Présent	Gabriele Fiachetti, Centre Commercial Signy	1274	gcollin@bluewin.ch		022 361 18 45		•			•
	Sirnach	Wullwerk	Fischingerstraße 26	8370	wullwerk@bluewin.ch		0041 71 960 06 90		•			•
	St. Gallen	Boutique Tonja Mode mit Wolle	Vadianstrasse 22	9000			071 223 12 71		•			•
	Steffisburg	Silvia Heller	Oberdorfstrasse 31a	3612	info@strickbar.ch		079 219 67 54		•			•
	Steffisburg	Hinkel Pinkel Folmer Winkel	M. Folmer, Thunstr. 57	3612	mfolmer@bluewin.ch		033/437 08 80		•			•
	Sursee	strick-art	Mühleplatz 2	6210	strick-art@gmx.ch		041 921 66 31		•			•
	Teufen	Presto-Lana	Sammelbuehldtrasse 11	9053			071 335 75 55		•			•
	Thun	we love wool	Charlotte Schmid, Obere Hauptgasse 25	3600	charlotteschmid@gmx.ch		033 222 54 46		•			•
	Uster	Fallmasche GmbH	Poststrasse 6	8610	info@fallmasche.ch		044 942 38 58		•			•
	Visp	Web and Wollstube	Hildegard Margelist, Kantonsstr. 14	3930	web-wollstube@bluewin.ch		027 946 47 06		•			•
	Weinfelden	Wollring	Rathausstrasse 14	8570			071 622 19 27		•			•
	Zürich	Hand-Art	Neumarkt 10	8001	guldenschuh@tuttolana.ch		0041/4455757		•			•
	Zürich	Vilfil	Kreuzstrasse 39, Beim Kreuzplatz	8032	office@vilfil.com	www.vilfil.com	0041/443839903	•	•			•
	Chur	Z Khurer Wundertrüggli	Reichsgasse 52	7000					•			
				TAIWAN								
Taiwan, R.O.C.	Taipei	Cactus Quality Co. Ltd (Distributor)	7FL-2, No. 140, Sec.2 Roosevelt Rd	10084	cqcl@ms17.hinet.net	www.excelcraft.com.tw	00886-2-23656527		•			
				THAILAND								
Bangkok		Global Wide Trading (Distributor)	10 Lad Prao Soi 88	10310	TheNeedleWorld@yahoo.com / global.wide@yahoo.com		00 662 933 9019		•			
				USA								
North Carolina	Hickory	Sirdar USA Inc (Distributor)	406 20th Street SE	28602	sirdarusa@sirdar.co.uk	www.sirdar.co.uk	001 828 404 3705	•	•			•
Alahabma	Birmingham	In the Making	4232 Dolly Ridge Road	35243	orders@shopinthemaking.com		(205) 298 1309		•			•
Alaska	Anchorage	Southside Knitting Nook	12201 Industry Way Unit 3	99515	deeknit12201@gmail.com		(907) 317 0484		•			•
Arkansas	Rogers	Mockingbird Moon	315 N. Second	72756	mockingbirdmoon@gmail.com		(473) 202 5640		•			•
California	**Danville**	**A Yarn Less Raveled**	**730 Camino Ramon**	**94526**	**info@ayarnlessraveled.com**		**(925) 263 2661**	•	•			•
California	Encinitas	Common Threads	191 North El Camino Real	92024	invoice@fiberartshop.com		(760) 436 6119		•			•
California	Eureka	Yarn	518 Russ Street	95501	sunshineyarn@gmail.com		(707) 443 9276		•			•
California	Little River	Mendocino Yarns	7901 N. Highway One	95456	yarnshop@mcn.org		(707) 937 0921		•			•
California	**Los Altos**	**Uncommon Threads**	**293 State Street**	**94022**	**info@uncommonthreadsyarn.com**	www.uncommonthreadsyarn.com	**650-941-1815**	•	•			•
California	Los Angeles	The Little Knittery	3195 Glendale Boulevard	90039	thelittleknittery@gmail.com		(323)663 3838		•			•
California	Napa	Yarns on First	1305 First Street	94559	contact@yarnsonfirst.com		(707) 257 1363		•			•
California	Oakland	Piedmont Yarn & Apparel	4171 Piedomnt Avenue	94611	info@piemontyarn.com		(510) 595 9595		•			•
California	Pacific Grove	Monarch Knitting	529 Central Ave	93950	ann@monarchknitting.com		(831) 647 9276		•			•
California	Redondo Beach	L'Antelier Inc.	1722 S Catalina Ave	90277	kddamskey@gmail.com		(310) 540 4440		•			•
California	Sacramento	Rumpelstiltskins	1021 R Strret	95811	rumpel@yarnyarnyarn.com		(916) 442 9225		•			•
California	San Anselmo	Atelier Marin Inc	217 San Anselmo Ave	94960	ateliermarin@gmail.com		(415) 256 9618		•			•
California	**San Francisco**	**Atelier Yarns**	**1945 Divisadero Street**	**94115**	**atelieryarns@gmail.com**		**(415) 771 1550**	•	•			•

County	Town / City	Stockist	Address	Postcode	Email	Website	Telephone	Rowan At	Yarn	Fabric	Online	Instore
California	**San Francisco**	**Imagiknit**	**3897 18th Street**	**94114**	**info@imagiknit.com**	**www.imagiknit.com**	**415-621-6642**	•	•			•
California	San Rafael	Dharma Trading Company	1604 Fourth Street	94901	store@dharmatrading.com		(415) 456 1211		•			•
California	Santa Cruz	The Swift Stitch LLC	402 Ingalls St. #12	95060	kmh@cruzio.com		(831) 427 9276		•			•
California	Santa Cruz	Yarn Shop Santa Cruz	765 Cedar Street Suite 103	95060	corymeyers@mac.com		(831) 515 7966		•			•
California	Santa Rosa	Cast Away	100 4th Street	95401	justine@castawayandfolk.com		(707) 546 9276		•			•
California	Studio City	La Knitterie Parisienne	12642 Ventura Boulevard	91604	info@laknitterieparisienne.com		(818) 766 1515		•			•
California	Tarzana	Zoe's Knit Studio	18596 Ventura Boulevard	91356	info@zoesknitstudio.com		(818) 881 9637		•			•
California	Ukiah	Heidi's Yarn Haven	180 South School Street	95482	hyhyarn@pacific.net		(707) 462 0544		•			•
California	Ventura	Anacapa Fine Yarns	4572 Telephone Rd #909	93003	lois@anacafineyarns.com		(805) 654 9500		•			•
Colorado	Colorado Springs	Ewe and Me…	1045 K Garden of the Gods Road	80907	debbiegray@eweandmeyarnbou.com		(719) 203 5240		•			•
Colorado	**Denver**	**Lamb Shoppe**	**3512 E 12th Ave**	**80206**	**info@thelambeshoppe.com**	**www.thelambshoppe.com**	**(303) 322-2223**	•	•			•
Colorado	**Fort Collins**	**Lambspun of Colorado**	**1101 E Lincoln Ave**	**80524**	**shirley@lambspun.com**	**www.lambspun.com**	**(800) 558 5262**	•	•			•
Colorado	Fort Collins	My Sister Knits	1408 West Moutain Ave	80521	julie@mysisterknits		(970) 407-1461		•			•
California	Littleton	Colorful Yarns	2001 East Easter Ave #101	80122	colorfulyarns@gmail.com		(303) 798 2299		•			•
Connecticut	Granby	Marji's Yarncrafts	381 Salmon Brook Street	06035	marjisyarn@sbcglobal.net		(860) 653 9700		•			•
Connecticut	Ridgefield	Nancy O'Connell LLC	23 Catoonah Strret	06877	nancyo.nancyo@gmail.com		(203) 431 2266		•			•
Connecticut	New Haven	Knit New Haven	26 Whitney Avenue	06510	kniynewhaven@att.net		(203) 777 5648		•			•
Connecticut	**Glastonbury**	**Village Wool LLC**	**2279 Main Street**	**06033**	**marion@villagewoolyarnshop.com**		**(860) 633 0898**	•	•			•
Connecticut	Westport	Wesyport Yarns	582 Post Road East	06880	danni@westportyarns.com		(203) 454 4300		•			•
Connecticut	Woodbridge	The Yarn Barn LLC	1666 Litchfield Turnpike	06525	yarnbarn@optonline.net		(203) 389-5117		•			•
Delaware	Bethany Beach	Sea Needles	780 Garfield Parkway	19930	gb@seaneedles.com		(302) 539 0574		•			•
Delaware	Newark	Stitches with Style	16-E Polly Drummond	19711	knitsws@comcast.net		(302) 453 8130		•			•
District of Columbia	**Washington**	**Looped Yarn Works**	**1732 Connecticut Avenue NW, #200**	**20009**	**web@loopedyarnworks.com**	www.loopedyarnsworks.com	**202-714-5667**	•	•			•
Florida	Hollywood	Raging Wool	1850 NW 122nd Terrace	33026	Alice@raginwoolshop.com		(954) 385 0861		•			•
Florida	Lake Worth	Just Imaginknit	6663-B Lake Worth Road	33467	justimaginknit@comcast.net		(561) 433 3444		•			•
Florida	Lady Lake	The Yarn Lady	304 Oak Street	32159	theyarnlady@comcast.net		(352) 775 7779		•			•
Florida	**Miami**	**The Kniting Garden**	**1923 Ponçe de lEon Blvd**	**33134**	**info@theknittinggarden.org**		**(305) 774 1060**	•	•			•
Florida	**Naples**	**Knitting with Nancy**	**3804 Tamiami Trail East**	**34112**	**knittingwithnancy@comcast.ent**		**(239) 7938141**	•	•			•
Florida	Tampa	Roxy's Yarns	3347 South Westshore Blvd	33629	bnjventures@verizon.net		(813) 839 7699		•			•
Georgia	Atlanta	Yarning For Ewe	3220 Cobb Parkway Suite 102	30339	yarningforewe@gmail.com		(678) 909 4963		•			•
Georgia	Clarksville	Bumbleberry LLC	1345 Washington Street	30523	bumbleberry@windstream.net		(706) 754 0462		•			•
Georgia	**Roswell**	**Cast On Cottage**	**Coleman Village, 860 Marietta Hwy**	**30075**	**info@castoncattage.com**	**www.castoncottage.com**	**(770) 998-3483**	•	•			•
Georgia	Saint Simons Island	The Stichery of St Simons	3411 Frederica Road	31552	ulladesigns@gmail.com		(912) 638 3401		•			•
Georgia	Savannah	The Frayed Knot LLC	6 West State Street	31401	thefrayedknotsav@yahoo.com		(912) 233 1240		•			•
Georgia	Savannah	Unwind LLC	7710 Waters Avenue	31406	to.unwind@yahoo.com		(912) 303 3970		•			•
Gerorgia	**Woodstock**	**The Whole Nine Yarns**	**8826 Main Street**	**30188**	**info@thewholenineyarns.com**		**(678) 494 5242**	•	•			•
Illinois	Chicago	Yarnify	47 West Polk Street Suite G2B	60605	barbaraofyarnify@gmail.com		(312) 583 9276		•			•
Illinois	**Downers Grove**	**Knitche**	**5221 Main Street**	**60515**	**kathy@knitche.com**		**(630) 652 5648**	•	•			•
Illinois	Evanston	Close Knit	1630 Orrington Avenue	60201	closeknit@sbcglobal.net		(847) 328 6760		•			•
Illinois	**Forest Park**	**Knit Nirvana**	**7453 W Madison**	**60130**	**sue@knitnirvana.com**	**www.knitnirvana.com**	**708-771-5232**	•	•			•
Illinois	**Galena**	**Fiber Wild**	**304 South Main Street**	**61036**	**amy@fiberwild.com**	**www.fiberwild.com**	**815-777-3550**	•	•			•
Illinois	Herrin	The Yarn Shoppe	105 N 16th Street	62948	herrinyarnshoppe@gmail.com		(618) 988 9276		•			•
Illinois	**Saint Charles**	**Wool And Company**	**107 West Main Street**	**60174**	**neil@woolandcompany.com**	www.woolandcompany.com	**630-444-0480**	•	•			
Illinois	Urbana	Klose Knit	311 West Springfield Avenue	61801	brigittepieke@hotmail.com		(217) 344 2123		•			•
Indiana	**Fort Wayne**	**Knitting off Broadway**	**1309 Broadway**	**46802**	**yarn@knittingoffbroadway.com**	www.knittingoffbroadway.com	**280-422-9276**		•			•
Indiana	**Indianapolis**	**Broad Ripple Knits**	**6510 N. Cornell Avenue**	**46220**	**www.broadrippleknits.com**		**317-255-0540**	•	•			•
Indiana	**Indianapolis**	**Mass Avenue Knit Shop**	**862 Virginia Avenue**	**46203**	**massaveknitship@ameritech.net**	www.massaveknitshoponline.com	**317-638-1833**	•	•			
Indiana	Valparaiso	Sheep's Clothing Knitting	60 West Lincolnway	46383	paula@knitdoctor.com		219 462 1700		•			•
Indiana	Zionsville	Village Yarn Company	209 South Main Street	46077	maryvaughn@villageyarncompany.com		(317) 873 0004		•			•
Iowa	Ankeny	Knitting Next Door	704 SW 3rd Street	50023	knittingnextdoor@yahoo.com		(515) 963 0396		•			•
Iowa	Iowa City	The Knitting Shoppe	2141 Muscatine Avenue	52240	theknittingshoppe@etherbiz.net		(319) 337 4920		•			•
Iowa	**West Des Moines**	**Yarn Junction Company**	**132 5th Street**	**50265**	**yarnjunction@gmail.com**		**(515) 277 2770**	•	•			•
Kansas	**Lawrence**	**The Yarn Barn**	**930 Mass Ave.**	**66044**	**info@yarnbarn-ks.com**	**www.yarnbarn-ks.com**	**(800) 468-0035**	•	•			•
Kentucky	Lexington	Magpie Yarn LLC	513 East High Street	40502	magpieyarn@windstream.net		(859) 455 7437		•			•
Louisiana	Baton Rouge	Knits By Nana	7612 Old Hammnd Hwy	70809	missy@knitsbynana.com		(225) 216 9460		•			•
Maine	Bath	Halcyon Yarn	12 School Street	04530	purchasing@halcyonyarn.com		(207) 442 7909		•			•
Maine	Belfast	Heavenly Socks Yarn	82 Main Street	04915	hsy@myfairpoint.net		(207) 338 8388		•			•
Maine	Camden	The Cashmere Goat	20 Bayview Street	04843	info@tegknit.com		(207) 236 7236		•			•
Maine	**Freeport**	**Grace Robinson & Co**	**208 US Rte 1, Ste 1**	**4032**	**grandco@gwi.net**	www.yarnandneedlepoint.com	**(207) 865-6110**	•	•			•
Maine	Glenburn	Essentially Felt Studio	865 Pushaw Road	04401	sandy@essentiallyfelt.com		(207) 942 0365		•			•
Maine	Portland	KnitWit Yarn	247A Congress Street	04101	yarnbain@gmail.com		(207) 774 6444		•			•
Maryland	**Annapolis**	**Woolwinders**	**709 Skippers Lane**	**21401**	**info@woolwinders.com**		**(240) 632 9276**	•	•			•
Maryland	Annapolis	Yarn Basket Inc.	53 Maryland Avenue	21401	yarnbasketmaryland@gmail.com		(410) 295 7000		•			•
Maryland	Baltimore	Woolworks	6117 Falls Rd	21209	info@worksbalt.com	www.woolworksbalt.com	(410) 377-2060	•	•			•
Maryland	**Bethesda**	**Second Story Knits**	**4706 Bethesda Ave**	**20814**	**info@secondstoryknits.com**	**www.secondstoryknits.com**	**301 652-8688**	•	•			•
Maryland	Catonsville	Cloverhill Yarn Shop	77 Mellor Ave	21228	temptingewe@cloverhillyarns.com		(410) 788 7262		•			•
Massachusetts	Beverly	Yarns in the Farms	641 Hale Street	01915	info@yarnsinthefarms.com		(978) 927 2108		•			•
Massachusetts	Boston	Newbury Yarns Inc	2 Milk Street	02108	knitting@newburyyarns.com		(617) 572 3733		•			•
Massachusetts	Brookline	Uncommon Yarn	PO Box 1899	02446	uncommonyarn@gmail.com		(857) 352 4281		•			
Massachusetts	**Burlington**	**Another Yarn LLC**	**15 Cambridge Street**	**01803**	**distrib@anotheryarn.com**	**www.anotheryarn.com**	**781 570 2134**		•			•
Massachusetts	Dennis	Yarn Houd LLC	620 Rt. 6A	02638	yarnhound@comcast.net		508 385 6951		•			•
Massachusetts	Dorchester	Stitch Hurse	846 Dorchester Ave	02125	info@stitchhousedorchester.com		(617) 265 8013		•			•
Massachusetts	Hingham	Yarns in the Square, LLC	400 Lincoln Street Unit #2	02043	info@yarnsinthesquare.com		(781) 749 2280		•			•
Massachusetts	Lenox	Colorful Stitches	48 Main Street / Rear	02140	bonnie@colorfulstitches.com		(413) 637 8206		•			•
Massachusetts	Mendon	Yarn Garden	3 Maple Street	01756	cheryl.leider@gmail.com		(617) 599 6922		•			•
Massachusetts	Natick	Fabric Place Basement	321 Speen Street	01760	peter@fabricplacebasement.com		(508) 655 2000		•			•
Massachusetts	Natick	Iron Horse Inc.	3 Pond Street	01760	ironhorsefiberart@gmail.com		(508) 647 4722		•			•
Massachusetts	Needham	Black Shhep Knitting Co.	1500 Highland Ave	02492	nancy.shulman@blacksheepknitting.com		(781) 444 0694		•			
Massachusetts	Northbourgh	Craftworks	243 West Main Street	01532	craftworks.coop@gmail.com		(508) 393 9435		•			•
Massachusetts	**Northampton**	**Webs**	**75 Service Center Road**	**01060**	**webs@yarn.com**	**www.yarn.com**	**(413)584-2225**	•	•			•
Massachusetts	Plainville	In The Loop Company	60 Man Mar #3	02762	intheloop@comcast.net		(774) 847 7977					
Massachusetts	Salem	Circle of Stitches	66 Wharf Street	01970	info@circleofstitches		(978) 745 9276		•			•
Massachusetts	Williamstown	The Spin-Off Yarn Shop	130 Water Street	01267	beth@spinoffyarnshop.com		(413) 344 6257		•			•
Michigan	**East Lansing**	**Woven Art Inc.**	**325B Groove Street**	**48823**	**wovenartshop@gmail.com**		**(517) 203 4467**	•	•			•
Michigan	East Tawas	Tawas Bay Yarn Co. Inc.	1820 East US-23	48730	misso@att.net		(989) 362 4463		•			•
Michigan	**Grand Blanc**	**Beyond The Rain Forest**	**12830 South Saginaw**	**48439**	**slord41496@aol.com**		**(810) 953 0089**	•	•			•
Michigan	Grosse Pointe	Knotted Needle	20229 Mack Avenue	48236	knottedneedle@gmail.com		(313) 886 2828		•			•
Michigan	**Macomb**	**Crafty Lady Trio**	**15401 Hall Road**	**48044**	**contact.us@craftyladytrio.com**		**(586) 566 8008**	•	•			•
Michigan	Holland	Garenhuis Yarn Studio	27 W 9th Street	48423	Yarn@garenhuis.com	www.garenhuis.com	616-294-3492		•			
Michigan	Holland	Lizzie Ann's Wool Co.	54 E. 8TH Street	49423	llzgraff@aol.com		616 392-2035		•			•
Michigan	Niles	Red Purl LLC	207 N. 2nd Street	49120	redpurl@att.net		(269) 684 0411		•			•
Michigan	**Royal Oak**	**Ewe-Nique Knits**	**515 South Lafeayette Avenue**	**48067**	**amy@ewe-niqueknits.com**		**(248) 584 3001**	•	•			•
Michigan	**Traverse City**	**Lost Art Yarn Shoppe**	**741 Woodmere Avenue**	**49686**	**gerhilduhl@centurytel.net**		**(231) 941 1263**	•	•			•
Minnesota	Duluth	Yarn Harbor Inc	4629 East Superior Street	55804	yarnharbor@yahoo.com		(218) 724 6432		•			•
Minnesota	**Lakeville**	**Unwind Yarn Shop**	**10460-170th Street West**	**55044**	**unwindyarnshopmn@gmail.com**		**(952) 303 6617**	•	•			•
Minnesota	Mendota Heights	3 Kitten Needle Arts	750 Main Street Suite 112	55118	laura@3kittensneedlesarts.com		(651) 457 4969		•			•
Minnesota	Minneapolis	5814 Excellsior Boulevard	(952) 303 3895	55416	chrisknits@lindenyarn.com		(952) 303 3895		•			•
Minnesota	Saint Cloud	Bonnie's Spinning Wheel	16 21st Avenue SO	56301	bonnies@integra.net		(320) 253 2426		•			•
Minnesota	**St Paul**	**The Yarnery**	**840 Grand Ave**	**55105**	**yarnery@gmail.com**	**www.yarnery.com**	**(651) 222-5793**	•	•			•
Minnesota	**Still Water**	**Darn Knit Anyway**	**423 South Main Street**	**55082**	**aimee@darnknitanyway.com**		**(651) 342 1386**	•	•			•
Minnesota	**White Bear Lake**	**A Sheepy Yarn Shoppe, Inc.**	**2185 3rd Street**	**55110**	**info@sheepyyarn.com**	**www. sheepyyarn.com**	**651 426-5463**	•	•			•
Minnesota	Winona	Yarnology LLC	65 E 3rd Street	55987	info@yarnologymn.com		(507) 474 9444		•			•
Missouri	Independence	Angelika's Yarn Store	500 Dodgion Street	64050	angelikas@yarn-store.com		(816) 461 5505		•			•
Missouri	Nixa	Lowlander Knitwear	205 North Main Street	65714	jacqui@lowlanderyarnshop.com		(417) 414 8240		•			•
Montana	**Eureka**	**The Woolery Mammoth LLC**	**576 US Highway 93 North**	**59917**	**woolerymammoth@gmail.com**		**(406) 297 7403**	•	•			•
Montana	**Hamilton**	**The Yarn Center**	**110 Pinckney**	**59840**	**threeyorkiesyarn@aol.com**		**(406) 363 1400**	•	•			•
Montana	**Missoula**	**Joseph's Coat Yarn**	**115 3rd St W**	**59801**	**josephscoatyarn@gmail.com**		**(406) 549 1419**	•	•			•
Nebraska	**Lincoln**	**Knit Paper Scissors**	**6701 Vanderslice Circle**	**68516**	**knitandpaperandscissors@gmail.com**		**(402) 429 8029**	•	•			•
Nebraska	**Omaha**	**Personal Threads Boutique**	**8600 Cass Street**	**68114**	**sales@personalthreads.com**	**www.personalthreads.com**	**402 391-7733**	•	•			•
Nevada	**Reno**	**Jimmy Beans Wool**	**4850 Joule Street Suite A1**	**89502**	**support@jimmybeanswool.com**	**www.jimmybeanswool.com**	**(775) 827-9276**	•	•			•
New Hampshire	Concord	The EleganT Ewe	75 South Main Street Unit #3	03301	info@elegantewe.com		(603) 226 0066		•			•
New Hampshire	Dover	Spinning Yarns	511 Central Avenue	03820	margoterdmann@comcast.net		(603) 740 6476		•			
New Hampshire	Harrisville	Harrisville Designs Inc	PO Box 806	03450	dmiller@harrisville.com		(603) 827 3333		•			
New Jersey	Madison	The Blue Purl	60 Main Street	07940	thebluepurl@gmail.com		(973) 377 5648		•			•
New Jersey	Hazlet	Moore Yarn LLC	1366 Route 36	07730	mitzy@mooreyarn.com		(732) 847 3665		•			•
New Jersey	Hillsborough	The Yarn Attic	5 Layton Court	08844	rhonda@theyarnattic.com		(908) 864 5311		•			•
New Jersey	Mount Holly	Woolbearers LLC	90 High Street	08060	woolbearers@verizon.net		(609) 914 0003		•			•
New Jersey	Princeton	Pins And Needles	8 Chambers Street	08542	pinsandneedlesinfo@gmail.com		(609) 921 9075		•			•
New Jersey	Summit	Wool and Grace, Inc	102 Summit Avenue	07901	info@woolandgrace.com		(908) 277 1431		•			•
New Mexico	Albuquerque	The Yarn Store at Nob Hill	120 Amherst Drive NE	87106	teresa@theyarnstoreatnobhill.com		(505) 717 1535		•			•
New York	Barrytown	Fabulous Yarn	117 Barrytown Road	12507	fabulousyarn@gmail.com		(917) 226 5074		•			•
New York	Brooklyn	M & M Yarn Connection	1766-46th Street	11204	em1766@gmail.com		(718) 436 5262		•			•
New York	Canton	The Celtic Knot Textiles	17 Main Street	13617	theceltickno t@hotmail.com		(315) 714 3206		•			•
New York	**Farmingdale**	**Infinite Yarns Inc.**	**34 Hemstead Turnpike 3B**	**11735**	**customerservice@infiniteyarns.com**	**www.infiniteyarns.com**	**(631) 750 1790**	•	•			
New York	Ithaca	Homespun Boutique	314 East State Street	14850			(607) 277 0954		•			•
New York	**Jamesville**	**Yarn Cupboard**	**6487 East Seneca Turnpike**	**13078**	**info@yarncupboard.com**		**(315) 399 5148**	•	•			•
New York	Kauneonga Lake	Knit One Needlepoint Too	140 Lake Street	12749	k1n2@aol.com		(845) 583 5648		•			•
New York	Nyack	Knitting Nation	30 North Broadway	10960	knittingnation@gmail.com		(845) 348 0100		•			•
New York	**Sayville**	**Rumpelstiltskin**	**22 Main Street**	**11782**	**milton2@optonline.net**		**(631)750-1790**	•	•			•
North Carolina	Apex	Downtown Knits	12 North Salem	27502	info@downtownknits.com		(919) 249 5638		•			•
North Carolina	Franklin	Silver Threads & Golden Needle	41 East Main Street	28734	franklinncyarn@yahoo.com		(828) 349 0515		•			•
North Carolina	Nags Head	Yarn and More	4104 S Virginia Dare Trail #21	27959	deanna@yarnandmoreinc.com		(252) 715 2244		•			•
North Carolina	Swansboro	The Salty Sheep Yarn Shop	101-4 Church Street	28584	thesaltysheep@gmail.com		(910) 325 0018		•			•
North Carolina	Winston Salem	Knit One Smock Too	4003-A Country Club Road	27104	knitonesmocktoo@gmail.com		(336) 765 9099		•			•
Ohio	**Cincinnati**	**Hank Yarn LLC**	**2651 Observatory Avenue, Suite 101**	**45208**	**hankyarn@me.com**	**www.hankyarn.com**	**513 386-9869**	•	•			•
Ohio	Cincinnati	Keepsake/Patternworks	10151 Carver Road Suite	45242	lynne.lounsbury@fwcommunity		(603) 253 8148		•			•
Ohio	Dayton	Strings Attached Yarns	225 North Main Street	45402	kristen@stringsattachedyarns.com		(937) 221 9585		•			•
Ohio	**Dublin**	**Knitting Temptations**	**35 South High Street**	**43017**	**knit2temptations@gmail.com**		**(614) 734 0618**	•	•			•
Ohio	**Lakewood**	**River Colors Studio**	**1387 Sloane Avenue**	**44107**	**orders@rivercolors.com**		**(216) 228 9276**	•	•			•
Ohio	Mason	Main Street Yarns	126 West Main Street	45040	liseporter@ymail.com		(513) 204 0078		•			•
Ohio	Springboro	Wooly Bully Yarn Company	1355 Main Street	45066	woolybullyyarnco@aol.com		(937) 748 1002		•			•
Oregon	**Ashland**	**The Web-Sters**	**11 North Main St**	**97520**	**info@yarnatwebsters.com**	**www.yarnatwebsters.com**	**(800) 482-9801**	•	•			•
Oregon	Bandon	The Wool Company	990 2nd Street SE	97411	woolco@mycomspan.com		(541) 347 3912		•			•
Oregon	**Beaverton**	**For Yarns Sake**	**11767 SW Beaverton**	**97005**	**anne@foryarnssake.com**	**www.foryarnssake.com**	**(503)469-9500**	•	•			•
Oregon	Eugene	The Knit Shop	2811 Oak Street	97405	jean@knit-shop.com		(541) 434 0430		•			•
Oregon	Hillsboro	Black Sheep at Orenco	6154 NE Brighton Street	97209	tina@blacksheepatorenco.com		(971) 732 5391		•			•
Oregon	Hood River	Knot Another Hat	16 Oak Street, Suite 202	97031	customerservice@knotanotherhat.com		541-308-0002		•			•
Oregon	McMinnville	Oregon Knitting Company LLC	309 north Baker	07128	oregonknittingco@gmail.com		(971) 261 9608		•			•
Oregon	Portland	Dublin Bay Knitting Co.	1227 NW 11th Avenue	97209	info@dublinbay.net		(503) 223 3229		•			•
Oregon	Portland	Northwest Wools	3524 SW Troy	97219			(503) 803 6076		•			•
Oregon	**Roseburg**	**Knotty Lady Yarns, LLC**	**642 SE Jackson Street**	**97470**	**knottyladyyarns@yahoo.com**	knottyladyyarns@yahoo.com	**541-673-2199**	•	•			
Pennsylvania	Belthlehem	The Knitters Edge	1601 West Broad Street	18018			(610) 419 9276		•			•
Pennsylvania	Doylestown	Forever Yarn	15 W. Oakland Ave	18901	foreveryarn@yahoo.com		(215) 348 5648		•			•
Pennsylvania	Emmaus	Conversational Threads Inc	6 South 4th Street	18049	cfitzpa289@aol.com		(610) 421 8889		•			•
Pennsylvania	Ligonier	Bo Peep Fien Yarn	221 West Main Street	15658	michelleg411@hotmail.com		(724) 238 4040		•			•
Pennsylvania	Lititz	Ewebiquitous LLC	39 East Main Street	17543	ewebiquitous@yahoo.com		(717) 568 8890		•			•
Pennsylvania	New Holland	The Speckled Sheep	423 Diem Woods Drive	17557	info@thespeckledsheep.com		(717) 435 8359		•			•
Pennsylvania	Newtown Square	Slip Knot	3715 West Chester Pike	19073	info@slipknotknit.com		(610) 359 9070		•			•
Pennsylvania	Phoenixville	Purls of Wisdom	2208 Kimberton Road	19460	purlsofwisdompa@gmail.com		(610) 933 5010		•			•
Pennsylvania	**Pittsburgh**	**Knit One**	**2721 Murray Avenue**	**15217**	**lknoopvery@gmail.com**		**(412) 421 6666**	•	•			•
Pennsylvania	Sewickley	Sewickley Yarns	Sewickley Yarns LLC	15143	sewickleyyarns@gmail.com		(412) 741 8894		•			•
Rhode Island	Barrington	Knit One Quilt Too LLC	10 Anoka	02806	info@knitonequilttoo.com		(410) 337 5578		•			•
South Carolina	Beaufort	Coastal Knitting LLC	900 Port Republic	29902	judyalgar@yahoo.com		(843) 470 0148		•			•
South Dakota	**Sioux Falls**	**Athena Fibers**	**3915 S. Hawthorne**	**57105**	**athenafibers@gmail.com**		**(605) 271 0741**	•	•			•
Tennessee	Brentwood	Bliss Yarns	127 Franklin Road	37027	info@blissyarns.com	www.blissyarns.com	615-370-8717	•	•			
Tennessee	Knoxville	Loopville	5204 Kingston Pike	37919	jinka@loopvilleyarn.com		(865) 584 9772		•			•
Texas	Austin	Red Beauty Textiles	PO Box 153216	78715	redbeautytextiles@gmail.com		(512) 900 1092		•			•
Texas	Austin	Yarnbow	1310 Ranch Road 620 South, Suite B202	78734	mail@yarnbow.com	www.yarnbow.com	512-777-1703	•	•			•
Texas	Comfort	The Tinsmith's Wife	405 7th Street	78013	tinsmithwife@hctc.net		(830) 995 5539		•			•
Texas	Dallas	Holley's Yarn Shoppe	5211 Forest Lane, Suite 115	75244	info@holleysyarn.com	www.holleysyarn.com	972-503-5648		•			•
Texas	Dripping Springs	The Sated Sheep LLC	100 Commons Road Suite 5	78620	thesatedsheep@gmail.com		(512) 858 2053		•			•
Texas	Fort Worth	West 7th Wool	3612 West 7th	76107	info@west7thwool.com		(817) 731 5044		•			•
Texas	Houston	Nimblefingers	12456 Memorial Drive	77024	nimblefingerstx@gmail.com		(713) 722 7244		•			•
Texas	Novasota	WC Mercantile	201 East Washington Avenue	77868	info@wcmercantile.com		(936) 825 3378		•			•
Utah	**Ogden**	**The Needlepoint Joint LLC**	**241 Historic 25th Street**	**84401**	**npj@xmission.com**		**(801) 394 4355**	•	•			•
Utah	**Provo**	**Wasatch and Wool Yarns**	**1635 West Redstone Ctr Drive**	**84098**	**wasatchandwool@outlook.com**		**(435) 901 0525**	•	•			•
Utah	Provo	Harmony LLC	315 East Center Street	84606	lauratharmon@gmail.com		(801) 615 0268		•			•
Vermont	Chester	Six Loose Ladies Yarn	287 Main Street	5143	6looseladies@gmail.com		(802) 875 7373		•			•
Vermont	Norwich	Northern Lights Yarn Shop	289 Main Street	5055			(802) 649 2000		•			•
Vermont	Woodstock	Whippletree Yarn Shop	7 Central Street	5091	whippletreeyarnshop@gmail.com		(802) 457 1325		•			•
Virginia	Fredericksburg	Hidden Purls	PO Box 142	22404	shop@hiddenpurls.com		(800) 285 1605		•			•
Virginia	Fredericksburg	Untangled Purls LLC	2561 Cowan Blvd.	22401	untangledpurls@gmail.com	www.untangledpurls.com	540-479-8382	•	•			
Virginia	Haymarket	Needles in the Haymarket	15125 Washington Street	20169	needlesinthehaymarket@gmail.com		(703) 659 1062		•			•
Virginia	Henrico	Knitting B LLC	8801 Three Chopt Rd	23229	info@knittingb.com		(804) 484 6005		•			•

County	Town / City	Stockist	Address	Postcode	Email	Website	Telephone	Rowan At	Yarn	Fabric	Online	Instore
Virginia	North Chesterfield	GotYarn	723 Boulder Spings	23225	yarnie@gotyarn.com		(804) 300 115		•			•
Virginia	Middleburg	Hidden Country Yarns	PO Box 1206	20118	hcy@skeins.com		(540) 253 9990		•			
Virginia	**Midlothian**	**Dances With Wool**	**1229 Sycamore Square**	**23113**	**shop@danceswithwoolrva.com**		**(804) 690 2978**	•	•			•
Washington	**Bainbridge Island**	**Churchmouse Yarn and Teas**	**118 Madrone Lane**	**98110**	**info@churchmouseyarns.com**	www.churchmouseyarns.com	**704-373-7442**	•	•		•	•
Washington	Burien	Town Square Fabric & Yarn	445 S.W 152nd Street #100	98166	cnouits@hotmail.com		(206) 246 9276		•			•
Washington	Carnation	Tolt Yarn And Wool LLC	PO Box 33	98014	kimberley@toltyarnandwool.com		(425) 333 4066		•			
Washington	Issaquah	The Nifty Knitter	317 NW Gilman Boulevard	98027	theniftyknittershop@gmail.com		(319) 512 9834		•			•
Washington	Kennewick	Sheep's Clothing	3311 West Clearwater Ave B120	99336	latisha@aknottyhabit.com		(509) 734 2484		•			•
Washington	**Mount Vernon**	**Wildfibers**	**706 South First St**	**98273**	**sparker@wildfibers.net**		**360-336-5202**	•	•			•
Washington	Olympia	Canvas Works	525 Columbia Street SW	98501	canvasworks@aol.com		(360) 352 4481		•			•
Washington	Renton	Knittery	601 S Grady Way	98057	gramwin1@hotmail.com		(425) 228 4694		•			•
Washington	Seattle	Acorn Street Shop	2818 NE 55th Street	98105	shop@acornstreet.com		(206)525 1726		•			•
Washington	Seattle	The Fiber Callery	8212 Greenwood Avenue North	98103	megan@fibergallery.com		(206) 706 4197		•			•
Washington	Seattle	The Tea Cozy Yarn Shop	5816 24th Avenue	98107	jean@teacozyyarn.com		(206) 783 3322		•			•
Washington	**Seattle**	**The Weaving Works Inc.**	**6514 Roosevelt Way NE**	**98115**	**info@weavingworks.com**		**(206) 524 1221**		•			•
Washington	Seattle	Tricoter	3121 E. Madison Street	98112	tricoter@tricoter.com		(206) 328 6506		•			•
Washington	Seattle	Bad Woman Yarns	1815 North 55th Street, Suite 202	98103	mail@badwomanyarn.com		206 547-5384		•			•
Washington	Vancouver	Blizzard Yarn and Fiber	6924 NE Fourth Plain Blvd	98661	irina@blizzardyarnandfiber.com		(360) 991 5350		•			•
Wisconsin	Appleton	Iris Fine Yarns	132 E.Wisconsin Ave	54911	info@irisfineyarns.com	www.irisfineyarns.com	(920) 954 9001		•			•
Wisconsin	Bayfield	Brown Stone Centre	121 Rittenhouse Avenue	54814	brownstonecentre@gmail.com		(715) 779 3400		•			•
Wisconsin	**Brookfield**	**Cream City Yarn**	**15565 W. North Avenue**	**53005**	**info@creamcityyarn.com**	**www.creamcityyarn.com**	**262 923-7014**	•	•			•
Wisconsin	Delafield	Knitch	608 Milwaukee Street	53018	Knitch@knitch.net		262-646-9392		•			•
Wisconsin	Green Bay	Silver Thimble Quilt & Yarn	2475 University Avenue	54302	silverthimble@tds.net		(920) 468 1495		•			•
Wisconsin	**Madison**	**The Knitting Tree**	**2636 Monroe Street**	**53711**	**knittingtree@yahoo.com**	**www.knittingtree.com**	**608-238-0121**	•	•			•
Wisconsin	**Milwaukee**	**Knitting Knook LLC**	**6858 North Santa Monica Blvd**	**53217**	**knittingknook@me.com**		**(414) 540 4080**	•	•			•
Wisconsin	Saint Germain	Just Yarnin LLC	446C Hwy 70 East	54558	justyarnin@gmail.com		(715) 479 9276		•			•
Wisconsin	Sturgeon Bay	Spin LLC	108 South Madison Ave	54235	Spin@att.net	www.spinofdoorcounty.com	(920) 746 7746	•	•			•
Wisconsin	Verona	The Sow's Ear	125 South Main Street	53593	sylvie@knitansip.com		(608) 848 2755		•			•
		Craftys			**alex@sympoz.com**	**www.craftys.com**	**304-477-1099**	•	•		•	•
		Fiber Wild				**www.fiberwild.com**		•	•		•	•
		Got Yarn			yarn4u@gmail.com	www.gotyarn.com	804-300-1155		•			
		Keepsake Quilting				**www.keepsakequilting.com**		•	•		•	•
UNITED KINGDOM												
West Yorkshire	*Huddersfield*	*MEZ Crafts UK Ltd. (Distributor)*	*Unit 17F, Brooke's Mill, Armitage Bridge,*	*HD4 7NR*		*www.mezcrafts.com*	*01484 950630*	•	•	•	•	
Aberdeenshire	Aberdeen	John Lewis	George Street	AB9 1BT			01224 625000	•	•	•		•
Aberdeenshire	Aberdeen	Wool for Ewe	83-85 Rosemount Place	AB25 2YE	info@woolforewe.co.uk	www.woolforewe.com	01224 643738	•	•			•
Aberdeenshire	Fraserburgh	Mary Bobbins	31 Commerce Street, Fraserburgh	AB43 9AQ		www.marybobbinsshop.co.uk	01346 510 784		•			•
Aberdeenshire	Banchory	Meg's Attic	70 High Street, Banchory	AB31 5SS		www.megsattic.co.uk			•			
Avon	Bristol	John Lewis	Cribbs Causeway	BS12 5TP			0117 959 1100	•	•	•		•
Bedfordshire	Leighton Buzzard	The Spotted Sheep	1 - 4 Peacock Mews	LU7 1JH		www.thespottedsheep.co.uk	01525 376456		•			•
Berkshire	Reading	John Lewis	Broad Street	RG7 4AH			01189 575955	•	•	•		•
Berkshire	Windsor	C & H Fabrics	King Edward's Court, Service Road	SL4 1DW	windsor@candhfabrics.co.uk	www.candh.co.uk	01753 850688	•	•			•
Berkshire	Wokingham	Sew Not trading as Stitchery Do	31/35 DENMARK STREET	RG40 2AY	dreelanm@googlemail.com	www.stitcherydo.co.uk	01189 770 181		•	•		•
Buckinghamshire	Marlow	Lady Sew and SEW	Institute Rd	SL7 1BN	info@ladysewandsew.co.uk		01628 890532	•	•	•		•
Buckinghamshire	Milton Keynes	John Lewis	Central Milton Keynes	MK1 1NN			01908 679171	•	•	•		•
Cambridgeshire	Barton	Backstitch	Burwash Manor Barns, New Road	CB23 7EY					•			•
Cambridgeshire	Cambridge	John Lewis	10 Downing Street	CB2 3DS			01223 361292	•	•	•		•
Cambridgeshire	Cambridge	The Sheep Shop	72 Beche Road	CB5 8HU	sarah@sheepshopcambridge.co.uk	www.sheepshopcambridge.co.uk	01223 311 268		•			•
Cambridgeshire	Peterborough	John Lewis	Queensgate Centre	PE1 1NL			01733 344644	•	•	•		•
Cambridgeshire	Ely	Sew Much To Do	7 High Street Passage, Ely	CB7 4NB		www.sewmuchtodo.co.uk			•			•
Carmarthenshire	Whitland	Colourways	Market Street	SA34 0AJ	shop@colourway.co.uk	www.colourway.co.uk	01994 241333	•	•			•
Carmarthenshire		Esgair Fibres							•			•
Ceredigion	Lampeter	Calico Kate	36 High Street	SA48 7BB	kate@calicokate.co.uk	www.calicokate.co.uk	01570 422866	•		•	•	•
Ceredigion	Aberystwyth	Clare Wools	13 Great Darkgate Street	SY23 1DE	cynthia@clarewools.co.uk	www.clarewools.co.uk	01970 617786		•			•
Cheshire	Cheadle	John Lewis	Wilmslow Road	SK9 3RN			0161 491 4914	•	•	•		•
Cheshire	Cheshire	Sew-In of Marple	46 Market Street, Marple	SK6 7AD		www.myknittingyarnandwool.co.uk	0161 427 2529	•	•			•
Cheshire	Nantwich	Stitch	3 Mill Street	CW5 5ST	nfo@StitchNantwich.co.uk		01270 625318		•	•		•
Cheshire	Warrington	Black Sheep Wools	Glaziers Lane, Culcheth	WA3 4AQ	orders@blacksheepwools.com	www.blacksheepwools.com	01925 764231	•	•			•
Cheshire	Warrington	Hobbycraft	Alban Retail Park	WA2 8TP			01925 237470		•			•
City of Edinburgh	Edinburgh	Hobbycraft	Fort Kinnaird Shopping Park	EH15 3RD			0845 051 6561		•			•
City of Edinburgh	Edinburgh	Jenners	48 Princes Street	EH2 2YJ			07703 750974	•	•			•
City of Edinburgh	Edinburgh	John Lewis	St James Centre	EH1 3SP			0131 556 9121	•	•	•		•
City of Edinburgh	Edinburgh	McAree Bros	19 Howe Street	EH3 6TE	sales@mcadirect.com	www.mcadirect.com	0131 558 1747	•	•			•
Clackmannanshire	Alloa	Wee County Yarns			clare@wee-county-yarns.co.uk	www.wee-county-yarns.co.uk	01259 759000		•		•	•
Conwy	Abergele	Snowdonia Wools	2 Pen Y Bont House	LL22 7HA	glenys@snowdoniawool.co.uk		1745823835	•	•			•
Conwy	Llanrwst	Ar-y-Gweill	24 Station Road	LL26 0EP	arygweill@aol.com		01492 641149		•	•		•
Cornwall	Bude	Coastal Yarns	The Old Forge, Lower Warft	EX23 8LG	info@coastalyarns.co.uk		01288 350304	•	•			•
Cornwall	Truro	Truro Fabrics	Lemon Quay	TR1 2LW	info@trurofabrics.co.uk	www.trurofabrics.com	01872 222130	•	•	•		•
Cornwall	Penzance	Harbour Crystals and Wools	25 Causewayhead,			www.harbour-wools.co.uk	01736 874455		•			•
Cumbria	Carlisle	Hobbycraft	Unit A2 Kingstown Retail Pk, Parkho	CA3 0JR			8450516595		•			•
Cumbria	Ulverston	Blue Moon Yarns t/a Loopy	51 Market Street, Ulverston			www.loopywool.co.uk	01229 480080		•			•
Derbyshire	Buxton	Sew-In of Buxton	1 Spring Gardens	SK17 6BJ		www.myknittingyarnandwool.co.uk	01298 26636	•	•			•
Devon	Bovey Tracy	Spin A Yarn	26 Fore Street	TQ13 9AD	info@spinayarndevon.co.uk	www.spinayarndevon.co.uk	01626 836203	•	•			•
Devon	Modbury	Hulu	Sentinel House, Poundwell	PL21 0XX	sales@hulucraft.co.uk	www.hulucrafts.co.uk	01548 831911	•	•		•	•
Devon	Dartington	The Wool Merchant	The Shops at Dartington, Shinners Bridge	TQ9 6TQ			01884 243569	•	•			•
Devon	Totnes	Creative Crafts & Needlework	18 High Street	TQ9 5RY		www.creative-crafts-needlework.co.uk	01803 866002		•			•
Devon	Exeter	Exeter Sewing Machine Company	7 Heavitree Road, Exeter	EX1 2LD		www.exetersewing.co.uk			•			•
Dorset	Bournemouth	Carly's Crafts	Shop 1, 1a Cardigan Road, Winton	BH9 1BJ	michelek1964@hotmail.com		01202 512106		•			•
Dorset	Wimborne	Golden Hands	41b East Street	BH21 1DX			1202639360		•			•
Dorset	Christchurch	The Crafty Knitter	103 Bargates, Christchurch	BH23 1QQ		www.thecraftyknitter.co.uk	01202 474449		•			•
Dumfries & Galloway	Castle Douglas	Art 2 Go	130-132 King Street	DG7 1LU	sarah@outbackyarns.co.uk	www.outbackyarns.com	01556 504900	•	•	•		•
East Sussex	Brighton	C & H Fabrics	179 Western Road,	BN1 2BA		www.candh.co.uk	01273 321959	•	•	•		•
East Sussex	Eastbourne	C & H Fabrics	82/86 Terminus Road	BN21 3LX		www.candh.co.uk	01323 410428		•			•
East Yorks	Driffield	C Foster & Son	Little Houndale Knits, Little Houndale Farm	YO25 4LF	kath@littlehoundaleknits.com		01377 255093					•
Essex	Billericay	Craft Arena	Studios 48-50, Barleylands Craft Village, Barleylands Road,	CM11 2UD		www.craftarena.co.uk	01268 523780		•			•
Fife	Pittenweem	The Woolly Brew	39 High Street	KY10 2PG			01333 312042		•			•
Flintshire		Yarn O'clock	2 Earl Road, Mold	CH7 1AJ	yarnoclock@gmail.com	www.yarnoclock.co.uk	01352 218082		•			•
Flintshire	Mostyn	Abakhan	Coast Road	CH8 9DX			01745 562 100		•	•		•
Glamorgan	Cardiff	John Lewis	The Hayes	CF10 1EG			029 2053 6000	•	•	•		•
Glamorgan	Penarth	Yarn & Yarns	22 Cornerswell Road	CF64 2UZ			02920 712097		•			•
Glamorgan	Swansea	Red House Quilting	4 Cornwall Place	SA3 4DP	mail@redhousequilting.com	www.redhousequilting.co.uk	01792 368 080		•	•		•
Glamorgan	Swansea	Swansea Bay Yarns	88. St Helens Avenue	SA1 4NN	info@swanseabayyarns.co.uk	www.swanseabayyarns.co.uk	01792 469171	•	•			•
Gloucestershire	Gloucester	The Bluestocking Wool Shop	20 George Street, Stroud	GL5 3DP			01453 763490	•				
Gloucestershire	Stroud	Haberdashery Twist	28 High Street	GL5 1AJ			01453 297639		•	•		•
Greater Manchester	Manchester	John Lewis	Peel Avenue, The Trafford Centre	M17 8JL			0161 491 4040	•	•			•
Gwynedd	Dolgellau	Knit One	Maes Gwyn	LL40 1RB	angharad.jones4@btinternet.com		01341 422194	•	•			•
Hampshire	Basingstoke	Pack Lane Wool Shop	171 Pack Lane, Kempshott	RG22 5HN	enquiries@packlanewool.co.uk	www.packlanewool.co.uk	01256 462590		•	•		•
Hampshire	Rowlands Castle	Handmade Studios	4 The Green	PO9 6BN	info@handmadestudios.org	www.handmadestudios.org	02392 412901		•	•		•
Hampshire	Southampton	John Lewis	West Quay Shopping Centre	SO15 1GY			0238 021 6400	•	•	•		•
Hampshire	Winchester	C & H Fabrics	8 High St	SO23 9JX		www.candh.co.uk	01962 843355		•	•		•
Hertfordshire	Watford	John Lewis	The Harlequin, High St	WD2 8HL			01923 244266	•	•			•
Hertfordshire	Welwyn Garden City	John Lewis	Bridge Road	AL8 6TP			01707 323456	•	•	•		•
Hertfordshire	Walkern	Hearts and Crafts	69 High Street, Walkern	SG2 7NT					•			•
Hertfordshire	Buntingford	Crafty Angel	Unit 2b, Hyde Hall Farm, Sandon, Buntingford	SG9 0RU		www.craftyangelshop.myshopify.com			•			•
Isle of Man		JJ Ribbons							•			•
Jersey	St Helier	Rachel's Textiles Studio	47 La Colomberie	JE2 4QA	rachel@rachelstextilesstudio.com	www.rachelstextilesstudio.com	01534 878877			•		•
Kent	Broadstairs	C Wools	17 High Street	CT10 1LP	info@cwool.co.uk		01843 862848		•			•
Kent	Canterbury	C & H Fabrics	20-21 St Margarets St	CT1 2TH		www.candh.co.uk	01227 459760	•	•	•		•
Kent	Greenhithe	John Lewis	Bluewater	DA9 9SA			01322 624123	•	•	•		•
Kent	Tenterden	Hoop	92 High Street	TN30 6JB	vanessa@hoopandloop.co.uk		1580388011	•	•			•
Kent	Tunbridge Wells	C & H Fabrics	113/115 Mount Pleasant	TN1 1QS		www.candh.co.uk	01892 522618	•	•	•		•
Kinross-Shire	Kinross	Skeins and Bobbins	120 High Street, Kinross	KY13 8DA					•			•
Lanarkshire	Glasgow	John Lewis	Buchanan Galleries	G4 0BZ			0141 353 6677	•	•	•		•
Lanarkshire	Glasgow	The Wool Haven	21 Langside Place, Glasgow	G41 3DL		www.thewoolhaven.com			•			•
Leicestershire	Leicester	John Lewis	2 Bath House Lane, Highcross	LE1 4SA			0116 242 5777	•	•	•		•
Lincolnshire	Cleethorpes	A Good Yarn	53 Cambridge Street	DN35 8HD	kate@agoodyarn.co.uk	www.agoodyarn.co.uk	01472 508707		•			•
Lincolnshire	Louth	M&G Designs	14 Eastgate	LN11 9NE	mandgneedleworkdesigns@btconnect.com	www.mandgdesignsneedlecraft.co.uk	1507604923		•	•		•
Lincolnshire	Stamford	Ewe Wool Shop	4 Stamford Walk	PE9 2JE	i_love_ewe@ymail.com	www.i-love-ewe.com	01780 763838		•			•
London	Central London	John Lewis	300 Oxford Street	W1C 1DX			020 7629 7711	•	•	•		•
London	Central London	Liberty	Regent St	W1B 5AH			020 7734 1234	•	•			•
London	Central London	Peter Jones	Sloane Square	SW1W 8EL			0207 881 6364	•	•			•
London	Crouch End	Nest	102 Weston Park	N8 9PP	info@handmadenest.co.uk	www.handmadenest.co.uk	2083408852		•			•
London	Herne Hill	Sharp Works	220 Railton Road	SE24 0JD			2077387668	•	•			•
London	London	Fringe	108 Alexandra Park Road	N10 2AE			0208 8839478		•			•
London	London	Stitch Up Sewing Ltd	130 Arthur Road, Wimbledon	SW19 5PN	sandiebon@btinternet.com		0208 9446488		•			•
London	North London	John Lewis	Brent Cross Shopping Centre	NW4 3FL			020 8202 6535	•	•			•
London	Stratford	John Lewis	101 The Arcade, Montfichet Road	E20 1EL			020 8532 3500	•	•	•		•
London		The Knitting Shop			office@theknittingshop.co.uk	www.theknittingshop.co.uk			•		•	•
London		Really Maria							•			•
Merseyside	Liverpool	John Lewis	70 South John Street	L1 8BJ			0151 709 7070	•	•	•		•
Monmouthshire	Abergavenny	The Wool Croft	9 Cross Street	NP7 5EH	info@thewoolcroft.co.uk		01873 851551	•	•	•		•
Monmouthshire	Chepstow	Undy Yarns	Unit 10 St Mary's Arcade, Chepstow			www.undyyarns.co.uk	01291 629797		•			•
Monmouthshire		Go Knit							•			•
Norfolk	Diss	Diss Wool & Craft Shop	2 Cobbs Yard, St Nicholas Street	IP22 4LB	sales@disswoolandcrafts.com	www.disswoolandcrafts.com	01379 650640		•			•
Norfolk	Norwich	John Lewis	All Saints Green	NR1 3LX			01603 660021	•	•	•		•
Norfolk	Norwich	Norfolk Yarn	11, Pottergate	NR2 1DS	norfolk_yarn@yahoo.co.uk	www.norfolkyarn.co.uk	01603 927034	•	•			•
North Yorkshire	Bedale	New Jersey	38 Market Place	DL8 1EQ			01677 427 746		•			•
North Yorkshire	Clapham	Beckside Yarn & Needlecraft	Church Avenue	LA2 8EA	info@becksideyarns.co.uk	www.becksideyarns.co.uk	01524 251122		•			•
North Yorkshire	Filey	Beachcomber	35 Belle Vue St	YO14 9HU			01723 514434		•			•
North Yorkshire	York	John Lewis	Unit C, Vangarde Way	YO32 9AE				•	•	•		•
North Yorkshire	Leeds	BaaRamEwe							•			•
North Yorkshire	North Allerton	Natural Knitter Wool Shop	1a Friarage Street, Northallerton	DL6 1DP		www.naturalknitterwoolshop.com			•			•
Northamptonshire	Northampton	Hobbycraft	Tyne Road	NN5 5AF			01604 591800		•			•
Northamptonshire	Rushden	Manfield Crafts	24 Griffiths Street	NN10 0RL	enquiries@manfieldcrafts.com		01933 314920	•	•			•
Northern Ireland	Cullybackey	The Glen Gallery	48 Fenagh Road	BT43 5PH			2825880354	•	•			•
Northumberland		The Hat Box							•			•
Nottinghamshire	Beeston	Yarn	55 Chilwell Road	NG9 1EN	info@yarn-in-notts.co.uk	www.yarn-in-notts.co.uk	0115 925 3606	•	•	•		•
Nottinghamshire	Nottingham	John Lewis	Victoria Centre	NG1 3QA			0115 941 8282	•	•	•		•
Oxfordshire	Bicester	Bicester Wools	86 Sheep Street	OX26 6LP	info@bicesterwools.com	www.bicesterwools.com	01869 322966		•	•		•
Oxfordshire	Burford	Burford Needlecraft	53 High Street	OX18 4QA	burfordneedlecraft@gmail.com		01993 822316		•			•
Oxfordshire	Oxford	Oxford Yarn Store	3 North Parade Avenue	OX2 6LX	karen@oxfordyarnstore.co.uk	www.oxfordyarnstore.co.uk	01865 604112	•	•			•
Oxfordshire	Oxford	The Fibreworks	10a Middle Row, Chipping Norton,	OX7 5NH		www.thefibreworks.co.uk			•			•
Oxfordshire	Witney	Witney Sewing & Knitting Centre	61 High Street	OX28 6JA		www.witney-sewing-knitting.co.uk	01993 702772		•	•		•
Pembrokeshire	Fishguard	Jane's of Fishguard	14 High Street	SA65 9AR		www.janes-fishguard.co.uk	01348 874443		•			•
Perthshire	Aberfeldy	Karelia House	Kenmore Road, Comrie Bridge	PH15 2LS			01887 822027		•			•
Perthshire	Perth	Great British Yarns LTD	Lermoos, Duncrievi, Glenfarg, Perth	PH2 9PD	info@greatbritishyarns.co.uk	www.greatbritishyarns.co.uk	01577 830742		•	•	•	•
Powys	Brecon	Bobbins	6 The Bulwark	LD3 7LB	bobbins-brecon@hotmail.co.uk		01874 622287	•		•		•
Roxburghshire	Kelso	The Kraftworks 3	2 The Square	TD5 7HL			01573 228623		•	•		•
Shropshire	Ludlow	The Wool Shop	13 Broad Street	SY8 1NG	thewoolshop.jean@hotmail.co.uk	www.ludlow-woolshop.co.uk	01584 872988	•	•	•		•
Shropshire	Much Wenlock	Ippikin	59 The High Street	TF13 6AE	ippikin@googlemail.com	www.ippikin.co.uk	01952 728371		•			•
Shropshire	Shewsbury	Anca	Unit 10, The Mall, Bank Farm Road	SY3 6DU	anne@anca-wools.co.uk	www.anca-wool.co.uk	01743 249504		•	•		•
Somerset	Bath	Wool LTD	19 Old Orchard Street	BA1 1JU		www.woolbath.co.uk	01225 469144	•	•			•
Somerset	Frome	Marmalade Yarns	11 Catherine Hill	BA11 1BZ	CatrionaandMaxine@marmaladeyarns.co.uk	www.marmaladeyarns.co.uk	01373 473557		•			•
Somerset	Ilminster	The Sewing Corner	26 Silver Street	TA19 0DR	thesewingcorner26@gmail.com		01460 259989		•			•
Somerset	Porlock	Jana Henrie	Bridge House, High Street, Exmoor National Park	TA24 8PY	jane.dyer2@btinternet.com		01643 862058		•			•
Somerset	Weston Super Mare	The Wool Sanctuary	68 Ashcombe Road	BS23 3DX	suziebeans@outlook.com	www.thewoolsanctuary.com	7805126078		•		•	•
Somerset		The Sewing Corner							•			•
South Yorkshire	Sheffield	John Lewis	Barkers Pool	S1 1EP			0114 2768511	•	•	•		•
Staffordshire	Leek	Bibelot	2 Sheepmarket	ST13 5HW	hello@bibelot.co.uk	www.bibelot.co.uk	01538 388764		•	•		•
Staffordshire	Lichfield	The Knitting Corner	Unit 3, Curborough Hall Farm, Watery Lane	WS13 8ES	theknittingcorner@btinternet.com		01543 415837	•	•			•
Staffordshire	Newcastle under Lyme	K2Tog	63 High Street, Wolstanton	ST5 0ER	sales@cucumberpatch.com	www.cucumberpatch.co.uk	01782 862332	•	•			•
Staffordshire	Burton on Trent	Chrissy's Crafts	104 Craythorne Road, Burton on Trent	DE13 0AZ					•			•
Suffolk	Bury	Sew Much To Do							•			•
Suffolk		Quilters Haven Ltd	68 High Street, Wickham Market	IP13 0QU	quilters.haven@btinternet.com	www.quilters-haven.co.uk	01728 746275			•		•
Surrey	Carshalton Beeches	Maxime Wools	68 Banstead Road	SM5 3NL	enquires@maximewools.co.uk		0208 66105625	•	•			•
Surrey	Caterham	The Knit Club	27 High Street	CR3 5UE	louise@theknitclub.co.uk		01883 345220		•			•
Surrey	Guildford	C & H Fabrics	7/8 white lion walk, Guildford	GU1 3DN		www.candh.co.uk	01483 301380		•	•		•
Surrey	Kingston	John Lewis	Wood Street	KT1 1TE			020 8547 3000	•	•	•		•
Torfaen	Blaenavon	Go Knit	35 Broad Street	NP4 9NF	jenny@goknit.co.uk	www.goknit.co.uk	7711616948		•			•
Tyne and Wear	Durham	The Woolly Workshop	Cottage 1, Fowlers Yard, Back Silver Street, Durham	DH1 3RA		www.thewoollyworkshop.co.uk			•			•
Tyne & Wear	Newcastle upon Tyne	John Lewis	Eldon Square	NE99 1AB			0191 232 5000	•	•	•		•
Warwickshire	Warwick	Warwick Wools	17 Market Place	CV34 4S	mail@warwickwools.co.uk	www.warwickwools.co.uk	01926 492853		•			•
West Midlands	Coleshill	Remember When	80 High Street	B46 3AH	info@rememberwhenshop.co.uk	www.rememberwhenshop.co.uk	01675 466418			•		•
West Midlands	Solihull	John Lewis	Touchwood	B90 4SH			0121 704 1121	•	•	•		•

County	Town / City	Stockist	Address	Postcode	Email	Website	Telephone	Rowan At	Yarn	Fabric	Online	Instore
West Midlands	Solihull	Stitch	Cedar Cottage, Notcutts	B94 4EN	sales@stitchsolihull.com		0121 3146888		✓	✓		✓
West Sussex	Chichester	C & H Fabrics	33/34 North Street	PO19 1LX		www.candh.co.uk	01243 783300		✓	✓		✓
West sussex	Horsham	C & H Fabrics	7 Black Horse Way	RH12 1NP	horsham@candhfabrics.co.uk	www.candh.co.uk	01403 242127		✓			✓
West Sussex	Shoreham by Sea	Shoreham Knitting	19 East Street	BN43 5ZE	sales@englishyarns.co.uk		01273 461029	✓	✓			✓
West Yorkshire	Brighouse	Baa Baa Brighouse	11 Church Street, Rastrick, Brighouse	HD6 3NF		www.baabaabrighouse.co.uk			✓			✓
West Yorkshire	Hebden Bridge	Attica	Unit 10E Top Land Country Business Park	HX7 5RW	info@attica-yarns.co.uk	www.attica-yarns.co.uk	07860 624240	✓	✓			✓
West Yorkshire	Leeds	Baa Ram Ewe	87 Otley Road, Headingley	LS6 3PS	info@baaramewe.co.uk	www.baaramewe.co.uk	0113 278 1788		✓			✓
West Yorkshire	Wakefield	Wool 'N' Stuff	12 Cross Square	WF1 1PH	woolnstuff@yahoo.co.uk	www.woolnstuff.co.uk	01924 565740		✓			✓
Wiltshire	Bradford on Avon	Nosek's Just Gems	4 Lamb Yard, Kingston Road	BA15 1FG	caron@noseks.co.uk	www.noseksjustgems.com	01225 706222		✓			✓
Wiltshire	Cricklade	Cricklade Needlecrafts	89a High Street	SN6 6DF	info@crickladecrafts.co.uk	www.crickladecrafts.co.uk	01793 750604		✓			✓
Wiltshire	Salisbury	Born To Knit	Studio 4, Fisherton Mill, Fisherton Street	SP2 7QY			07557 985935		✓			✓
Worcestershire	Broadway	Sew U Knit Crafts	2 Cotswold Court	WR12 7AA	sewuknitcrafts@outlook.com	www.sewuknitcrafts.co.uk	01386 852279		✓			✓
Worcestershire	Bromsgrove	Loopy Ladies	8 Worcester Road	B61 7AE	karen@loopyladies.co.uk	www.loopyladies.co.uk	07791 365253		✓			✓
Worcestershire	Droitwich	Emm's And Sew Much More	6-8 High Street	WR9 8EW	sales@iloveemms.co.uk	www.iloveemms.co.uk	1905778381	✓	✓	✓		✓
Worcestershire	Worcester	House of Haby	Market Hall, The Shambles	WR1 2RA					✓			✓
		A Bit Woolly				www.abitwoolly.co.uk			✓		✓	
		Art of Yarn			sales@artofyarn.co.uk	www.artofyarn.co.uk			✓		✓	
		Baa Baa Brighouse			info@baabaabrighouse.co.uk	www.baabaabrighouse.co.uk	01484 722662	✓	✓		✓	
		Biggar Stitches				www.biggarstitches.com			✓			✓
		Craft Supplies Store				www.knitting-supplies-store.co.uk			✓		✓	
		Deramores				www.deramores.com			✓		✓	
		English Yarns			sales@englishyarns.co.uk	www.englishyarns.co.uk	01273 461029	✓	✓		✓	
		Go Knit				www.goknit.co.uk	07711 616948		✓		✓	
		Great British Yarns LTD			info@greatbritishyarns.co.uk	www.greatbritishyarns.co.uk	01577 830742		✓		✓	
		Hobbycraft				www.hobbycraft.co.uk			✓		✓	
		Irene J Noad			jannette@btinternet.com	www.jannettesrareyarns.co.uk			✓		✓	
		Knitbliss Yarns			sales@knitblissyarns.co.uk	www.knitblissyarns.co.uk			✓			✓
		Knitters Needs				www.knittersneeds.co.uk			✓		✓	
		Knit UK			knituk@live.co.uk	www.knituk.com			✓			✓
		Laughing Hens				www.laughinghens.com			✓		✓	
		Love Knitting				www.loveknitting.com			✓		✓	
		Wise Badger Limited			customer.services@wisebadger.com	www.wisebadger.com	01789 773021		✓		✓	
		Once A Sheep			info@onceasheep.com	www.onceasheep.com			✓			✓
		Peachey Ethknits				www.ethknits.co.uk			✓			✓
		Poppy's			admin@poppys-holmfirth.com	www.poppys-holmfirth.com	07557 950935		✓			✓
		Sandcastle Yarns				www.sandcastleyarns.co.uk			✓		✓	
		Sew and Make			sales@sewandmake.co.uk	www.sewandmake.co.uk	01359 259659	✓	✓		✓	
		SMD Knitting			info@knittingwool.com	www.knittingwool.com	0800 622 6225		✓		✓	
		Spins and Needles			sarah@spinsandneedles.co.uk	www.spinsandneedles.co.uk		✓	✓		✓	
		Susie's Craft Basket			susan@artfuldodgers.co.uk	www.artfuldodgers.co.uk	0161 819 9933	✓	✓			✓
		Sweet Sheep Fine Yarns				www.sweetsheep.co.uk			✓		✓	
		The Knitting Village				www.knittingvillage.co.uk			✓		✓	
		The London Wool Company			info@londonwools.com	www.londonwools.com			✓			✓
		Wight Yarns				www.wightyarns.webeden.co.uk			✓		✓	
		Wool Warehouse Direct Ltd			sales@woolwarehouse.co.uk	www.woolwarehouse.co.uk	01926 882818		✓		✓	

·············

GALLERY

Our easy reference guide to the designs featured in this magazine.

·············

ROWAN

KINSHIP

| ALMONDBURY | OXTON | GRANSMOOR | WEETON SCARF | FARNLEY | SYKES | HUTTON SCARF | GREENWOOD | BRADSHAW |

Cocoon
Martin Storey
Pattern 110
Main image 4, 6, 7

Kid Classic
Sarah Hatton
Pattern 124
Main image 4, 9

Hemp Tweed
Lisa Richardson
Pattern 132
Main image 10, 11

Alpaca Merino DK
Lisa Richardson
Pattern 161
Main image 11

Big Wool
Emma Wright
Pattern 149
Main image 12, 13

Kid Classic
Martin Storey
Pattern 156
Main image 14, 15

Felted Tweed
& Kidsilk Haze
Lisa Richardson
Pattern 163
Main image 15

Felted Tweed
Galina Carroll
Pattern 135
Main image 16, 17

Kid Classic
Martin Storey
Pattern 148
Main image 19, 21

| THACKREY SCARF | COWLAM | FISHLAKE | BIELBY | WILSHAW | LUND | MARR | EASTBURY |

Felted Tweed
Martin Storey
Pattern 155
Main image 29

Hemp Tweed
Lisa Richardson
Pattern 120
Main image 30, 31

Felted Tweed
Marie Wallin
Pattern 128
Main image 33, 34

Felted Tweed
Martin Storey
Pattern 127
Main image 35

Big Wool
Georgia Farrell
Pattern 165
Main image 36, 37

Pure Wool
Superwash DK
Sarah Hatton
Pattern 140
Main image 39

Alpaca Merino DK
Lisa Richardson
Pattern 143
Main image 40, 41

Alpaca Merino DK
Emma Wright
Pattern 158
Main image 43

DAWN TILL DUSK

| EVENING | EVENING | DUSKY SCARF | DUSKY SCARF | MELLOW | MELLOW | AFTERGLOW | AFTERGLOW | SUNSET |

Kid Classic
Martin Storey
Pattern 119
Main image 53, 70, 75

Felted Tweed & Kidsilk Haze
Martin Storey
Pattern 112
Main image 54, 55, 73

Kid Classic
Sarah Hatton
Pattern 134
Main image 54, 55, 74

Kidsilk Haze & Fine Lace
Martin Storey
Pattern 108
Main image 56, 72

Kid Silk Haze
Marie Wallin
Pattern 162
Main image 58, 59

| ECLIPSE | HUTTON SCARF | TWILIGHT | TWILIGHT | SUBDUED | VEILED | VEILED | EVENTIDE | EVENTIDE |

Kidsilk Haze
& Fine Lace
Martin Storey
Pattern 164
Main image 66

Felted Tweed
& Kidsilk Haze
Lisa Richardson
Pattern 163
Main image 67

Kidsilk Haze & Fine Lace
Lisa Richardson
Pattern 138
Main image 67, 68, 80

Alpaca Merino DK
Emma Wright
Pattern 113
Main image 69, 82

Kid Classic
Martin Storey
Pattern 164
Main image 71, 81

Kid Classic
Lisa Richardson
Pattern 106
Main image 76, 77